The Industrial Ephemeral

ATELIER: ETHNOGRAPHIC INQUIRY IN THE TWENTY-FIRST CENTURY

Kevin Lewis O'Neill, Series Editor

The Industrial Ephemeral

LABOR AND LOVE IN INDIAN
ARCHITECTURE AND CONSTRUCTION

Namita Vijay Dharia

UNIVERSITY OF CALIFORNIA PRESS

The publisher and the University of California Press Foundation gratefully acknowledge the generous support of the Richard and Harriett Gold Endowment Fund in Arts and Humanities.

University of California Press
Oakland, California

© 2022 by Namita Vijay Dharia

Library of Congress Cataloging-in-Publication Data

Names: Dharia, Namita Vijay, 1980– author.
Title: The industrial ephemeral : labor and love in Indian architecture
    and construction / Namita Vijay Dharia.
Other titles: Atelier (Oakland, Calif.) ; 7.
Description: Oakland, California : University of California Press, [2022] |
    Series: Atelier : Ethnographic inquiry in the twenty-first century ; 7 |
    Includes bibliographical references and index.
Identifiers: LCCN 2021061564 (print) | LCCN 2021061565 (ebook) |
    ISBN 9780520383098 (cloth) | ISBN 9780520383104 (paperback) |
    ISBN 9780520383111 (epub)
Subjects: LCSH: Urbanization—Social aspects—India—Delhi—
    21st century. | Labor—Anthropological aspects—India—Delhi. |
    Construction workers—India—Delhi. | Architecture and
    anthropology—India—Delhi. | BISAC: SOCIAL SCIENCE /
    Anthropology / Cultural & Social | SOCIAL SCIENCE / Sociology /
    Urban
Classification: LCC HT147.I4 D47 2022 (print) | LCC HT147.I4 (ebook) |
    DDC 307.760954/560905—dc23/eng/20220114
LC record available at https://lccn.loc.gov/2021061564
LC ebook record available at https://lccn.loc.gov/2021061565

31 30 29 28 27 26 25 24 23 22
10 9 8 7 6 5 4 3 2 1

Dedicated to
Madhusudan, Malati, and Mandakini,
forever in my heart

Contents

Illustrations

TABLE

Acknowledgments

The labor and love of many formed this book. Thank you to my committee members: Michael Herzfeld for fostering my love for anthropology; Mary M. Steedly for nourishing my writing voice and ethnographic passion; and Ajantha Subramanian for honing my political stances, knowledge, and arguments through insightful criticism. My partners-in-academic-arms Sa'ed Atshan, Sai Balakrishnan, Naor Ben-Yehoyada, Vivien Chung, Eda Cakmakci, Lizzy Cooper-Davis, Richard Delacy, Gangsim Eom, Alex Fattal, Ben Gaydos, Bronwyn Isaacs, Nancy Khalil, Damina Khaira, Neelam Khoja, Julie Kleinman, Ekin Kurtic, Veronika Kusumaryati, Andrew Littlejohn, Jared McCormick, Andrew McDowell, Anh Thu Ngo, Jyoti Natarajan, Chiaki Nishijima, Andrew Ong, Juno Parreñas, Federico Perez, Sabrina Peric, Ramyar Rossoukh, Ivette Salom, Benjamin Siegel, Claudio Sopranzetti, Nick Smith, Nicolas Strensdorff-Cisterna, Noah Tamarkin, Anand Vaidya, Tom Vogl, Julia Yezbick, Dilan Yildirim, and Emrah Yildiz, whose feedback, spirit, and constant love nurtured this book and me to our fullest selves.

I am grateful for my South Asian studies community for their friendship and firm grounding in context: Elise Burton, Rohit De, Hardeep Dhillon, Abbas Jaffer, Sadaf Jaffer, Dan Majchrowicz, Deonnie Moodie, Dinyar Patel, Shayan Rajani, Mircea Raianu, Arafat Razzaque, Aarti

Sethi, Dan Sheffield, Chitra Venkataramani, Leilah Vevaina, and Namita Wahi. Thank you to the many companions who joined my intellectual journey, infusing it with friendship and fierce intellect: Begum Adalet, Hayal Akarsu, Piyali Bhattacharya, Kerry Chance, Nejat Dinc, Vineet Diwadkar, Sahana Ghosh, Radhika Govindarajan, Huma Gupta, Khalid Hadeed, Sohini Kar, Jennifer Mack, Alykhan Mohammed, Liza Oliver, Caterina Scaramelli, Jeremy Schmidt, Anoo Iyer Siddiqui, Tariq Thachil, Nishita Trisal, and Sarover Zaidi.

Thank you to Sarah Pinto, Vyajayanthi Rao, Jesse Shipley, Tulasi Srinivas, Chris Walley, and Mary Woods, whose astute inputs transformed this book at its critical development phases. Mentors whose work, teachings, and support are invaluable to this research include Asad Ahmed, Steven Caton, Maya De, Shubhra Gururani, Nicholas Harkness, Cornelia Herzfeld, Meena Hewett, Kajri Jain, Smita Lahiri, Rahul Mehrotra, and Lawrence Ralph. I am indebted to Ramnarayan Rawat, Anand Yang, Susan Wadley, and participants at the AIIS dissertation to book workshop for their inputs. The support of my RISD colleagues Alero Akporiaye, Jennifer Prewitt-Freilino, Lindsay French, Jung Joon Lee, and Damian White and my many students proved invaluable in the process of writing this book. My gratitude toward the staff at Harvard Anthropology and RISD Liberal Arts for tackling administrative bureaucracy for me: Anna Cimini, Susan Farley, Marianne Fritz, Gail Hughes, Cristina Paul, and Linda Thomas.

I am grateful to the Political Ecology Working Group at Harvard and the many people who offered me opportunities to workshop and enhance my research, including John Anjaria, Sarah Besky, Debjani Bhattacharyya, Lisa Björkman, Iftikhar Dadi, Gareth Doherty, Moises Lino e Silva, Nikhil Rao, and Llrena Searle. Am grateful to Daniel Barber, Ikem Okoye, and Peg Rawes for sustaining my interdisciplinary interests. Thank you to Aromar Revi, Gautam Bhan, and the Indian Institute for Human Settlements for hosting the research in India. This work was supported by the Wenner-Gren Foundation, the Radcliffe Institute for Advanced Study and the Lakshmi Mittal and Family South Asia Institute at Harvard University, the Cora Du Bois Charitable Trust, the Rhode Island School of Design, IJURR Foundation, and the Department of Anthropology at Harvard University. Excerpts from this book appeared in "Embodied Urbanisms: Corruption and the Ecologies of Eating and Excreting in India's Real

Estate Economies," in *Cultural Anthropology*; "Labour and the Temporalities of Indian Design and Construction," in *The Journal of Architecture*; "Artifacts and Artifices of the Global: Practices of US Architects in India's National Capital Region" in *The Global South*, and *The Routledge Companion to Architectural Education in the Global South*. Kevin O'Neill's astute insight and unwavering support gave me the strength and courage to write the book I want. The wonderful Kate Marshall, Enrique Ochoa-Kuap, Emily Park, and the staff and faculty at the University of California Press guided this book through the seas of publishing. I am grateful to Jon Dertien and Sharon Langworthy at BookComp, who helped produce this book. Thank you to my two anonymous reviewers for their valuable critiques and inputs and to Philip Sayers for his developmental edits.

I would be nowhere without Neelkanth Sir, the staff and workers at Haveli and Wandering Woods, and the many people who generously shared their knowledge of construction and urbanism with me. I am grateful to Andrew Amstutz, Anamika Bagchi, Hoda Bandeh-Ahmadi, Siddharth Mishra, Ankon Mitra, Rajendra Parihar, Arjun Rajagopal, Tarun Sharma, and Sahil Warsi, whose friendship sustained me in the field. Thank you to Harshal Ajani, Jude D'Souza, Christine D'Sa, Niti Gourisaria, Afshan Hussain, Girisha Keswani, Himashee Khanna, Komal Kotwal, Nidhi Mathur, Kevin Pereira, Shamli Sakhare, Advait Sambhare, Vrinda Seksaria, and Santosh Thorat for sharing my love of architecture. And to friends who stood by me through the highs and lows of academia: Ameya Balsekar, Akshay Bajaj, Sunayana Banerjee, Ritwik and Rahee Dahake, Mayura Deshpande, Mehul Gandhi, Shweta Gidwani, Shimul Melwani, Vishu and Gayatri Rao, Rohit Reddy, Krupa Shandilya, and Tahira Thekekara.

I am grateful to Kaushalya and Jaiprakash Bhojak, Aruna and Mohan Monga, and Kanak and Sid Pandey for opening up their homes to me in Delhi. Thank you to Saraswathy and Kumar Nochur for their support in writing this book. This book owes its first thanks to my parents Ratna and Vijay Dharia for raising me to be all I can be, and to my sister Neha Dharia for her steadfast belief in my abilities. She and Shail Bhojak look after our family, giving me the invaluable space to write this book. Last but not least, to Aditya Nochur, whose constant cheerleading and love guides me across the finish line.

Note on Anonymity

All the names of people, places, companies, and institutions are fictitious pseudonyms, except for public figures and those mentioned in publications quoted. I have blurred, obscured, or substituted some identifying details in order to further protect identity.

Map 1. Central cities and districts in India's National Capital Region. *Source:* Created by author.

Introduction

CONSTRUCTION'S URBANISM (GURGAON, DECEMBER 2011)

It is a cold December evening in Gurgaon, a city within India's National Capital Region (NCR), and I stand on an elevated Delhi Metro platform. My train into Delhi is still five minutes away, and I watch the sun set over the growing urban region. The station, close to the southwestern border of India's National Capital Territory (NCT) of Delhi, is busy with commuters heading home. Gurgaon, a city-suburb soon to be renamed Gurugram, stretches before me in the gentle light of dusk. From my vantage, I see the city as it dissolves into the gray-blue shadows of the night. This is the first of fifteen months that I will spend in NCR—a region that comprises multiple cities and states that surround the NCT—doing research on the construction industry and the urban development it has brought about. I plan to interview developers, laborers, architects, and allied groups across the production chain of the construction industry and just met a friend from my days as an architecture undergraduate to talk about urban development.

The setting sun illuminates construction work in the area; light speckles across brand-new highways and glints in the delicate lattices of electric

Figure 1. Sunset over buildings under construction, Gurgaon, 2012. Photo by author.

poles. The long rays of a December sun extend across empty tracts of land that await construction and diffuse through the incomplete windows of concrete apartment blocks. Sunlight percolates a landscape of circling tower cranes and half-finished building frames. Clouds of cement and sand hang over the city and turn the air opaque and asthmatic. The sun hovers behind the hazy towers, a glowing, orange ball tamed by the construction dust in the sky.

The city space below the station platform I stand on overflows with the armatures of construction work. *Mazdoors* (laborers) return home from construction sites, their *fantis* (planing tools) and ploughs slung over their shoulders, their saws, hammers, and *dors* (plumb lines) held in plastic bags. Pedestrians hop, agile and limber, over the ups and downs of curing cement roads and dug-up pipes; they navigate around new trenches and climb over the mud mountains that cover the old. Scaffolding rises from the pavement. Dump trucks full of cement or gravel ply the streets,

Figure 2. A cement mixer in Gurgaon, 2012. Photo by author.

interspersed with large flatbed trucks with steel bars that threaten to run through the windshields of the cars that follow. An occasional cement mixer stands patiently among clogged traffic, its concrete drum cease-lessly swirling to protect its semiformed cargo.

The rumbling belly of the cement mixer is iconic of the euphoric energy and atmospheres that construction generates: the dynamic sounds, smells, and all-encompassing sensory quality of construction. The liquid con-crete that will solidify into architecture's permanence reflects the indus-try's mobile and fluid material-scapes, and the rotating drum evokes the very cyclicality of construction's operations. The cement mixer's state of turmoil, its relentless churning, seeps into the sensibilities of all those in construction. It highlights the puzzle that seemingly permanent, concrete architectures and infrastructure are sustained through the nonendurance of people, machines, and materials.[1]

If construction is read as a heightened transient atmosphere, then what implications does this transience have for the permanence it gives rise to? In the pages that follow, I explore the fundamental dilemma at the heart of

Figure 3. View of Gurgaon from train platform at Sikanderpur metro station, 2013. Photo by author.

India's urban development politics: the relationship between the ephemeral and the durable. This book studies ephemeral atmospheres—understood as atmospheres generated by the temporary presence, transformation, and circulation of people, materials, and objects in construction—to question habitual ways of depicting Indian urbanism in architecture and anthropology.[2] I examine the political work aesthetically heightened atmospheres of construction do. In doing so, I argue that ephemeral atmospheres in construction act as a political economic tool through the enabling and disabling of specific kin, social, and material relations, a configuration I term the *industrial ephemeral*. Ephemeral atmospheres are fleeting and temporary, but they produce durable socialities and materialities that support both industrial accumulation and political mobilization.

Construction and urban development, then, despite the commonsense assumption that they deal in permanence, are actually characterized by the ephemeral, in many forms: movement of people, materials, and machines; material states; sounds; and emotions. The ephemeral manifests in the transforming material and aesthetic states of architecture under construction, which allow the rapid reshaping of social and political relations. It also names the disappearance of state support that gives rise to conditions of economic precarity. The active circulation of drawings and documents across the region and the sounds, smell, and textures of changing architecture, as well as the affects and emotions that accompany them, can likewise be viewed as instances of the ephemeral. The deliberate mobility and displacement of people in construction is an ephemeral that can be experienced not only as aspirational and enabling but also as violent and exclusionary. Together, these forms of the ephemeral consolidate and produce long-term relations; they generate the potential for exploitation and liberation through their active emergence and dissipation.

In *The Industrial Ephemeral* I capture this dynamism through ethnographic observations and interviews conducted at two construction sites: one a large-scale commercial real estate project I call Wandering Woods and the other a residential bungalow project I call Haveli. The former helped me analyze private, industry-led real estate and its production chains; at the latter, I was able to interact more closely with workers and foremen on site. Wandering Woods was representative of several large-scale residential and commercial real estate developments that dotted the fringes of Gurgaon in 2012. It was a developer-led operation and had over three hundred workers and about fifty supervising staff. Behind Wandering Woods was a large tract of land where workers were housed, known as the labor colony; it was gated and guarded. Haveli, on the other hand, was a smaller project, with thirty-odd workers, several of whom lived on site. It was an architect- and contractor-led bungalow development and is representative of the smaller-scale construction activity that takes place across the region. The pace of work was slower and less regimented than at Wandering Woods, allowing me more time with workers.

Construction is omnipresent in Gurgaon, a region that seems to have been under construction for over three decades.[3] In the fifteen months following my arrival in December 2011, my research on the industry would take me beyond these two construction sites, into engineering and architectural firms, factories and material supply shops, and workshop spaces. People from the two sites would guide me to farms and temples, to village homes and law firms. I would spend time at developers' offices and speak with journalists, investment bankers, planners, and politicians and visit buildings under construction in the region. This situated and circulatory methodology revealed the profound scalar, social, and spatial effects of the construction industry as it interdigitates with the region. While these fifteen months, between 2012 and 2013, constituted my official ethnographic fieldwork in the construction industry, my research is informed by a longer involvement with construction. I am a daughter of a landscape architect, a friend of architects, a trained architect who then practiced and taught architecture, an anthropologist who studied construction, and an educator who teaches artists and designers. In this introduction, I provide an account of key aspects of the construction industry by way of five time periods in my life. Eschewing a linear trajectory, I revisit these moments of reflection in order to highlight the ephemeral durabilities that drive construction work. These periods allow us to dwell in the production of Indian urbanism; they also demonstrate how my understandings of architecture, infrastructure, and construction have accreted through a life path immersed in the industry.

TRANSIENT ATMOSPHERES (GURGAON, FEBRUARY 2013)

MD and I take a break on a sun-dappled afternoon in February. We sit together on a patch of lawn in one of the many gated communities that make up Gurgaon's new wave of urban development. I am here conducting ethnographic fieldwork on the construction industry, and MD is a small-scale contractor and carpenter on the Haveli construction site.[4] We have spent the morning on the grimy construction site opposite the lawn and are happy to relax on the cool green grass of the neighborhood park. We chat as we open our lunches of vegetables, rotis, and rice, aware of the steady bangs and clangs emanating from the site across from us. The bangs merge with the noise of the Delhi Metro under construction and the sounds of construction sites around us. India's NCR is a colosseum of construction, and Gurgaon, a once-sleepy military and industrial town on the outskirts of New Delhi, feels like the epicenter.

On the peripheries of Gurgaon, tracts and tracts of former agricultural land are dotted with real estate in various stages of construction. Billboards shine brightly, promising fresh constructed paradises, palatial architectures, and verdant living. Sitting in the quiet colony park, MD and I observe Haveli under construction. It is dominated by sounds, smells, and movement: clouds of dust, the screeches of machines, the repeated motions of workers and supervisors across the site, and the intermingled smells of cement and sawdust. We watch as the architecture transforms, knowing that each day brings something new. There will come a time when the foundation is covered by mud; later the steel bars of columns will be encased by cement, the walls will then be plastered and painted, and finally, all the workers will be gone. Construction as an industry encodes an ephemeral logic: not only does it depend on its workers' ability to disappear from one site and move to another, but its constitutive processes—from site surveying to construction to project completion—are based on a set of continuous transformations that displace and erase previous atmospheres, materials, and work.

The effect is intense: this multisensory, ephemeral experience is typical of construction, where atmospheres of construction are understood as techno-aesthetic conditions: a mix of humans and nonhumans who produce changing and magnified sensoriums.[5] These continuous atmospheric transformations produce a "lived affect" and form a "force field" that organizes and disciplines people, materials, and space within industrial operations.[6] The sounds of machines, the movement of people, money, and drawings, the transforming architectures as staircases rise and walls fall produces an encompassing atmosphere that in my analysis is not a mere condition nor a diagnostic of technological and urban change, but is a "form of capital" and a form of politics both dominant and marginal.[7] Interpreting these construction atmospheres, would require a common theory of the environment produced by bringing together theories of affect, atmospheres, new materialisms, and aesthetics.[8] A focus on affect theory and new materialisms reveals the intimate workings of industrial political economy in construction.[9] Emphasizing these within aesthetic theory and tying them to a theory of atmospheres allows us to understand the sociopolitical relations ephemeral atmospheres engender.[10] I draw these together to argue that atmospheres are not epiphenomenal to the construction industry: they feed the accumulative dynamics of construction and the struggles against them. Ephemeral atmospheres are not universal; they are localized and differentiated, experienced and felt differently by those within them. It is this differential experience that leads to challenges to the industry's political economic might.

MD is short for Mohammed, but he prefers to initialize himself. I call him "MD ji," using a suffix for elders as a marker of respect and kinship. The nomenclature is strange given that we are likely of a similar age, but it is perhaps apt given MD's years of construction experience. As a Bihari Muslim man from the governmental Other Backward Classes (OBC or marginalized caste) category, MD paved his way into contracting through labor: he started by making ice cream, before moving into tailoring and then cement work, finally learning carpentry fifteen years ago. As a dominant-caste and -class, Baniya-Brahmin, Maharashtrian-Gujarati woman, I studied architecture in one of India's top public universities and worked in a firm with a global presence, only to return to sites as a PhD in training from Harvard University. The "ji" I use is juxtaposed against the "Madam" he uses; the two terms embed social hierarchies and a constructed but distanced kinship.

Everyone on site is a little afraid of MD, as he often curses people out. His boldness, however, makes him insightful and unafraid in his commentary on construction. Today we talk about human presence on construction sites and the circulation of people through urban architectures. "It is like this," he says. "You do the drawing, I will do the work or get the work done, someone else will come stay here, and someone else will break it." He traces the transitory states that construction requires, emphasizing the temporariness of both people and architecture. "The person who is breaking it will bring a machine, attach it to a generator, and *dhun dhun dhun dhun*"—he mimics the speed and sound of a jackhammer—"will break it all." I nod in response: I have seen the previous building on this site shatter under the claw of the excavator. MD goes on: "The owner of this house . . . he does not want the tree cut [down], as his father planted it." MD talks about the homeowner's ancestry and inheritance. He highlights the privilege of memorializing a tree: "When I die, will I tell my children, 'do not touch my body'?" He contrasts the tree, the property, and home against his own body, pointing out that he has no material legacy to be remembered by: "I worked my whole life to feed them." With characteristic directness, MD reiterates his own fleetingness, juxtaposing it against the permanence of the property he constructs. He highlights the central work of construction economies: to render people, environments, and even life ephemeral for material gain.

The idea that architecture, infrastructure, and construction are ephemeral is counterintuitive.[11] We are taught to recognize construction as a permanent process of spatial and social change, rather than to dwell on its temporality; we focus on architecture and infrastructure as an end and not on the means through which they are produced. Construction's ability to turn humans and material landscapes into transient entities, however, is the source of the industry's political-economic power. As the following chapters demonstrate, an ephemeral atmosphere produces heightened affective conditions of change that allow success for some and create precarity for others (chapter 1). The ephemeral materialities of money and drawings—their transformation, appearance, and disappearance—embed networks of knowledge and practices of power (chapters 2 and 3). Ephemeral construction sounds and atmospheres produce disciplinary environments that emphasize efficiency and rationality but often result in resistance and rebellion (chapters 4 and 5). Construction harnesses ephemeral emotions toward the making of real estate (chapter 6) and creates a system of economic and spatial precarity for migrant workers who must live in a state of continuous motion that denies them rights to the spaces they build. As MD puts it, "I finished the work, . . . even if I go to site, how will I go in? Is there any of our staff? All our staff has gone." The ephemeral names the host of temporary workers and the transient, processual material and sensory phenomena that characterize construction, from labor to aesthetics to emotions. It is a bodily, sensory, and aesthetic approach to understanding urban development that presents urban knowledge as absorbed, attuned to, and immersed in rather than meta-narrativized or quantified. The ephemeral as a temporary, nonpermanent state channels human transience, aesthetic transformations, and shifting material states into forms of subjugation but simultaneously holds the potential of agency and rebellion. To analyze the ephemeral is to analyze the heart of social and political struggle.

Four descriptions of the ephemeral—dictionary definitions of the term, official Hindi translations, academic studies of the ephemeral, and descriptions of the ephemeral by workers—provide insight into the spectrum of ephemeral occurrences in construction. In common parlance, *the ephemeral* is used to depict that which is fleeting, transient, or temporary, or that which appears and disappears, such as the temporary life of insects or anomalies in the atmosphere.[12] Ephemera or quickly destroyed materials in art (posters, flyers) and architecture (street stalls, informal settlements, refugee camps, festivals) have been the other of art history and architecture.[13] Even in anthropology, where *ephemera* references ghosts, media worlds, or temporary sensory phenomena, the ephemeral is an understudied concept.[14] The marginality of the ephemeral, however, can also be its strength. Ephemera can be "a mode of proofing and producing arguments" by minoritarian culture and criticism makers and produce subjectivity.[15]

The ephemeral as a concept appears in India. The high-register Hindi of government documents codes the ephemeral as *shanbhar* (fleeting) or *alpakaalik* (short-term, temporary). The latter form is used to describe temporary work and transit camps; in this form, the ephemeral describes the state of being temporary within a space (as a migrant worker) or a temporary material state (as in a transit camp or informal settlement). Both of these senses characterize the experience of construction workers. The ephemeral manifests on construction sites in the language of erasure (*gayab*, disappear) or dissolution (*miti mein mil jaana*, lit. to dissolve into the dust) that workers use to critique the industry. In this form it highlights the fleetingness of workers displaced from the sites they build. In all four instances, the ephemeral is a transitory state of people, materials, and objects in construction and becomes a tool for political comment. It is important to note too that the ephemeral is not a natural feature but one that is deliberately constructed.[16]

To be within a construction site is to inhabit a thriving space of work and life: alive with activity, half-formed and half-destroyed, occupied by myriad communities and classes, and overflowing with a multiplicity of work. It is to be immersed in construction atmospheres. Atmospheres saturate the senses and seep into all those who dwell within the space and are connected to the politics of labor. The immersive atmospheres of construction work, as with most industrial work, are environments generated through labor and its accompanying social relations. The shared experience and relations that atmospheres engender are tied to forms of laboring subjectivity, as the next section describes.

Construction's Kin (New Delhi, May–June 2010)

The summer before the Commonwealth Games sees a hectic pace of construction. The cityscape mutates as roads are dug up and repaved, new overpasses constructed, and bus stops completed. The Delhi Metro is under construction, and every day brings fresh heaps of gravel, stands of scaffolding, and machines. A Commonwealth Games Village grows on the banks of the river Yamuna, and laborers move in and out of the region, following work opportunities. I too travel in North and Northeast India, from Lucknow to Delhi and Gangtok to Indore, wanting to know more about India's urban change as I conduct preliminary fieldwork for my dissertation. NCR is the seat of construction activity for the region, I am told, where all the large decisions for small towns are made; it is where the headquarters of the developers and contractors and even the state ministers who make decisions are located, so I come to the city to investigate.

It is an unforgiving Delhi summer, potent with the dry heat that saps energy and water with equal intensity. One cannot walk—much less labor—for long in this weather. Yet workers dig and weld, cement and stack all around me as I walk the streets. The sudden sound and smell of water provides temporary relief and a source of joy only the thirsty can feel. I hear children laughing: Bandana and Rinki, two young girls, play on the side of the street as their mother washes dishes and bathes next to a small pipe pumping up water. This family, like many of those working on small-scale road construction, lives on the pavement next to the trenches they dig, and their home is a blue tarp tent supported by bamboo sticks.

The home is meager and bare, but their mother Heera knows her life priorities. "You should have children too," she advises me, perhaps knowing that the answer to my curiosity about her temporary home lies in an understanding of family; Bandana goes to a public school nearby, accessing a better education than the one available in the village. "Home is home, no matter how far you go," she says; you can live in a temporary state, by the side of a road, if it ensures long-term success or survival for your family.

Heera and her children are not the only ones living on the streets. As I move around the city, I hear machines backing up, dodge cascades of gravel, and am startled by loud crashes of falling metal. Workers remake the area, often living where they work. Architecture and infrastructure are no longer static and material objects but in a continuous process of transformation, one state forever morphing into a new one. Such was the dynamism of this scale of urban construction that everything and everyone seemed to be on the move. Ramesh, a mason working on an apartment building, describes the process: "We build huts (*jhuggis*) wherever we go. Wherever the work goes on, that is where we stay. Sometimes we are a hundred different men. We all come from different villages. We cook together and eat together. We break [down] our own homes and then move to the next worksite."

A hundred different people brought together through construction, eating together, living together, and working together, experiencing both the construction work on site as well as continuous displacement as they complete work. The breaking and constitution of materials, the dissolutions and concretizations, the movements and mediations—these conditions generate ephemeral atmospheres that comprise heightened aesthetic and affective states; atmospheres stimulate increased intimacies and emotions that forge social bonds. The temporality of construction—its physical demands, its surreptitious workings, and its urgencies—requires social networks and constructs social relations. The ephemeral builds kinship relations.

Kinship has long been a site of study for anthropologists, and South Asian studies have examined the agencies, contestations, and frictions that kinship networks produce.[17] Few authors, however, extend their consideration of kinship into business and agrarian development.[18] Ephemeral atmospheres deploy and facilitate a politics of kinship in two ways. First, ephemeral atmospheres of construction are part of what Kancha Ilaiah Shepherd calls a "casteization of capital," in that they replicate caste hierarchies and operate through caste-based affiliations and networks and are deployed to produce capital through the maintenance of caste hierarchies.[19] This effect is seen, for example, in the way that real estate developers populate their administration with kin members to keep profits in familial and community hands. Second, the proximities and atmospheres of labor on construction sites can also contribute to the formation of new social relations, constructing a relatedness through the intimacies and shared solidarities of work environments.[20] MD, for example, speaks fondly of many workers he has met on different sites and calls them and me on a regular basis to explore opportunities for work. The durability of kinship entangles with the ephemeral, as in both cases it is the ephemeral that feeds the strength of the durable. Ephemeral atmospheres facilitate the construction of social relations in order to accumulate capital; they provide cover for the construction and maintenance of hegemonic kin-based accumulation and thus are perpetuated by long-term kin relations; and they even harness the intimacies of kinship in labor solidarity and struggle.

Ephemeral atmospheres of construction, insofar as they facilitate political-economic power, are a site of caste dominance and struggle. Real estate, like other sectors of business in India, operates on strong kin relations and is for the most part dominant-caste and Hindu controlled. By using the terms *dominant-caste* and *non-dominant-caste*, I adopt Suraj Yengde's language and call to disown the upper-lower signifiers of caste, noting that this use isn't the same as M. N. Srinivas's use of the term, in which dominant caste represents a caste that is numerically strong in a village (such as Jats).[21] The bulk of developers, architects, and engineers, in construction, tend to be from dominant castes (Brahmin, Kshatriya, and Baniya), socially mobile castes, or religions with an affinity to Hinduism (e.g., Jain, Sikh). The bulk of construction laborers are from the Scheduled Castes and Tribes of India (SC and ST) or Other Backward Classes (OBC)—two governmental categorizations for affirmative action in India—many of whom prefer political self-identifications such as Dalit or Bahujan, Dalitbahujan, and Adivasi or Indigenous people. Historically, workers came from kin groupings such as Lohars (steelworkers), Sutars (woodworkers), Mistris (masons), Banjaras (nomadic tribe), and Kadiyas (masons); these groupings correspond to communities listed within the SC and ST or OBC categories, and many workers on site prefer to use their kin grouping.[22] The construction boom later expanded to include wider sections of Adivasi labor and more members of non-dominant-caste and Dalit communities.[23] Many of them are Muslim. Together, these groups constitute construction's force of laboring, sometimes landless workers.

Caste hierarchies in India form a complicated terrain, and changes to localized hierarchical relations occur through time as well as through infrastructures of social change such as affirmative action. While some laborers climb economic ladders to become small-time contractors and foremen themselves, the positions of site supervisor and construction manager are often reserved for individuals with engineering degrees or familial connections (often these are individuals from small-town, lower-middle-class backgrounds, yet who have greater caste privilege). The changing landscape of Hinduism and shifting trends in landownership, however, have challenged caste hierarchies and allowed for caste mobility.[24] In the context of Gurgaon, this is especially true in relationship to caste communities such as Jat and Ahir (understood as historically marginalized) landowners, who are often the majoritarian caste in their villages, whose kinship networks facilitated the growth of Gurgaon, and who gained political economic capital through the real estate boom. Sometimes, though, this caste mobility exacerbates caste hierarchies rather than eliminating them, as mobile castes strive to render themselves visible, often through additional discrimination or violence against Dalits and Adivasis.[25]

Ephemeral atmospheres—the stepped-up activity and constant material transformation, the speedy work, and mobile workers—facilitate kin-based networks of capital and shape caste positionalities in the political economy of urban development. Atmospheres help sustain accumulative oppressions and the dominant-caste face of Indian industries: vocal agitators are fired or moved to different sites, money is laundered or pilfered among social groups, and friends and kinspeople are given employment opportunities when work steps up. Ephemeral atmospheres harness kinship in construction work, highlighting the importance of kinship for infrastructural and urban development politics.

THE LABOR PROBLEM (MUMBAI, JULY 2003)

The monsoon has turned Mumbai green and cool, and I stick my head out of the train door as it speeds northward. I revel in the exhilarating experience of open space in one of the densest cities in the world. Urban spaces of the former island of Bombay unfold like a panorama as the train moves at a rapid pace through Mumbai's industrial core. It runs past the abandoned footprints of mill lands and factories. Tall skyscrapers under construction erase years of labor struggle and displacement, disorienting those who pass them. India's neoliberal economic reforms have been good to its real estate market; it is a fine time for architecture, and a fine time to be a new architect.

My architectural diploma is still fresh in my hand, but MD, though I do not know him yet, has already been a carpenter for five years now. He has rejected cement work as too grueling—it burned his hands and feet—and asked his uncle to teach him carpentry instead. He is married, has children, and has moved himself up the rungs of construction's production chain from being a helper to a skilled worker (*karigar*, lit. artisan). There are *karigars* on the site I am headed to supervise, but I don't know their names. My education never discussed the labor of producing architecture, and I am at a loss as to how to behave. Everything about this experience makes me feel alien and unprepared: moving from an education that emphasized urban and social change to a practice that designs spaces for the elite; talking to laborers who do not use the metric system I was trained in and instead use the language of *chauthai* and *chaudai*, inches and feet; arguing with older male contractors as a young woman and having my bag checked as I enter and exit the site, in case I steal; and giving instructions to carpenters who clearly know more than me, who were probably thinking what MD would say in anger years later: "If you didn't know, why didn't you just ask?"

This is the book I wish I had read in order to situate the architecture I was to practice and in order to better conceptualize my place and relations within it. Each chapter is a story of the construction industry that students are never told. The chapters of this book, following the stages of construction, depict the power and labor relations that shape urban architectural, infrastructural, and design work. It challenges architects and anthropologists to more carefully interrogate the politics of labor, unions, and industries often relegated to other disciplines.[26]

As an architecture student you are never taught to ask the people who belong to the communities you build in about what they want or to collaborate with the person building what you have designed. You are often unaware of the social histories—and presents—of the plot you draw upon, as well as the financial and production chains your work is a part of. You are the expert, the designer; the lines you draw upon a plan, the models you spend all night crafting, the clean walls and sleek marble floors are cathedrals of your own imagination constructed by invisible and unrecognized hands. Construction kills that purified imagination—as I found out while supervising elite spaces under construction, where wood splintered, designs failed, and aspirations fell through the communication gaps of a Bauhaus-inspired design education and familial lineages of labor. As we tried to concretize fluid forms and phantasmagorical designs in plywood, working with carpenters who had never constructed shapes like these before, design and construction turned into an exercise of mediation, of conversation, and of collectivity. As Peggy Deamer writes of architects, "we can only have a more fulfilling, less passive, and more disruptive role in capitalism if we don't think of construction and labor as conceptual 'others'" of architecture, and, I would add, embrace its production chains.[27]

Architecture's silence around its production chains is shared by anthropological studies of design. This exciting field of research on designers and the politics of design tends to neglect production chains and labor. This neglect is a form of violence: it erases the contributions of the working class to architecture and allied design fields. Ignoring labor politics also erases the diverse knowledge systems and exchange of knowledge that design relies upon, marginalizing non-dominant-caste or minoritarian knowledge in particular.[28] The detachment of construction from architecture is false and is a constructed division. As such, I present architecture, real estate, and construction as a site not of singular imagination and action but of entangled human and material collectivities—collectivities that do not lend importance to the fixed and the tangible in the masculine worlds of construction, but rather identify the importance of the ephemeral, the relational, and the intimate workings of construction worlds. I utilize ethnography as an embedded method that highlights the lived experiences of and power differentials between communities to bridge the gap between architectural/design training and the lived realities of construction work.

In *The Industrial Ephemeral*, I follow the people and pathways of construction in order to highlight the constitutive role of labor in the making of architecture and urban regions. The book's structure mimics the process of design and construction, beginning with surveying a region and understanding its social contexts, before moving to finance and money in construction, planning and design, and then following the stages of construction from excavation and commencement, to stepped-up activity, to concretization. The book, then, rewrites my own education in architecture and urbanism, embedding it in a larger labor chain and production process. Storytelling and language play a key role in my writing as a way to emphasize the experiences of those in construction. Through immersive storytelling in the main body of the book and theoretical discussions in the footnotes, I step back from the dominant style of analysis in contemporary anthropology.[29] For those who enjoy debates surrounding anthropological terms, the footnotes are for you.

THE INDUSTRIAL URBAN (MUMBAI, DECEMBER 2006)

I am driving home from Mumbai airport, excited to be back in the city of my childhood after six months away. The past year and a half have been a deep dive into urban and postcolonial theory, of reading about South Asian urbanism, but the texts and scholars are far from my mind today. Mumbai, the city of my childhood, wakes in its usual smog. I stick my head out into the iridescent dawn to take in the air. The density of the urban space aligns with the calibrations of human density my body is comfortable with, and I feel the rhythms of my body match the pulsations of the city.[30]

My drive takes me through central crossroads in Dharavi: the informal settlement turned poster child of developmental urbanism, and the talk of many architectural studios in the United States, is starting its day. I am reminded of the time I drove a herd of students from the United Kingdom around Mumbai; they kept pointing to buildings and asking if they were slums. No, I replied to each of their queries, amazed that they thought the whole city was a slum, amazed at their fascination with slums. Often referred to as the world's largest slum, Dharavi represented the temporary architectures of informal settlements. The early morning saw the road-facing storefronts of Dharavi open as pavement dwellers packed up their blankets to make space for the street traffic to come. The *chowk* (or crossing) was already starting to fill with laborers waiting to be hired for day work. The familiarity of this durable informal economy, however, was replaced with uncanniness as we passed by the former mill lands. Mammoth buildings towered over me, their gray concrete frames dominating the small streets we drove on. For years these working-class spaces had been a site of labor and urban struggle, as activists fought first against mill closures and later against the appropriation of lands for real estate. Large skyscrapers and office complexes had grown like aggressive weeds on the site of what once were stone and brick warehouses and green space. The surreal towers, built in the short time span of six months and rising out of the depths of narrow Mumbai streets, were, in their way, more transient than the durable Dharavi.[31]

Discussions of South Asian urbanism in the United States had thus far largely limited themselves to histories and informal settlements, and it is only in the next few years that writing on urban Indian infrastructure, redevelopment, and deindustrialization would emerge: a necessary push back against the representation that drove the constant search for slums among students in study abroad programs. Yet the scale and dominance of the towers felt like something had fallen through the gap—a new industry towered over me, yet none seemed to believe it existed. The fascination with informal spaces on the part of architectural studios swept the increasing impact and presence of transnational infrastructural capital under the carpet. The architectures and the real estate and construction industries that created them reshaped the landscape of ruro-urban India, yet none seemed to recognize the vitality of these operations as an industrial transformation of urbanism.

The construction industry is considered a top-ten industry in India.[32] It is the third largest employer in the country, providing jobs to more than forty-six million people.[33] Despite this scale, the operations of the construction industry are so piecemeal that it is not legible as an industry. This resonates with the changing face of industries as digital economies take over many an urban operation: rolling mills and smokestacks may be replaced by workers on the move, mobile applications, and dispersed production centers, but many of the same operating goals, treatment of labor, and profit margins remain. As big industries move out of cities and are replaced by service economies and informal labor, urban industries are still present—it is just that their look and feel is different.

An ephemeral form of the industrial shapes contemporary urbanism: its logics are erasure, displacement, rapid mobility, and precarity, and the construction industry is its most prominent face. The dynamic and sensory atmospheres of the ephemeral in construction distract from the industrial operations, accumulations, and labor struggles that accompany them. A spectrum of industrial struggles and opportunities is embedded in the ephemeral: from the refusal of people to be rendered ephemeral, to the role of the state in their displacement and migration, to spontaneous friendships and capital accumulations. The construction industry operationalizes the ephemeral in order to control the labor and profits of growing urban zones; it produces the industrial ephemeral.

The rising skyscrapers in Mumbai were not an anomaly but part of a boom in construction activity across Indian urban regions. The late 1990s and early 2000s were a period of rapid urbanization in India. A national debt crisis in the late 1980s forced the government to cut public funding and deregulate sectors to encourage foreign direct investment. The liberalization of sectors such as information technology, banking and finance, and pharmaceuticals brought about an exponential growth in gross domestic product (GDP), from $266.502 billion in 1991, to $478.965 billion in 2001, to $1.823 trillion in 2011, when I headed to NCR for fieldwork.[34] Urban growth was furthered by the relaxation of regulations on foreign private equity in real estate. These factors led to the rise of land financialization and speculative real estate and propelled the real estate sector.[35] In the North, the city of Gurgaon was already part of one of the world's fastest growing urban regions, and by 2012 the city's ruro-urban peripheries were a veritable large-scale construction site.[36] The urban area of Gurgaon district had expanded by approximately twelve times the size of the island of Manhattan from 2007 to 2012.[37] More broadly, the years from 1991 to 2011 had seen the addition of 160 million urban residents. More than sixty new airports and 417 special economic zones (SEZs) had sprung up across the subcontinent.[38] This was not a creeping informal urbanism, but sweeping private industry–led development that was part of a wave of change that moved 77 percent of India's wealth into the hands of 10 percent of its population.[39] The dynamic and the ephemeral are not only qualities of informal architectures in postcolonial worlds; they are also tools of global and national political economies.

I present a local story of a multinational real estate and construction industry and emphasize the ephemeral in the industrial: how a multimillion-dollar industry utilizes the ephemeral to perpetuate itself in one of the world's most populous nations. The real estate and construction industry is doubly embedded in industrial violence: it perpetuates the erasure and displacement of both workers and industries from fast-financializing land while propagating itself. I follow the construction industry in the wake of the 2008 Euro-American real estate crash and trace the movement of global real estate, investment, and construction firms into India, focusing not only on the operations of global capital through real estate but also on the sensibilities through which global real estate operates, the locales it necessitates, and the socialities and spatialities it has constructed in NCR.

GENDERED CONSTRUCTIONS (MUMBAI, 1986)

The material realities of construction first came into my dreams at six years old, buried in the profuse smell of cement and sawdust in my landscape architect mother's hair. If I have to trace the beginnings of my fieldwork in construction, they can be found in the site visits my sister and I took with our mother, playing with material samples and tools in her office after school, traveling to bungalows under renovation, and visiting gardens that were heaps of mud and stacks of stones waiting to be shaped.

MD and I are children of India's construction boom. Growing up at very different speeds and in very different societies that paved divergent life paths, we witnessed and participated in different dimensions of the last three decades of rapid urban growth and the formalization of the construction industry. We came into construction with different kin networks and constructed new connections as we moved through it. MD came into construction by going to live with his paternal uncle, who first got him a job in cement. MD's connections—family and friends—moved him from Bihar to Gujarat to Delhi and back, while mine brought me into Mumbai's construction sites. Urban India transformed at an unprecedented scale as MD and I grew older. The ephemeral atmospheres that we came of age in were the site of an intimate reworking of society: construction came to govern the life experiences of forty-six million workers and their families, including MD's and mine.[40] The churnings, transformations, and rapid urban change facilitated by construction between the 1990s and the period of my fieldwork allowed bodies and behaviors to be disciplined and controlled, forged social and familial bonds, and embedded us all in a web of unequal social relations. Ephemeral atmospheres are intimate and affective. Herein lies their power.

Construction in India, especially NCR, is understood as a male-dominated field. In the classic divisions of studying labor, production was considered a masculine realm and reproduction a femme one, effectively dividing the spheres of work and home.[41] The contributions of scholars of feminist and queer studies to urban political economy and political ecology have been central to muddling this binary; authors have studied domestic concepts such as kinship, intimacy, and affect, drawing them into the spheres of production, labor, and work.[42] This has served to deconstruct and blur the gendered binary of labor and industrial studies. This holds even more true in construction as the work often means building someone's home. The social relations that are produced within the sphere of the home are present and at play in the dimensions of real estate work; there are no stark divisions between domesticity and industry. By studying the ephemeral and nonenduring, the intimate and affective, I deconstruct the masculinity of the industry and challenge the boundaries between home and work. I take a political ecological lens to the study of the construction industry. This highlights femme concepts such as kinship, intimacy, affect, and atmospherics, exploring how they work within production chains.[43] Ephemeral atmospheres are intimate and feminized in the sense that they create social relations and govern and control intimate aspects of the self and society such as love, behavior, and desire; they draw kinship into capitalism and collapse the spheres of home and work. In drawing on these intellectual threads, my work is indebted to scholars of women, gender, and sexuality studies in anthropology and political ecology.

At the same time, this stance on gender relations is also a personal reminder that construction and maternal love are, for me, intertwined. I was born into construction—indeed, perhaps experienced construction, like the many children I met on sites, in a prenatal stage, seeing, hearing, and absorbing the materials of construction through my mother's blood, smelling them in her hair as she put me to bed each night. The smell of sawdust and cement in my mother's hair orients me toward the delicate and inconspicuous intimacies that construction works through. A transitory moment of materials mingling with the body, occupying the intersubjective space between mother and daughter—this moment embeds the labors of her day, the labors of her night, and the interdependencies and entanglements construction demands. It marks a political economy of construction, one that performs an intimacy so hard to articulate yet profoundly felt. One that embeds our angers, anxieties, and loves within the transforming environments around us and is ripe with kin-based love. It is a reminder of the workers and women erased from the histories of Indian construction and lingers thirty years later as a reminder to look, smell, and listen for invisible durabilities within the ephemeral atmospheres of construction.

1   Ephemeral Infrastructures

AT HOME ON THE ROAD

The Indian National Highway 8 (NH8, now renamed NH48) is an expansive length of highway that leads out of India's NCR toward Jaipur, the capital of the state of Rajasthan. Beginning near Delhi's diplomatic enclave—Chanakyapuri—the highway runs past the capital city's international airport and through the city-suburb of Gurgaon (renamed Gurugram) into the state of Rajasthan, from which it moves into Gujarat. The highway rose to prominence in 2012 when the NH8 became part of the Delhi-Mumbai Industrial Corridor (DMIC), a $90 billion infrastructural endeavor that spans 1,483 kilometers.[1] The construction vision of the DMIC includes plans for industrial townships and heavy industries, a high-speed freight line, three ports, six airports, a six-lane intersection-free expressway, and a 4,000 MW power plant.[2]

The sheer size and scale of the DMIC proposal indexes the triumph of the Indian road as the public-private pathway (literal and metaphorical) to India's developmental vision. If during the colonial era railways in India formed the infrastructural intervention of social progress, in the late twentieth century this responsibility shifted onto the infrastructural shoulders

23

of Indian roads.[3] While railroads serve as important channels of migration, as the DMIC proposal outlines, road infrastructures are accompanied by large-scale construction visions, building not only highways but also planned commercial projects, industrial zones, and residences along them.

How does infrastructural construction shape the sociality and spatiality of a region and affect the lives of those who build it? Durable road infrastructures, I argue, are formed by an ephemeral core, a core that is the primary site of class, caste, religious, and gender struggle. This ephemeral core is produced through the industrial workings of construction. The construction industry relies on and perpetuates a social and physical ephemeral. A social ephemeral is understood as the affects and relations between people and the circulation and erasure of a labor force, and a physical ephemeral is understood as the transformation of land, architecture, infrastructure, and ecology, keeping in mind that the social and material are not separate but entangled processes. Building on conversations of materiality of infrastructures in anthropology that view infrastructure as a "a social-material assemblage," I demonstrate that ephemeral workings such as erasures, material conversions, conjurings, and atmospherics form an important dimension of materiality and play a vital role in the politics of infrastructures.[4]

The chapter presents a brief overview of the region, the construction industry, and its people. This overview format resonates with the first stage of construction processes known as site survey, wherein engineers, architects, and developers will examine a region to understand both terrain, infrastructural connections, and social life. At the same time, I introduce different forms of the ephemeral in the construction industry that appear across the book. State actors enact an ephemeral through the withdrawal of state support in strategic spaces, thus creating conditions of economic precarity. Transforming material and aesthetic states, ecologies, and atmospheres can be viewed as instances of the ephemeral that allow social and political relations to be reshaped. The ephemeral manifests in the dematerialization of land into capital and property and drives real estate speculation. The deliberate mobility and displacement of people in construction is an ephemeral that is both aspirational and exclusionary. Construction is accompanied by ephemeral affective states that shape subjectivity and social relations.

Figure 4. Unfinished road in Gurgaon district, 2012. Photo by author.

By focusing on the construction of infrastructure and the social constructions that infrastructure stimulates, I present how a privatized construction industry deploys the ephemeral in the politics of urban development.
Unlike studies in anthropology that examine the complexity of state-society
relations that surround infrastructures, I emphasize the role of private
operators in the urban and infrastructural development of India.[5] While the
state does loom large in construction, the decades since the 1990s have seen
a deliberate rescinding of the Indian state from infrastructural construction
and key sectors of governance related to it, such as labor welfare. This has
allowed for the traction and growth of a privatized construction industry
that governs the social and spatial landscapes of urban India.

A DISAPPEARING STATE

It is 8:00 a.m. on a cold January morning. Neelkanth Sir (a retired planner) and I are driving along the NH8. The winter's cold has brought about
a dense fog that does not deter Neelkanth Sir as he steps on the gas. The
world around us accelerates. Dust-covered factory sheds and half-built
private housing complexes appear and disappear in a sequenced haze. A
plot of telephone towers rises like a field of metallic stalks from the fog. The
fairy lights of yellow *sharab-theka* shops (liquor shops) twinkle through

the smog, and ghostly tendrils of the dissipating fog weave through the wheat fields. Neelkanth Sir drives me to an industrial estate on the NH8. He wants to show me what planned development in the region looks like, and the area we pull up to is one he helped plan.

The industrial estate is a large stretch of land adjacent to the NH8, and we drive into its quiet streets. Large gridded roads and accompanying infrastructure indicate that the space is state controlled.[6] The strong planning gesture, however, has had strange results; I am surprised to see no factories or buildings but only barren land. The rectangular plots are empty, save signposts stating warnings not to trespass. Crops grow in the building plots. The estate is a ghost town.

The Haryana State Industrial and Infrastructure Development Corporation Limited (HSIIDC) developed this industrial estate, as well as many others along the NH8. The HSIIDC is a parastatal organization that envisions projects, acquires land for them, takes responsibility for the infrastructural development of the land, and controls the bidding or allocation processes for companies. Often the HSIIDC also defines the nature of the industrial estate and accompanying township (e.g., car city, leather city) and reserves a greater percentage of land for select industries. As we drive through the industrial estate with no industries, however, I am reminded that many consider parastatals public entities that act in private interests; parastatals are accused of supporting corporate rather than citizen interests. This sentiment extends to the widespread belief among construction workers about the inconsistency of state welfare and regulatory protections. The life stories of Yusef, Ahmed, and Chandra describe how the contemporary state creates an ephemeral presence: it selectively extracts itself from public protections while exerting its power in other arenas, opening avenues for privatized development.

The life history of Haryana town planner Yusef is an example of state welfare in the years before privatization. A fifty-year-old Muslim man, Yusef enjoys a comfortable post in the Department of Town and Country Planning in Haryana. I interview him in his home, a two-story bungalow, filled with plants Yusef cares for. His early childhood, he narrates, was structured by landlessness, agriculture, and India's educational and land reform policies. His two daughters move through the bungalow, playing, as he talks about his life.

"I was born in Rajasthan. My *mummy* and *papa* were uneducated landless laborers," Yusef reminds me that his middle-class life had humble beginnings. Yusef's father was bullied out of his share of ancestral land by Yusef's uncle, and the family was forced to migrate to Yusef's mother's village. Schooling was important to Yusef's mother, and she insisted her two sons be educated; the two brothers enrolled in public school. As Yusef grew older he helped bolster family income through sharecropping and other forms of manual labor; due to this he struggled to stay in school. He worked in brick kilns with his family one summer: "The conditions were not conducive there. And I was a child. For five to seven days, I fell ill. But then I thought we have to work hard. . . . So very good, the highest amount one lakh five thousand bricks were made by us—the full family."

The family struggled in absolute poverty until a government scheme for landless laborers gave Yusef's father 5 *bhigas* (approximately 3 acres) of land in the early 1970s. This stability was, however, short-lived, as Yusef's father passed away from a snake bite in 1976, shifting responsibility onto the shoulders of the schoolgoing brothers. Once again Yusef struggled to make ends meet. "I was a laborer lifting stones for one rupee a day. But I ran off after half a day. I bought a few vegetables and started selling them in the market. After that I started selling ice candy." Yusef and his brother did odds jobs to keep the family afloat and stay in school. Well-meaning educators stepped in and paid Yusef's school fees in the ninth grade and bought him a uniform. "That was the turning point. In the tenth grade I was thirteenth in the state. . . . I got a fellowship to go to college. I used to send money home and pay for instruments [tools] for the fields."

Yusef's intelligence, and the social and state structures around him, served him well. He got a degree in geography and was offered a scholarship to the Centre for Environmental Planning and Technology in Ahmedabad. He supported his family with his scholarship money, returned to Haryana to take the state exam for planners, and entered the state's town planning department. State-led land reforms, technological subsidies, and educational scholarships moved a landless Yusef into middle-class comfort.

The pathways the state constructed for Yusef are different in contemporary times. Younger site workers argue that the many scenarios of economic mobility provided through state aid require equal amounts of financial investment and social capital (though Yusef too had a degree of social capital). Workers complain that they need to bribe officials to get into the army, to gain governmental jobs such as those of schoolteachers, to access developmental funds, and to work for projects initiated under the Mahatma Gandhi National Rural Employment Guarantee Act (NREGA).[7] In contrast now, the private sector emerges as a new pathway to social mobility. Workers believe that learning skills on construction sites and making contacts will help them move up the economic ladder faster. They see the new technologies brought in by private companies as something that will pave their way to economic mobility; private companies tend to have greater budgets and a transnational presence, allowing them to be equipment-heavy construction firms. This allows companies to become a pathway of economic mobility where English, skilling (construction training), and technological prowess hold force. The rise of the private sector has seen a replacement of state support with a mobile, entrepreneurial dream. The ephemeral manifests as the rescinding of state welfare, tossing workers into the vagaries of privatization, ensuring the marginalization of some and success of others, as Ahmed and Chandra's stories depict.

In the contemporary construction industry, road construction has moved from state built (from the 1950s to 1990s) to public-private partnerships (PPP) and privatized management. Special state parastatals, created to build highways, hand over build-operate-transfer (BOT) contracts to infrastructural firms. Infrastructural firms are given development rights for tracts of land along the highway as incentives. The mega-scale brings an influx of multinational construction firms and technologies. Important highways in India are now built with advanced technological equipment that can construct four to five kilometers per day. These machines create concrete roads far more durable than the traditional bitumen ones. Some new expressways between cities are built with paver technology. In this construction process, concrete is cast in 3.5–3.74-meter by 7-meter (or custom-sized) blocks. A machine guides the layout out of concrete and is continuous in motion. The concrete is smoothened on site with the help of guide rails and sensors to ensure the mix falls into place at the right angles, heights, and curvatures. This creates a seamless and smooth highway where technology controls the levels and path of the road, as well as facilitating a higher speed of construction. The technology, known as "slip-form pavers," produces new highways at a faster pace.

Ahmed is a tremix contractor on the Wandering Woods site and a vocal proponent of privatization. Ahmed's generation cannot rely on the public supports that Yusef had, but learning new technologies gave Ahmed a step up in life. Tremixing is a form of casting concrete floors that allows them to harden in far more durable ways than ordinary casting processes. The resultant floors are ideal for heavy-use spaces such as factory floors and parking garages. Floors are cast in bays of 2 by 2 meters, and a machine sucks the water out of them to quickly cure and harden them with the help of additional chemical applications.

Ahmed stands apart from other workers; he is always exceptionally well-dressed for someone who works with cement-concrete. His usual dress code consists of ironed shirts and clean blue jeans. He sits by the side of the square panel under concretization and supervises his staff as they pour concrete and even it out. He then removes his own shirt, lays it on cement bags nearby, and rolls up his jeans before he gets to work. He swooshes an aluminum bar (*fanti*) across the concrete to level its surface and attaches the tremix cloth and pump to the finished panel. One day, after much cajoling, he tells me of his experiences. His class category reads very differently from other workers', and so I am taken aback when he tells me he has very little education.[8]

Ahmed's father is a tailor in their village, and he is one of eight children: five sons and three daughters. A landless, non-dominant-caste tailor, Ahmed's father could barely make enough to feed them all. As Ahmed describes it, this financial pressure left his father ill and stressed (*pareshani*), and the elder, male children stepped in to help. Ahmed's elder brother was the first to leave their village in the tribal areas of the new state of Chhattisgarh; he became a mason in Gurgaon. Ahmed speaks of the family's absolute poverty: he worked the fields from 6:00 a.m. to 9:00 a.m. before school but eventually was too ashamed to go to school because of his lack of clothes. "I did not have clothes to wear. I used to go to school in only underwear or torn shorts. . . . I did not have a decent notebook, or pen, or a pencil. At that time a pencil cost 10–25 paisa. I did not even have that."

The constant beatings he received at school and his lack of clothes, books, and tools eventually took their toll. Ahmed stopped going, in an act of shame and rebellion. After he "roamed" around in the village for a few years, his family encouraged him to join his brother. He came to Gurgaon.

"For two, three months, I just looked and roamed around, and then went back to the village. Then I came back from the village and slowly, slowly learnt." He found the work to be "OK" (*theek*). His brother taught him a mason's work bit by bit. He would correct Ahmed on the proper usage of tools. Sometimes he would stop working on a project and ask Ahmed to take over. "After six months I said that I want to work on my own." Ahmed went to Chandigarh and on from Chandigarh to Varnala. He used his kinship networks and moved through information gained from friends and acquaintances. He received his first contract job to tremix a power plant. He got himself two helpers to work for him. Confident from that experience, he returned to Delhi and asked his brother to buy him a tremix machine. They borrowed money from family and friends, looked for a cheap machine, cajoled a dealer for a discount, and bought one. He has been working on his own since; that was in 2003.

Smart and quick-witted, Ahmed has an opinion on everything. He derides public schools and hospitals, critiques class hierarchies in India, and dreams of leaving the city and returning to his village. "I will open some small business of my own." Ahmed describes his plan to me: "I will live on my own terms/will, so that there is no pressure on me. . . . Invest one or 1.5 lakhs [about $2,250] and start a gift item or clothes store that sells shoes, jeans, and things." Store or not, Ahmed and his brother have done well by their family. They educated their younger brothers, who also became masons; they rebuilt their mud house in the village into a seven-room, brick and mortar home; and they paid the marriage expenses of two sisters and are sending the youngest to college. The once-shirtless young boy now says that he cannot wear unironed clothes.

Ahmed's narrations stand apart from Yusef's in terms of state presence. A steady stream of governmental schemes supported Yusef's career trajectory. State-sponsored schemes—land distribution, scholarship programs, and agrarian technological subsidies—provided a support structure. These state-led mobilities are now fading. Years later, a much younger Ahmed struggles. Entrepreneurialism runs high and state support conscribes individuals to rural locations, lending funds to construct a home toilet, providing temporary work in the area, and offering agrarian subsidies. Ahmed's narrations convey a distrust of public services and faith in private technological development; they highlight individual entrepreneurialism and kin networks.[9] This is paralleled by the shift into PPPs in road development. As workers move back and forth on the roads, their faith in and support of India's shifting grid of state support diminishes. A faith in state support is replaced by a growing faith in the private technological realm. The irony of infrastructure is that its contemporary construction represents the receding of state presence and increasing reliance on privatized development, development that may have improved Ahmed's life but proved difficult for those such as Chandra, for all roads are not created the same.

Driving through a village on the eastern periphery of Gurgaon, we see state infrastructure decay. Sir and I find the road undrivable: the car bogs down in sludge dissolved by the pouring rain. I get out, and Sir asks me to step aside, before asking a few men sitting on the threshold of a local store to give the car a boost onto sturdier ground. The men step up and heave. Their practiced behavior reminds me that specific communities have benefited from the making of roads and others have not. The back roads of the NH8 move through tiny villages that dot the landscape around Gurgaon. Mirroring the state jurisdictional boundaries, the roads in the village stand in contrast to the NH8. They are made of a mixture of mud and sand, and they expand and shrink with the seasons. Roads are often so muddy that repeat tire tracks have transformed the center of the road into a series of solidified waves, parallel crests, and troughs of mud. At other points the desert sand envelops the road and erases the thinning asphalt from sight.

Road networks, while appearing continuous, are in reality piecemeal and broken into jurisdictional components. The NH8 is part of several interstate highways constructed and controlled by the National Highway Authority of India (NHAI). The NHAI constructs national highways, but its jurisdiction often overlaps with several other authorities. Each urban local body (ULB) or municipal council is responsible for road construction and maintenance in its own urban area; for example, parts of the NH8 that pass through Gurgaon are subject to the jurisdiction of the Gurgaon Municipal Corporation (now Municipal Corporation of Gurugram). Regional development authorities or authorities for SEZs— airports, sugarcane production, or irrigation—build roads in the areas under their jurisdiction. In some cases, a special authority is created to build specific highways. This is the case for the DMIC. Unless they fall under one of these authorities, villages and towns are responsible for their own roads. Jurisdictions overlap, and construction failures often involve an incessant game of shifting responsibility across the various authorities. The movement of individuals across geographies produces similar elisions of responsibility, an institutional story Chandra is well acquainted with.

The medical camp at Wandering Woods operates once a week, and I meet Chandra among the line of workers waiting to see the doctor. I sit in the clinic, invited there by site supervisors, who show me the company initiatives. Chandra comes to the doctor with a forearm bandaged with a grubby bandage. He waits his turn, in the dingy space, as the doctor moves through the laborers in line. In broken Bangla, I ask Chandra where he is from, and he identifies himself as a Malda worker. A tiny district of Bengal that borders Bangladesh, Malda is a catchall space where Indigenous populations and minority communities coalesce to find work in north India. Labor contractors channel them toward cities. Chandra tells me that he heard that they gave you work in Malda, so he went there with some friends. He arrived in Delhi on a train with thirty-odd workers and was assigned to work here for three months. He is twenty years old, if that, and says he works in the fields when he does not do construction work. Uneducated, he also lacks Hindi speaking skills and is hired as a manual laborer on site. He does *helperi* (helper) work: mixes concrete, carries things, shovels, and cleans.

The doctor sees Chandra for all of two minutes. He records his name and his age, prescribes Combiflam, an anti-inflammatory pill, and recommends his fracture for further investigation. The instructions are written in English, a language that Chandra does not understand. When I ask his supervisor what will happen to Chandra's hand, he says that they are not required to treat it, as the fracture did not happen on the site. "If they get injured at work they come running; they are very clever that way."

Just as roads like the NH8 are subject to multiple jurisdictions, people too have spatial affiliations that circumscribe their political and social positionality. Chandra's citizenship and political rights are only recognized in the areas he travels from. As a temporary out-of-state worker living in a temporary labor camp (the name for temporary worker housing on site, as opposed to a semilegalized informal settlement or *jhuggi-jhopdi*), Chandra has no voting rights in Gurgaon, no political support, and no backing from locals, who cannot meet and get to know him within the time of his ninety-day contract. The site and camp division too shape his experience: illnesses and injuries not occurring on site are not required to be treated by his employer. Being injured in the temporary settlement provided to workers, as Ahmed was once, does not allow a worker access to employer-provided treatment, as it is not a work-related injury. The state operates through geographic conscription insisting on the stability of spaces, the boundaries of which are challenged and dissolved by road and rail infrastructures and those who travel on them.[10] State authorities allow migrants to fall through the cracks.

For several who stand in line at the medical camp with Chandra, roads have been harsh. The chronic diseases they carry in their bodies (as the doctor describes)—asthma, rheumatoid arthritis, tuberculosis, low immune systems, and skin infections—are compiled effects. They represent people deprived of nutrients throughout a life of poverty and years of work in difficult environments. They carry home these chronic diseases, often adding bronchial diseases, cancer, STDs, and liver cirrhosis to the mix. The shifting mobilities of a life on the road in construction do not allow Chandra a chance to make his historical and political claim in the area that he helps build.

The ephemeral nature of state support gives rise to a migratory population as more individuals look to supplement their meager agricultural incomes through labor in aggressive construction markets. The life stories of Yusef, Ahmed, and Chandra describe the removal of state support from certain aspects of social welfare. Faith in public services falls as entrepreneurialism is emphasized. Individuals leave home to look for lucrative work. This mobility allows multiple jurisdictions to evade responsibility for worker well-being, simply by claiming it is the responsibility of another authority. Roads expand forms of connectivity and bring social mobility for some but also bring exploitation and violence upon many as they move across districts and states. The ephemeral manifests in the strategic withdrawal of state support and the creation of a minority citizenry in a state of being forever on the road.

THE RISE OF PRIVATE INFRASTRUCTURES

Traffic slows down and gathers as Neelkanth Sir and I drive onto the NH8 one morning. Smoke and loud sounds ahead signal that the road is under construction. A yellow steamroller, turned a dust-covered mustard, urges itself up onto the sloped-mud embankment meant for the new road. Puffs of dust rise as the steamroller's heavy barrel compacts the layers of earth and stone into a new foundation. Up ahead workers pour asphalt on the already consolidated parts. The acrid smell of fresh tar wafts up from the still-warm and gleaming jet-black surface.

Asphalt construction is a popular road technology in urban India due to its speed and low requirements in terms of costs and skill of construction. It begins with a soil engineer conducting a CBR (California bearing ratio) test to determine the existing strength of the soil. The thrust of the soil and materials for the road are calculated on the basis of the results. Workers mound and tamp the existing soil and raise the road level above the surrounding area to safeguard against floods. Additional soil and stone are added to marshy areas. Installing pipes through the embankment and configuring slopes ensure adequate water drainage. This forms the subbase, on top of which is laid the base layer. The base layer, known as a "metalled layer," is thirty to fifty centimeters deep. It consists of small stone aggregates that are crushed and compacted. Compaction or vibration rollers are dragged over this layer to give it strength. The final layer is a bitumen layer, which fills the voids between the base layers and is further compacted and rolled down.

This is not the first nor the last layer to be added to the NH8. The road itself is a product of a longer transnational history that involved both large-scale infrastructural development and small-scale repair work. The construction history of Indian roads can be traced to the reign of the Mauryas in the early seventh century.[11] Arterial corridors laid down by Guptas, Sher Shah Suri, Mughals, and the British were successive overlays upon these ancient roads.[12] The NH8, from Delhi to Jaipur, forms part of a historic path that connects two ancient capitals of India to each other. It has seen metalled layer work from the British, the asphalt of post independence, and the contemporary processes of concretization. Roundabouts and overpasses have been added to its linear path, and new connectors flow from its grand, trunked body.

Like the puffs of smoke ahead of us, each new road and stage of construction brings with it a different atmosphere. At times mounds of mud and their dispersal will create an atmosphere of haze, only to be destroyed by the weight of water sprinkled to settle the mud. At others the heat and smell of tar will rise to be gradually tamed by the movements of the roller. These atmospheres of road construction are not just moments of transience that result in infrastructures but are sites of constitution of the construction industry. As the material environments of the NH8 transform, they also enable the social mobility of some groups and increase precarity for others. In the processes of making lie the making and remaking of kin relations that drive the expansion of the industry.

Infrastructural development jump-started India's real estate industry as it built expertise, brought equipment, and lowered costs of construction. As an independent India sought to increase its infrastructural capabilities, building dams, industries, electric lines, railways, and then roads, it brought groups together, created friendships, and consolidated kin relations. From the construction sites and planning offices rose a networked conglomerate of dominant-caste developers and contractors with close personal ties. Prominent among them was the Baniya caste, a trading caste that many industrialists draw from; Pran Singh's family forms an example.

Singh's father was one of the first large-scale building services contractors in postcolonial North India. The firm, set up almost fifty years ago, has several offices across the country. I visit their large five-storied Delhi office, where an expansive, open-floor plan and spiraling stairwell greet me as I enter. I walk to Singh's office on the top floor. The floors are filled with more than one hundred staff members, working on, as I would come to realize, the biggest development projects in the region.

"I did my civil engineering and completed in [1981] and as soon as I completed my engineering I joined the company. Me and my brothers run the company." Mr. Singh talks to me about his family business. In 1977, Singh recalls, his father had contracts across India, including in the states of Maharashtra and Jammu and Kashmir. Their presence in construction prior to India's real estate boom gave the contracting company an advantage as the sector grew. The firm had long-established friendships with several prominent developers; the companies grew in tandem.

Singh and his brothers were educated as engineers and took over their father's business. The brothers split the business a few years earlier, but their combined teams service the portfolios of prominent developers in the region. The brothers now run some of the most powerful services firms in India. "Our business has grown up so we do not face any challenges anymore. People get the challenges from us," boasts Pran Singh. The next generation builds new branches for the family business. I meet Kiran, a nephew who became an architect and started his own firm. The walls of his office are full of plans for hotels, airports, and public parks. Photos of him with big-name developers and leaders hang next to pictures of the elaborate architecture his firm designs. The colorful drawings and congenial photographs act as reminders of the social networks of familial construction conglomerates in India.

Several of NCR's large-scale contracting, engineering, architectural, and developer firms shared the road to economic success; their paths and businesses grew with each new construction site. As sites expanded, so too did family-led firms that added more kin to the ranks. Younger generations expanded the industry: contractors trained architect sons, and informal money lenders produced developer children. New sites and connections spawned a series of contracting, architectural, engineering, and developer businesses who made friends and strengthened their dominant-caste networks, with notable exceptions. This sociality, while ephemeral—as it is set up by fleeting encounters, personal favors, and temporary work contracts—creates a durable but transforming social infrastructure of people, and these networks emerge in local populations, too.

Drive past the patchwork of industries and apartments under construction and past the toll-booth on the NH8, and you will drive through the town of Virgaon. This area was once a village but is now a town. Two- and three-story structures front the highway, their façades painted blue, yellow, green, and bright red with signs in bold type that advertise cell phones, money transfers, Coca Cola, dentists, and cures for sexually transmitted diseases. Small cement and brick shops sit next to restaurants that serve hot *roti-sabzi*; plastic garbage and discarded waste from packed goods are piled on the streets; and cows, dogs, and goats roam free among the people, who motorbike, bicycle, drive, or walk through the narrow, muddy streets.

The mess surrounding Virgaon indexes not urban decay but rapid transformation and speculative land economies. Virgaon is a rich and fast-urbanizing village due to its location on the NH8. The farmlands of Virgaon were sold to the HSIIDC or to real estate developers years ago; the HSIIDC built an industrial estate on the NH8, while developers constructed apartment complexes to provide housing for nearby industries. Several landowning families made good money, and a few invested this in apartments in the area, land farther down the highway, or near villages of their kin.

Neelkanth Sir is a Virgaon man. He was born and raised in this village. A son of a farmer with several siblings, Sir is from the Ahir caste. Ahirs once owned the majority of land in Gurgaon, in contradistinction to the rest of Haryana, where much of the land was owned by the Jats.[13] The Ahir community trace their ancestry to Krishna and make proud claims that their clan was adopted by the Hindu God after the mythical battle of the Mahabharata. Their traditional occupation was cowherding, but they are recorded as historical cultivators in the region.[14] Many Ahirs pride themselves on their dairy consumption and vegetarianism.

Sir's family farmlands were sold to the Haryana Urban Development Authority (HUDA) years ago, but his ancestral home in the village still remains. He is the youngest son in his family and was educated by his brothers, who remained farmers. Unlike them, but with their help, he won scholarships to Delhi's premier university—Jawaharlal Nehru University—to study geography and later went to the prestigious School of Planning and Architecture (SPA) to study planning. Appointed planner in the Department of Town and Country Planning, Neelkanth Sir has not just planned urban areas for the state of Haryana; his career has changed the social and material future of his kinship network.

Neelkanth Sir's trousers and shirts contrast with the kurta-pajamas of his brothers, and the extended family often gives him a hard time for succeeding but not helping them enough, as Neelkanth Sir has benefited from the roads in and out of Gurgaon. Over the years he has crafted a network of individuals—academics, planners, ministers, lawyers, brokers, farmers—mobilized through his professional and kinship ties. Through his urban development and agrarian network, Neelkanth Sir says, he helps his nephews' and family friends' economic prospects. Several of his family members run construction equipment businesses. One nephew works as a watchman for a housing complex built on village land, while another runs a car-parts business. Some relatives work as facilitators for developers or real estate brokers and mimic Sir's drives across the region. On an average day, Sir moves across Gurgaon meeting with people, he facilitates connections (as he did for me), and his phone rings with people asking for advice: where to buy property, how to transfer property, or how to acquire permissions for construction. Through his family, friends, and acquaintances, and his movements around Gurgaon, he forges new kin and construction connections for the region.

If the friendships of NCR's construction elites and their political ties enable the policy changes and planning of infrastructure and real estate, then the networks of individuals such as Neelkanth Sir form the armatures for land acquisition and construction. Their life pathways involve brokering across the social worlds they are embedded in and mediating disparate personal, corporate, and bureaucratic terrains. It is locals who enable piecemeal land acquisitions and convince farmers to buy and sell land, settle land disputes, and appease local politicians. Their histories of connection to the land, as well as their kin networks, allow them to navigate the complex terrain of landownership, jumbled land records, and layered bureaucracies to gain economic mobility themselves. Resonant yet differential forms of social networks also extend among the construction workers who build roads and real estate.

I meet Mahaab and Mohamed, a young mason and helper couple, on a small construction site in NCR. Mahaab and Mohamed are from West Bengal and arrive in NCR through Mahaab's parents. Theirs is a family of masons, and each son learned the trade from his parents. During the 2000s construction boom Mahaab and Mohamed, now married and well established in NCR, bring their acquaintances to sites. They are joined on site by two families from nearby villages, allowing them not only to serve as masons and helpers on site but also to contract for small work. Now acting as the principal masonry team on a small-scale construction site, Mahaab and Mohamed receive accolades and higher pay for their ability to supply labor to construction sites. Mahaab's parents work on a site in Dwarka, New Delhi, and the young couple keep their network alive by moving across sites on rare days off to meet with her parents and other masons. Mahaab's and Mohamed's social connections expand to enable the growth of infrastructure and real estate. Their changing networks grow the region materially and spatially.

Networks hold true for architect-anthropologists as well. It is 2001, and I sit on the *katta* (platform) of the Sir J.J. College of Architecture workshop.

It is around three in the afternoon, and classes on the art and design campus are winding down. The boys working in the canteen run cups of *chai* and *missal pao* to the students who lounge out front. Twenty years later, our life paths will lead us in different directions within the fields of architecture and design: two of us will move to the West and East coasts of the United States to do PhDs in anthropology and design technologies, while others will work for developers and be the project managers of some of the largest towers on Mumbai's skyline. Some will start their own firms and development ventures, while others will go to business school and join the entrepreneurial digital economies of construction. Today, as I meet the people who sat on the *katta* with me, I think of my own research, produced from my own networks. My fieldwork began with meeting friends of friends who introduced me to their friends. These connections from friends and mentors in both India and the United States, substituting the enunciation of anthropology student for the qualification of architect, as well as the Harvard University name, opened and produced networks that grew this book. Growing up with an architect not only made me comfortable with the language of construction but also created the uncanny association of construction sites with maternal love, lending me comfort in spaces where middle-class women rarely appear. My landscape-architect mother draws my own kinship networks into my career path, making me the daughter who learned about the politics of construction through her mother's work.[15]

To dwell in the processes of constructing infrastructure is to understand that these conditions of heightened temporality are also the site of transforming social relations. Within the rapping of the drill, the smell of hot tar, and the stacking of metal pipes grow intangible, social solidarities and fractures. While kinship relations, in particular those of caste, are durable, construction binds a temporality to them. It allows for quicker friendships and abets the creation of temporary family and friends, some of which dissipate once work ends. Other social relations become durable through ephemeral atmospheres and spur construction work. Infrastructure then is produced through the play of the ephemeral and durable. A road might exist as a permanent line on a map but is under constant construction and reconstructs social relations: road construction is grounded in the ephemeral, where the shifting space of construction and the kin relations they make grow private infrastructure and real estate.[16]

THE SHIFTING STATES OF PEOPLE AND PROPERTY

The Kundli Manesar Palwal (KMP) expressway runs through Gurgaon district and cuts perpendicular to the NH8. The NCR transportation master plan proposed the KMP expressway as a ring road around the entire footprint of NCR. Only part of it was approved and constructed. The bypass is designed to divert traffic toward Punjab and Himachal Pradesh. The expressway has been in the news; it was scheduled to be completed over a year ago.

The KMP intersects the NH8 as an elevated highway, and Sir and I drive to access it. Sir tells me this area is formed from five villages, and each has its separate *panchayats* (village governing councils). There are fields and small shops around us. Once in awhile we pass a set of small shanties with villagers sitting around offering chai and other services. A group of old men (often village elders) sit at the intersection (*chaupal*) smoking hookah, their heads swathed in the loose, white, turbaned style classic of local Haryanavis. An aunty will occasionally join them, spreading her skirted *theel* (*thel*) wide as she leans into the hookah, claiming her own social authority. Some of them yell "Ram Ram" to Sir, and he holds his hand out of the window to hail them.

The KMP rises a good four to five meters above the NH8. Neelkanth Sir and I head up a dirt road that will be a ramp for the KMP. The car struggles; I hear its wheels scrape and slide, but we make it onto the concrete surface to investigate. The KMP is in various stages of completion. Parts of it already have a concrete floor, while some stretches consist of tamped-down mud. We drive across loose gravel, which hits the bottom of the car in a continuous, ossified shower. We come to a bridge that is concrete and finished. Its connection to the rest of the road, however, is a set of open steel bars that cause the car to jump as we drive. An occasional motorcyclist passes us. Sir tells me that the expressway is supposed to be a bypass, but the government has proposed eleven "theme townships" along the expressway. These include an education city, a world trade center city, a fashion city, a leisure city, and a leather city. So many cities, I think, staring at the region full of small-scale farms, their fields brown and fallow as they wait the summer out.

Gurgaon is a region of SEZs. Created through the Special Economic Zones Act, SEZs are demarcated spaces with duty, customs, and tax exemptions that facilitate "ease of doing business" to attract foreign investment.[17] More often than not, they are catalysts for urban development in agrarian areas. In 2019 there were seven operational SEZs in Gurgaon district alone, with several others approved and notified.[18] Numbers are expected to rise along the DMIC. The development rights and incentives offered to SEZs allow for large-scale land acquisition and rapid real estate growth. Many argue that SEZs serve as a mechanism for rural land grabs and promote land financializaton by turning agricultural land into real estate.

Buildstrong, a real estate developer firm upon whose site I conducted research, is well acquainted with SEZs. In 2012 the firm owned six properties under construction, several of which were in SEZs. Like most real estate developers, the firm would use income generated from the presale of property under construction to buy land on which to build a second real estate project. In 2012, when I encountered it, this five-odd-year-old firm was valued at millions of dollars in capital but had yet to finish a single building.

The KMP expressway and the rampant acquisition and conversion of agricultural lands along it are part of the bullish behavior of the real estate market in the early 2000s. Real estate prices quadrupled in one decade, and the NH8 artery saw some of the highest surges in property prices in the region.[19] In the 1980s, land in "New Gurugram" on the NH8 was ₹50,000 ($1,000) per acre. This rose to ₹6,40,000 ($13,000) per acre in the 1990s; in 2015, land was acquired for ₹25,00,000 ($50000) an acre.[20] Real estate speculation made property more lucrative than agriculture and gave rise to a local economy of flipping land parcels. The price tag of real estate was tied to infrastructural development, since transportation corridors allow access to commercial and residential real estate. The areas we drove through on the KMP were already in several stages of financialization.

As with the story of Buildstrong, developers would begin the foundations for a project, then advertise the proposal, only to move the money received from the presale of the project to acquire new land parcels. This gave rise to a real estate house of cards in the region, with several projects under construction and very few completed. The extension of roads into green field lands and the repeat flipping of land and property through the travels of brokers and developers dislocate property from the sociality and history of land upon which it rests. Construction enables this conjuring. Floor plates and concrete slabs are disinterred from their locationality, and land itself becomes ephemeral as it transforms from land to property to capital: commodified, shuffled, distributed, and churned in the buffeting winds of speculative real estate.

The whirlwind politics of speculative economies—the rise and fall of prices and the predictions embedded in them—produces a house of cards of subdivided and divided properties across urbanizing India. Many of these properties have dissolved into unfinished architectures, promised but never delivered. Land lifts away from those who owned it, divides and multiplies, only to merge into speculative clouds and enable division, displacement, and accumulation. The financialization of land in India has led to its dematerialization: land has transformed into myriad states of capital and grown ephemeral.

Land financialization, however, has another face. The financialization of land and accompanying rapid urbanization of the early 2000s is also a story of agricultural decline. While areas around Gurgaon are affluent farming strongholds due to the region's production of basmati rice and history of green revolution initiatives (including electrification, tube-well drives, and high-yielding seed varieties), stories about real estate speculation in the region are matched by stories of diminishing landholdings and increased debt in the areas construction workers migrate from.[21] Veer, the young and charming layout mason on a Buildstrong construction site, explains these struggles. He tells me of his familial network and claims to land.

"We are of the *lohar* [metalworkers] caste. This does not mean that we beat on metal the whole day. It means working with any metal tool—a *karni* [cement scraper], the hammer, and . . . furniture work too." Veer's family are furniture makers, and his uncle works with a furniture manufacturer nearby. It is a large family. "My father, he is one of seven brothers. And each one of them has five-five, six-six, [repeats number for emphasis]—my family has the least [children]. Even then we are five brothers and one sister," describes Veer. "When I was a child, they counted the family: it was over a hundred people. We do not need a village." The family is big enough to form a village itself.

The Zamindari Abolition Acts, passed across Indian states in the 1950s, gave landless tenants and non-dominant-caste farmers claim over the lands they tended in an attempt to even out stilted landownership. The act itself had differential success and passed small and often infertile landholdings to tenanted families along caste lines, reworking or consolidating caste hierarchies.[22] Some grew rich with the lucrative real estate locations of their property, while others were not so lucky. Decades of population growth, with joint families and families with large numbers of children, as well as changing property laws left farmlands divided and subdivided down, shrinking the livelihood of agricultural workers.[23] Surviving by farming small plots becomes difficult as industrial farming grows. Dependency on fertilizers, high-yielding seeds, and pesticides further reduces income; combined with the vagaries of climate change, this drives farmers into debt. Landholdings cannot offer the entire family food for the year, much less support the changing needs of families. Monetizing the price of ancestral land becomes more appealing than cultivation on it.[24]

In a story that resonates with many Indian families, Veer's uncles insisted on a division of familial holdings. Given the number of siblings, Veer's nuclear family was left with only enough land on which to build a small house. This, combined with Veer's father's alcoholism, brought about the nuclear family's downfall. "Of the entire family my father and I are the most behind. When I was born we used to eat and live together but by the time my youngest brother was born, everyone had separated. My father drinks a lot and lost a lot of money." Absolute poverty (*gareebi*) and the binding necessity (*majboori*) of feeding the rest of the family took Veer out of school and into the city to work. He quit school in the sixth grade and started working in the construction industry when he was about thirteen years old (by my estimate). They could not afford the fees of ₹35 (less than 50 cents) per month for the private English school in the village he wanted to go to. The public school did not teach anything, he insisted, highlighting the failure of public education. He moved to the nearest city—Ranchi— where he worked as an apprentice for a mason. He moved up the ranks in six months and now works as a *raj mistri* or layout mason, the top of the line for masons. He started his career in Ranchi but moved to Gurgaon with his family in 2006. He is only twenty years old (an approximate figure) and has already spent the last seven years of his life working. "My age is to . . . roam around. And here I am, I am working, I am earning."

Veer is not alone. The construction sites I visited were full of people both young and old, for whom agriculture is now only a supplementary occupation. The high cost of fertilizers and pesticides, high-yielding seed varieties, subdivision of land, and increased debt make living on agriculture difficult for small farmers. This only increases with climate change and government changes in policy.[25] Land financialization not only disinterred land from property but also rendered a whole body of people mobile, moving from sites to farm and back to sites again in search of employment opportunities.[26] It enhanced seasonal migration and created a mass of people whose life is marked by transience.

EXTRACTIVE ECOLOGIES

The flat and dusty ribbon of the NH8 flows into a different atmosphere as it rises into the Aravalli range. Beyond the village of Virgaon spread acres of protected forestland filled with trees, peacocks, hyenas, and other North Indian flora and fauna. The NH8 forms a thick strip through the *kikar*-filled forest. The *kikar*, a species of acacia, is a short, stubby, and resilient tree that reigns over NCR's forested area and forms an impenetrable cover. The thorny, brambly tree, introduced by the British, survived the rapid shrinking of Gurgaon's water table.[27]

Neelkanth Sir's school once stood within these ranges; there is a temple complex and a cowshed where his school once was, with an elaborate gate with statues of Hindu deities. Sir and I walk into the complex, past an old, dry tank filled with broken rubble and moss. Sir tells me how he jumped into this tank on hot summer days. A wheezing pump from a tube well releases a paltry stream of water, and a few birds perch atop the pipe, taking small sips. The scene was different in Neelkanth Sir's childhood. He describes alternate landscapes of dense trees that occupied the forests before the *kikar* took over. He narrates nostalgic tales of water tanks and lakes dotting the Gurgaon countryside. He even tries to reconstruct the lakes by pumping groundwater into old tanks, but to no avail. Gurgaon, the land of lakes, is now the land of water shortage.[28] Urban development and a burgeoning population have transformed the landscape.

Construction, unlike mining, does not have a strong reputation for being an extractive industry, but it is. It acquires greenfield, arable land and transforms it into paved and developed space. It is a resource-heavy industry relying on potable water, stone, sand, and cement, all of which have extractive footprints. Through this construction degrades

Figure 5. Ecologies of Gurgaon district, 2012. Photo by author.

Figure 6. Lake in Gurgaon district, 2012. Photo by author.

and transforms landscapes. Construction's extraction is not limited to the earth; its extractive politics extend to the humans who work in the industry, where the environments of construction reduce the span and quality of human life. The ephemeral manifests as an erasure of previous ecologies and the reduced temporality of life.

Haveli, a large bungalow project in Gurgaon, is under construction, and the site contractors—Shreelal, Shankarji, and Jai—explain the project plans to me. An eight-bedroom home, the house is designed with a central courtyard in the middle and is designed in such a way that it can be subdivided into smaller apartments or be amalgamated into a large, single-family home. On the rooftop next to the giant mulberry tree will be a swimming pool. Jai, the youngest contractor, is determined to use the pool before he hands over the site. "Sisterfucker, before I leave this site I will also sit by the pool. I will lie down on one of those chairs like they have in Goa. Like this! He folds his hands behind his head as if he is lying in the sun on a lounge chair. "Wearing black glasses [sunglasses]."

Jai didn't always want to be a site contractor; his dream was to be in the army (the armed forces are seen as a socially mobile career). Before embarking on his civil engineering career, he applied to the Jat regiment but was rejected. "My heart broke," he tells me. In his early days, Jai worked for the cement giant turned developer Jaypee Group and built an F1 racetrack in Uttar Pradesh. "I had to work twelve-twelve hours [repeats number for emphasis], even forty-eight hours, I used to work in Jaypee. There was no tree for fourteen kilometers. We made a canteen and fuel store for the racetrack." He boasts about his access to a now cordoned off and elite space. "We remember it. People need a ticket now, we saw it for free."

The racetrack was a few miles away from Delhi on the PPP-built Yamuna expressway that connects New Delhi to Agra (famous for the Taj Mahal). I drive past the F1 racetrack a few months later on the Yamuna expressway, built by the Jaypee Group in return for development rights on 25 million square meters of land along it, a footprint that is almost half the size of the island of Manhattan and could house 7,290 Taj Mahal mausoleums.[29] This triumph in land acquisition, on the fertile plains of the Yamuna and Ganges Rivers, is rumored to be facilitated by the developer's friendships in the state government.[30]

While Jai evokes his ephemeral presence in the projects he constructs, his narrative also speaks of erased ecologies. Construction work thrives on extraction. The two fundamental materials for construction—concrete and steel—require excavated limestone, sand, clay, and iron ore, which in turn require large-scale industrial processes. As construction grows, so does the demand for these materials. By-products of construction and allied industries create high levels of pollution. Construction destroys water reserves; not only does concrete require large amounts of nonbrackish water to cure, but the industry's emphasis on paving, cementing, and asphalting creates hard surfaces that do not allow water tables to recharge and interrupt drainage patterns. Experts have argued for a direct link between urbanization, floods, and the reduction of drinking water supplies.[31] The problem is exacerbated by the number of swimming pools, grass gardens, and golf courses in real estate.

Sir is insistent that the region needs to renew its attention to its one thousand-odd lakes. He wants to rejuvenate the water tank in his school complex to help grow more foliage in the hills. The ineffective pump and bore well were his idea and paid for from the community service requirement funds of a nearby industry. On days when I am not with him, he is known to walk into large factories in the area and demand to see managers, often coming back to them with funding requests for projects such as a natural gas plant and plantation drives. He and I make several trips to the water irrigation department, which he has asked to build three bunds in the protected forest area to hold rainwater runoff and feed the lakes.

Construction is an act of rapid transformation; it changes the site of development, often creating architecture and infrastructure where there was none, but it also transforms the environments and landscapes of areas where its materials come from. Small mining towns, forests, and deserts are altered as construction grows, resource reserves are depleted, and landscapes are devastated through the extraction of construction. This extraction takes a toll on humans as well, as MD explains.

A carpenter on the Haveli site, MD is outspoken and has a harsh tongue. His use of profanity and his tendency to snap make several younger workers afraid of him, and I notice even the supervisors avoiding confrontations. MD became friends with me in the belief that I could help create connections, but he also enjoyed talking about his life. He had had a bad spell of luck a few years earlier, which began with a near-death experience. "I myself was in [a] coma for three months. I fell from the third floor. The doctor said that I did not even have breath." MD describes being in a construction accident. He points at the Haveli construction site: "Just like this three-story home, that was a three-story school. And on the last floor at that level there was a gate that had only two columns." The shifting material states of newly cast concrete led to a horrible accident. While he worked, however, his coworker was not paying attention. "When the second roof was opening. I said, 'do not open up the first column.' He opened the support. The roof took us with it. We fell next to a very big DG [diesel generator]."

MD's coworker fell straight onto some metal plates and bars and was completely cut up. MD was luckier, as he fell further away. "One of the column supports fell on me. I was conscious that I was falling from two stories. I got up from it and ran in fright and fainted." MD's coworker died, and MD himself lay in coma. He survived and was able to work again, but he was lucky. "Each building takes one or two men with it," MD says in his atonal drawl. He remembers his friend, knowing well the Bengali's story easily could have been his. "The two of us worked together. The idiot, sisterfucker, I used to look out for him, he used to look out for me. We stayed together with love and affection. . . . We stayed in the same hut, ate together," he sighs. "The problem was that he drank alcohol."

Every single person I spoke with on construction sites had witnessed death on one of them. The construction industry drains human resources. Laborers, like Veer—the young, landless mason—start working as early as thirteen years old and by forty have deteriorated physically under the impact of the hard labor the industry demands. Cement and the chemicals applied to it to manipulate curing enter the lungs and skin as workers wade through them. The heavy manual labor extracts youth out of the bodies of workers, several of whom already bear the physical manifestations of generations of malnutrition. Death comes easy on construction sites. It walks behind workers as they step across gaping voids or under structures that cannot hold their own weight. It echoes in the sound of materials falling suddenly from a height and shines silent in the water that drips from haphazard electrical wires strung across the site. At Wandering Woods, a laborer dies on a hot summer night. He had a heart attack in his bed, I am told when I come to the site the next day. I cannot help drawing the connection between the heart attack and the hard day's labor yesterday under the almost 50°C (122°F) sun. The family received no compensation, as he died off-site.

The Yamuna expressway has not been a mere connector but rather a pathway for urbanization and transformation of agrarian lands. Its construction shifted the ecology of the region. Accompanying this ecological shift has been the transformation in ecologies of spaces where sand, cement, and stone come from; less traceable is the extraction of human life that the roads and architecture are built on. The work of water, sand, cement, electricity, and diesel and the labor of human beings are fused into the architecture and infrastructure we stand on. Construction as a site and source of extraction renders the environment and humans ephemeral in the starkest of ways.

EPHEMERAL AFFECTS

Somewhere along the NH8, the signs and sensibilities of the urban—that durable aesthetic spectrum so hard to pinpoint—dissolve. Gurgaon drifts into the distance. Small roads with abandoned warehouses, fields in varied stages of growth, and peacocks perched upon trees make their appearance. The neon lights of Starbucks and Coke signs; the metallic paneled architectures; and the swarms of cars, buses, bikes, and pedestrians fade into the motorbikes of villagers and the chatter of schoolkids walking home. Slow-moving tractors full of people, animals, and food pause as cars honk to overtake. There are no information technology offices here and no happy hours, but homemade *chaas*, butter, and milk from the family buffalos overflow. The NH8 is a connector: it brings together diverse people, objects, and practices. Moving onto the road is an exercise in navigating difference, and the ephemeral manifests as its affects. The construction of a road produces a multitude of affective spectrums, such as those of the aspirations and anxieties of a contagious Westernization: fears over the accompanying destruction of Indian culture, the excitement of collapsing social hierarchies with new economies and products, or the anger at being left out of economic change. Two oppositional figures often represent this struggle over urbanization: the patriarchal, Haryanavi man and the young, professional middle-class woman—represented, in part, by Sir and me. A lot lies unsaid between us.

As Sir and I drive along the KMP, I talk to him about a recent talk show and a series of news articles that derided the village Khap Panchayats in Haryana. Consisting of senior men in the villages, Khap Panchayats are traditional governing councils that set protocols of behavior for the villages they govern. They were recently under the national spotlight for their strong stand against cross-caste marriage, intravillage marriages, and statements claiming, for example, that chow mein (i.e., Chinese-style noodles) and other fast foods lead to rape.[32] A popular talk show featured a Khap Panchayat leader opposing marriages between young men and women from the same village; the film star who interviewed the leader derided this belief.[33] As I described it to Sir, he asked me my opinion. "People should marry whomever they want. I do not really care," I replied. Neelkanth Sir explained the logic behind the *panchayat*'s opinion. Boys and girls in the same villages are raised to be like brother and sister. That is why they should not marry. He says in fact even the Panchgaon kids are said to be brothers and sisters (for Virgaon villagers), and "we do not marry them." He tells me about a woman he met in a Norwegian airport who, he claims, had children with her brother.[34] He says these things are common in the Western world.

I speak with two daughters-in-law—Medha and Charu—young women who live in the middle of farm fields and tend to both cattle and children. Unlike their formidable mother-in-law, who still wears the traditional Haryanavi skirted *theel* and *dupatta*, these young women wear *salwar kameez* outfits cut in popular styles from Bollywood films. Medha, the elder of the two, tells me that she is doing her exams to become a teacher, as a new private school has opened a few miles from their home. Urbanism brings new cycles of social change: unlike their mother-in-law's generation, in which very few young women of Medha and Charu's status worked outside the household, younger women in agrarian Gurgaon now step out of the house; some to go to colleges in New Delhi and others to teach or tutor.[35] Sir asks me to counsel a steady stream of women who want career advice in academia. He insists they should do their PhDs and secure academic jobs. Many social protocols, however, are still in place. Both Medha and Charu will pull their *dupattas* over their faces and leave the room when Sir walks into the house. Only their mother-in-law and I will sit on *khats* with the men as they talk about how women must be educated and how their daughters are the pride of the house, waiting only a few minutes to talk about how their daughters-in-law (*bahus*) have been spoiled to death by their parents.

"*Samjho ye bhi meri bitiya hai*" (imagine that she, too, is my daughter), Neelkanth Sir tells locals, helping me skirt judgment and gain acceptance. I move from woman of the road to daughter of the house, and by extension of the village and district. Like other Ahir daughters of Virgaon, there is a silent understanding that I behave. The responsibility rests uneasily on my Bombay-girl shoulders as I strive to be unopinionated, vegetarian, a teetotaler, and asexual. The melded worlds, from Harvard to Haryana, Bombay to Boston, manifest in internal struggle, as the terminologies of my multiple worlds—good girl, simple, bourgeoisie, privileged, ambitious, unmarried, over-opinionated, difficult—whirl across my body. Navigating and moving on roads, for Medha and me, means negotiating and managing differential norms and readings that hold our spaces together, it means taking our *dupattas* on and off as we travel on our divergent roads.

Roads, and the urbanization they enable crystallize battles over gender, with women's honor and security as the central fault line. A migrant, professional crowd often criticizes local villagers for their alcoholism and patriarchal attitude, believing Haryanvi and Jat masculinity to be threatening. The villagers believe that the professionals are inhuman, heartless, and indecent (the professional *keeda* or insect), and that women in particular are corrupt and brazen. One of the chief fault lines of this mix is talk of the high rate of rapes in the area.[36] Working professionals in multinational companies blame "drunk, village men" and their misogyny. Migrant women on site speak of the lawlessness of the space. Khaps defend the men by deriding women's behavior and provocative clothing and even cite changing food habits. The roads into Gurgaon construct a spatial battle that manifest in the battle of control over women, especially over young women, a control that Riddhi, Medha, and I are well acquainted with.

Riddhi went to architecture school with me in Bombay. Her parents were part of the wave of Delhi-ites who moved to more spacious apartments in Gurgaon, and she moved back to live with them after she graduated. She works for a developer in Gurgaon. On one of my first days in NCR she shows me around. She explains the different plots and sectors to me and points out the original villages. Riddhi designs bungalows in the north of India; unlike Bombay, whose crowded footprint does not lend itself to opportunities for construction, Gurgaon has space to construct homes. "You can actually build architecture," Riddhi says; she does admit to me that Gurgaon is a little more restrictive than Bombay had been during our undergraduate years, but "you find ways around it." She echoes a sentiment I have heard from several middle-class women in Delhi: "Having a car changes everything."

The focus on the car as protection and the anxieties surrounding "letting women out of the house" and onto the public streets are telling.[37] For various categories of women, the road is the space both of new experiences and of risk. It is presented as the space outside the shelter of family and familiar ground, where they can be violated and harmed and/or culturally transformed. In the case of mobile women—be they construction workers who come to sites from villages, the wives of laborers who live in labor camps, young women who go to college in Delhi from Gurgaon, or middle-class women working or living in Gurgaon—the road and their movement along it represents both vulnerability and new experiences. The road not only brings physical risk but also paves the way for economic mobility, new solidarities, and opportunities. For women in Gurgaon, the road and its affective economies form the very space for transition and transformation, in which they enact their vulnerabilities but also experience new possibilities. The ephemeral as affect here serves to construct new emotive and intersubjective sensibilities that enable forms of deference and defiance, to transform social hierarchies, and give rise to new controls and nonconformities. These oppositions push at each other, often in angry, violent ways, upon Gurgaon's roads.

EPHEMERAL DURABILITIES OF THE ROAD

The NH8 is cordoned off one morning. A long line of traffic cones and string narrows the three lanes out of Gurgaon down to two. As we drive outward on the highway, we see a number of large, temporary pavilions constructed out of bamboo and cloth. Masses of young men, dressed in saffron shirts and shorts, run along the cordoned-off road. On their shoulders rest bow-like bamboo arches festooned with streamers and ribbons; a clay pot hangs from each end. I am mildly alarmed at the sheer number of devout men running on the arterial road. My companion explains to my non–North Indian self that this is the Kanwar Yatra.

The word *kanwar* indicates the bow-like structure and the two pots that the men carry on their shoulders, and *yatra* means to journey. The Kanwar Yatra is an annual pilgrimage in North India wherein devotees of the Hindu God of destruction, Shiva, collect water from auspicious sources of the Ganges such as the towns of Haridwar and Rishikesh, then walk or run with the water back to their own villages. Highways in the region cordon off areas and divert traffic to account for the millions of men.[38] Nongovernmental organizations (NGOs), patrons, and religious institutions build temporary pavilions along highways where devotees are given free food and shelter. The men are not to put the pots of holy water down and are given poles to hang them on. They run to meet the tight deadline: the auspicious night when they must pour the water at their neighborhood Shiva temple.

The highway is jammed. Streams of men walk and run around us. The road is washed over with saffron ribbons and discarded plastic cups. The cars jostle together, stuck. Trucks and tempos, cranes and cement mixers, motorcycles and Mercedeses sit entangled, with angry drivers, as the pilgrimage takes over the road. The shouts of "Bam Bam Bol" (say the name of Shiva) and the stream of men on the road emphasize the ephemeral complexities of the road: the mixes of people and objects, the high emotions and intersubjective navigations, the different atmospheres, the transience of people and materials, and the pathways they produce and remove.

Infrastructure is not often interpreted as ephemeral. The hardness of the concrete, the heavy weight of the metalled surface, and the burning smell of asphalt under the hot sun convince us of the durability of road infrastructures. Yet the very water, electricity, people, cars, and social life that run through the veins of networks; the material and sensory dynamics of construction; the material land transformations; and the movements and disappearances of people all remind us that these durable structures are constituted by the ephemeral. In a country like India, they are forever under construction as new repairs, flyovers, connectors, and surfaces are dug up and created. Road infrastructures are alive in their everyday. The liveliness of roads lends an ephemeral core to this permanent infrastructure, which enacts dynamic kin-making, speculative transactions, ecological and atmospheric transformations, and affective relations. The ephemeral in construction forms the site of social struggle: it displaces people and empowers some, enables capitalist accumulation as it renders workers mobile, and transforms ecology as it shortens the span of life. It forms the site of the struggle to survive. Road infrastructures would not exist without the material interactions of making them or moving on them, and it is this very play of the ephemeral-durable that enables the agency and exploitation of construction's operations.

2 The Financial Sublime

"You know where there is black money, there will always be rats." Mr. Kumar, an engineer on the Wandering Woods construction site, regales me with stories of wealth in the construction industry. He weaves seductive tales of mattresses full of cash and cupboards with hidden shelves and claims that the hordes of money will always be found by detective rats. He pauses for dramatic effect and flashes his charismatic wide smile: "They are attracted to the smell of the notes."

My eyes widen. The at once grimy and pungent smell of rupee notes wafts up to me from my childhood. I get a Bollywood flashback of villains exchanging thick wads of cash in unfinished concrete towers. The figure of the rat—the underground creature of grime and filth—metaphorically merges with the stereotypical image of traders and politicians who chase black money: the human rats who love to wallow in the filth that black money perpetuates.[1] Months earlier, during my dissertation prospectus defense, my committee members quizzed me in a windowless classroom about how I would inquire about corruption. Viewing it as a taboo topic, my answer was that it might be unethical to ask my informants about their practices: recording secret corruption practices could have repercussions on the lives of those I spoke with. My expectations of a shared silence evaporated as I discovered the public nature and ease of black money and corruption talk in the construction industry.[2] It was 2012, and the air hung heavy with the very real but ambiguous presence of black money; no one seemed to know all it encompassed, but everyone claimed to experience it. Those I met explained that black money was essential to the working of construction and real estate.

Mr. Kumar narrates his experiences with black money as we drive through the ruro-urban peripheries of NCR. His descriptions are pertinent: central Delhi burgeons with anti-corruption protestors led by Gandhian Anna Hazare as we speak.[3] Arvind Kejriwal (a member of Anna Hazare's team) accuses prominent politicians of hoarding black money and bleeding the common man dry. Real estate and construction are the central loci of this outcry. Just last week, Arvind Kejriwal accused Delhi Land and Finance (DLF), Gurgaon's premier real estate developer, of forming a "malafide nexus" with family members of leaders in the ruling Congress Party.[4] He drew Gurgaon, real estate, and corruption together through the register of black money. Kejriwal's corruption talk was reflected on the national scale and in the media. A governmental white paper stated that Indians were hoarding 1.94 billion Swiss francs in Swiss bank accounts.[5] A report published by *Economic Weekly* that year claimed that India is the fifth-largest exporter of black money in the world.[6] The black economy, it is believed, amounts to a shocking 75 percent of the country's GDP.[7]

The term *black money* is as elusive as the financial practices it indexes. In its most basic definition, black money is money exchanged and accumulated to avoid taxation. It often represents cash transactions that bear no account or accountability and is seen in opposition to money recorded in formal transactions, known as white money. It is understood as money gained from bribes or cash payments and is also produced through laundering schemes. Authors remind us that black money is an ambiguous term that indicates not only stashes of cash but also a networked system of activities or an economic ecosystem.[8] Black money forms part of a constellation of financial terms and practices related to real estate and construction, including cash hoards, corruption, bribes, informal payments, doctoring books, *hawala* (informal financial network), smuggling, offshore funds, gold markets, and cash property transactions. Black money is categorized within informal finance. A key characteristic of black money, however, is its surreptitious and ambiguous but also much-discussed nature in relation to property, real estate, and construction in NCR. As in Mr. Kumar's rat story, it emerges on the one hand in speculative and often mythical narrations, and on the other, in simple, everyday practices. It would not be an exaggeration to say that everyone in construction experiences a black money transaction in one of its material manifestations, and that informal financial practices surrounding the term *black money*—including bribes, laundering, and cash payments—make India's real estate boom possible.

I examine conversations around black money and accompanying financial practices in real estate and construction in NCR. Unlike chapter 1, which introduces different forms of the ephemeral that undergird construction, here I focus on the ephemeral as the transition between material-intangible states of capital required to further construction and real estate. The ephemeral capacities of finance—its ability to transform into myriad material and intangible states (cash, gold, drugs, coal, property, cement, steel, architecture, stock options, and bank accounts) as it moves within social networks—creates an atmosphere of magic, awe, and fear that furthers real estate accumulation and speculation in NCR. I describe this atmosphere as a financial sublime. The financial sublime is an ephemeral atmospheric experience produced through the circulations and transformations of property and capital. The financial sublime emerges alongside the speculative economy of real estate and relies on the intimacy of kin relations in order to pass capital through formal-informal and material-intangible states.[9] This fluidity highlights the mutual dependencies of formal-informal economies and the relationship of the ephemeral to the durable.

The financial sublime builds on the sublime as a Euro-American concept that described the experience of the enormity and power of the natural world as that which inspires both wonder and terror at the same time.[10] The sublime is an atmosphere on an all-encompassing scale. Like global systems of finance, the sublime embeds Eurocentric history and colonial power and is often used to describe technological innovations.[11] Spoken of by gentlemanly painters and writers, the sublime was awe- and fear-inspiring but also a site of erasure and masking; in the North American context the sublime indexed an attraction to the natural world that denied the simultaneous settler colonialism in action.[12] This violence known to both perpetrators and Indigenous peoples was erased by discussions of the transcendental sublime that perpetuated the myth of the natural, untouched world. Years later real estate financial systems, very much linked to this epistemology of North American land grabs, adopt similar logics of awe and scale to perpetuate the real estate market and enable land appropriation. While the workings of real estate finance in NCR are well known, and everyone and anyone tries to insert themselves into its logic, finance does take on a scale of its own. It holds promise of great wealth for many but only those within the right social networks succeed. At the same time real estate finance is accompanied by many horror stories of swindling, murders, and gunfights. The financial sublime is this experience of larger-than-life quality and the combination of horror and awe in real estate. The produced magical quality and scale of financial transactions related to NCR helps elite individuals accumulate.

Here I reground the financial sublime to present the ephemeral transactions that make the sublime possible, thus revealing its dirty and material side.[13] The sublime is "a necessary spectacle of colonial rule" that creates the "feeling of submission and prostration."[14] It is a relational and short-lived concept that enhances the limitless aspects of technological development and the transformation of land and landscape that occurs in tandem.[15] In a similar manner, the financial sublime in real estate enacts the power of Indian elites and their global financial partners. The fear, awe, and limitless quality of transforming landscape and money talk in Gurgaon allow its very perpetuation.

Money, black or white (as money involved in formal transactions is known), constitutes the structuring principle of NCR's construction industry. As a lithe electronic transaction, money, in all its lightness, moves through credit cards and bank checks. Its only register might be the changing numbers of the stock exchange or the electronic documents that register moments of transaction. In its heaviness, though, money emerges in wads of cash as they circulate across the area's new highways. They hide in suitcases and car trunks. Money dangles from car windows and sneaks in envelopes onto officials' desks. It speeds with luxury cars on the road and sits weighted at the feet of God. It moves from pockets to safes and from safes to sites.[16] In its financial circulations into various forms of capital, money percolates across state and national boundaries but then returns to its locale. I attempt to trace this mystical, mirage-like movement of finance in NCR's construction industry: the material states it occupies and moves between, the geographies it constructs, and the relationships it forms.[17] The fluidity of formal-informal, political-corporate, and legal-illegal operations in construction finance aids the growth of real estate. The rising architecture and circulating speculations feed the financial sublime. It is, however, the very intimacy of each transaction that reinforces the stickiness of kin. This chapter combines political economic theory and theories of the sublime, following rumor, humor, and metaphor in real estate and construction finance. I do not focus on the veracity of stories of bribes, black money, and corruption but instead emphasize the ephemeral materiality and movements of capital these stories describe, the power relations and struggle they index, and the obfuscations they create. Through this I argue that individuals in the construction industry (and likely beyond it too) experience a financial sublime in disparate and differential ways.

LANDSCAPES OF DESIRE

Mr. Kumar gives me a ride to the Wandering Woods construction site and back every day. We take the car to Sikanderpur at the heart of Gurgaon, leaving his small Maruti Swift in a parking lot overnight, and take the metro home. This shaves a vital 1.5 hours off what would be a 5-hour back-and-forth commute and allows Mr. Kumar to reach home before his children go to bed. His workday, like that of many middle-class commuters in the sprawling NCR, extends from 7:00 a.m. to 8.30 p.m.

The sun is setting as we drive out of the plotted industrial sector Mr. Kumar works in and onto rough roads surrounded by delicious golden-brown fields. The Sai Baba idol on the dashboard sits benevolent as Mr. Kumar swerves in cowboy-esque fashion through the evening's aggressive traffic.[18] It is harvesting season. Stacks of wheat glint like gold on the dark-brown alluvial soil of the agricultural landscape. A sepia-tinted geography of fields, thorny bushes, and occasional cattle unfolds. Fertile farmlands sprawl in every direction. I stare through the large expanses in happiness. Occasional arrays of skyscrapers block my gaze and remind me that this is a fast-urbanizing area. They emerge in clusters at regular intervals among the fields. The skyscrapers sit incongruously within this agricultural-scape, their exposed, concrete-metal insides in varied stages of construction. Signs and fences surround vacant land, promising serene and verdant apartment living. Their promises seem distant from the clouds of dust, grime, and honks that surround me and Mr. Kumar and the other commuters on the road.

Mr. Kumar often likes to describe how the entire area around us was just jungle when he first began construction work in the late 1980s. This narrative belies the fact that Gurgaon was a thriving town and agrarian region to begin with. Developer-led bungalow plots and the first housing colonies appeared in the 1990s. This urban development brought both prosperity and corruption as land financialization overtook the region. India's neoliberal economic restructurings in 1991–92 lent renewed energy to construction and development activity in peri-urban India.[19] Within this period, the state encouraged privatized foreign direct investment (FDI), allowing the government to cut public funding and make up the deficits of India's debt crises in the 1980s.[20] It is estimated that in the years between 2001 and 2012, over three hundred multinational companies opened up shop in Gurgaon.[21] As professionals and students began to populate the area, owning and renting property became a lucrative enterprise. Residential property often tripled and quadrupled in a short time span.[22]

Commercial real estate grew as well. Requirements for new office spaces increased from 3.9 million square feet in 1998 to over 16 million square feet in 2004–05, 70 percent of which was driven by the information technology sector.[23] New business increased the spending capacities and income stability of the emerging category of professionals, spurring a demand for both commercial and residential property. The average national income went from US$3,392 in 1992 to US$7,664 in 2012.[24] This was likely reflected in NCR with bulges at the higher and lower end as India's wealth distribution grew in inequality.[25] The liberalization of the banking sector brought several privatized banks into the housing finance sector and created a competitive mortgage and financing market, further supporting the rise of real estate.[26] Property ownership mania gripped the upper middle classes in Delhi.[27] An obsession with land came to outweigh a historic Indian obsession with gold; newspaper reports declared that

India, the world's largest consumer of gold, was shouting a new slogan: "buy land instead."[28] "Place your money in property and it will bear fruit of gold." "The returns on land investment in India are incredible. . . . [W]hy would we invest in anything else?"[29]

Gurgaon was transformed. The fields we drove through grew wedding cake–like cement-concrete towers. A bank of shimmering office towers and malls with façades of glass rose along the central highways of the area. The new buildings transported us into Dubai, Shanghai, or New York. The tremendous rise in real estate prices brought a seductive mix of awe and horror. Talk of stability and prosperity through property circulated, as did talk of the wrong (corrupt or uneducated) people getting rich, and too much growth too fast. Discussions of money made on investment properties accompanied stories of drunk local farmers in Audis and BMWs. Fieldwork comprised collecting rumors, advice, and encouragement on investing in real estate.[30] The alluvial soils of Gurgaon's peri-urban areas pulsated with the speculative energies of real estate. The promise of money soaked into emerging architectures and landscapes. The region glowed with the promise of a bountiful harvest.

MIND THE GAPS

The prolific growth of construction activity in Gurgaon was not a transcendental exercise; it involved hard work on the ground. Mr. Kumar often boasts about how construction is about the people who get their hands dirty. He compares the developer Buildstrong's staff and his own team on site with pride in his voice: "They work nine to five, we work eight to seven. We stand all day in the heat and dust. They sit in air-conditioned offices. They would not survive here one day." This narrative of occupying and working on the land is a popular one in Indian industry worlds, and many an industrialist will tell stories of their humble roots and diligent work in the field. K. P. Singh, chief executive officer of Delhi Land and Finance Ltd. (DLF), the company responsible for spearheading real estate in Gurgaon, narrates his own experience: "We never forced or arm-twisted a single farmer into selling his land. . . . Land has always been an emotional issue in India. . . . We understood this and to allay their fears we spent weeks and months on building a relationship with farmers." Since average landholdings were only four to five acres, Singh dealt with hundreds of families, each with five to six individual members, as he consolidated land parcels. "I must have visited at least 500 families. . . . I sat with them, discussed various topics and had endless glasses of milk, tea, or buttermilk," he describes his on-the-ground work.[31]

Doing business in India, like travel on the NH8, is about working across the complex social worlds of Indian society: urban and rural; skyscrapers and informal settlements; ethnic communities, classed spaces, and linguistic communities. Mediations grow construction and real estate. The ephemeral manifests in the shifting, unstable states and locations of capital and the constant brokering required to produce it. The fluidity of finance relies on a social network that makes and unmakes itself in response to the requirements of the industry. Similar to the work of scholars who argue for the impossibility of drawing a boundary between the formal and the informal in the context of urbanization, economies, industries, and labor organization, tracing black money as it weaves through Gurgaon reveals the fluidity of many categories, including informal-formal, legal-illegal, public-private, educated-uneducated, and professional-agrarian worlds.[32] Categories thought of as oppositional rely on and produce each other with no clear demarcations between them.

The head office of the developers of Wandering Woods, however, still maintains the pretense of divisions. It is located in a business district full of glass and steel towers built to house and attract multinational firms. As I walk through the marbled lobby with a dark, wooden desk and a glass-lined atrium, I am confused about which country I am in. A silent and efficient uniformed man wipes up the NCR mud that I tracked in with my dusty construction-site shoes. The muddy memory of the worksite is erased under his mop. The heat of the outside dissipates under the cool of the marbled floor, and I am very aware of my inexpensive *salwar kameez*. Mr. Reddy, the chief financial officer (CFO), awaits my arrival in his air-conditioned office replete with tasteful art on the walls.

Mr. Reddy is a light-eyed, balding man who gave up a career in investment banking to move to real estate. His crisp and direct mannerisms remind me of acquaintances at Harvard Business School. He cuts a distinguished figure, in seeming opposition to the tirade he launches on the conservatism of the Reserve Bank of India (RBI). The RBI, according to him, is the "jailor" of India's growth potential. His primary grouse is the blanket ban on loans to fund the purchase of land. "The banks don't actually fund land . . . the basic logic being that it will lead to speculation. A lot of people with money, chasing few pieces of land, and then there is the fear [of] inflation."

Mr. Reddy is frustrated: he wants to expand real estate operations but cannot fund land purchases. The RBI, India's financial regulator and watchdog, has a stringent stance on land; developers describe it as an "overly bureaucratic organization" and blame it for "inhibiting the country's growth potential."[33] In its 2009 Master Housing Circular, for example, the RBI gave individuals, cooperatives, and public authorities access to debt-based financing for housing projects but restricted this option for land acquisition and construction for real estate developers.[34] "The RBI only acts retroactively," explained the CFO, indicating that he felt the RBI takes action after the fact. I remind him that the cautious ways of the RBI protected the Indian real estate market in 2008 when the US economy crashed. He argues back: "But where there are genuine requirements— I think the banks should actually make the decision. They should have some kind of safeguards." Through this he emphasizes that the RBI should create specific policies allowing banks to fund developers buying land.

Like the office and construction sites, financial practices in real estate and construction are imagined as divided into two paths, the formal and informal path. White money, professionalism, banking, and transparency came to be attached to the formal path. A "white" route, for example, would involve a joint venture between the landowner and developer, allowing the landowner a defined share of profits, paying landowners a token amount with the contract for a tiered payment structure, or borrowing money from a non-banking finance company (NBFC). These strategies, Mr. Reddy tells me, are seen as unfair as they deny developers fair stakes or rule out small developers with no credit rating. "We do all the work in developing, the farmer is just sitting on the land, why should they benefit?" Developers attempt to raise finances to pay off farmers at the outset of the project in order to maximize their profit. White money, and its accompanying legal restrictions, as Mr. Reddy argues, could not have met market demands.

Mr. Reddy describes the industry's reliance on informal finance and how practices such as tax evasion, corruption, accumulation, and black money hoards emerge. "Now what that does is because there is no formal access to land finance . . . people resort to . . . informal finance." Informal finance is not external to but inextricable from the workings of formal finance. He describes the reasons for this situation: "Typically banks have margins: you need to put in so much before we will release our finances. Typically the requirement is 40% . . . at any stage the bearer's folder should not be more than 60%. . . . But they [developers] include customer money in that 40%." That is, developers presell unbuilt flats to fund other land purchases. "Unfortunately, if the customers don't come forward, then I will have to go to the moneylenders, the informal sector. That becomes the issue. . . . The rates of interest are pretty high. I pay 14.5%. . . . The market rate of borrowing if I go to a moneylender is as high as 24%, but [if] you are really desperate you pay as high as 36%." The high rates of interest from informal moneylenders cause many developers to seek other paths. "Most of the large developers . . . have financing from politicians. One developer is associated with X [name redacted] politicians. There are people like XX [name redacted], they say that he's got Dubai money.[35] So, there are these alliances." As Mr. Reddy outlines, formal finance produces informal finance: "That money may not be clean money, but it actually serves the purpose, because otherwise these guys cannot finance anything at the scale at which they are doing." The growth of real estate in the region could only have been possible through large reserves of informal cash, unaccounted for money, and informal moneylenders. Informal finance is a necessary part of the functioning of real estate finance.

The early 2000s saw a rise in the number of developers in NCR. Large-scale developers often began their empires in cash-heavy industries such as cement, coal, alcohol, or infrastructure development before moving to real estate. The giants in NCR, for example, include Jaypee InfraTech Ltd. (cement), Wave Infratech Ltd. (alcohol), Unitech Ltd. (civil engineering), and DLF Ltd. (real estate). The rise of developers was accompanied by a parallel rise in informal financing companies and the NBFC sector, who in turn negotiated the informal-formal boundary of investing and finance. Individuals with large amounts of cash from other sources (including jewelers, tradesmen, contractors, and moneylenders) began to fund small-scale developers. This was made possible through existing histories and infrastructures of moneylending.[36]

The fluidity of working between formal-informal finance, the intangible-material states of capital, and the worlds of white-black money in real estate and construction requires individuals to match the tempos of opportunity that rise and then quickly dissipate. This ephemeral mediation connects to the kin relations that grow real estate. A steady network of real and fictive kinship relations, embroiled in a politics of schooling-ethnicity-gender-class-caste, facilitates real estate growth. K. P. Singh describes the importance of networks in a story of a memorable dinner party. Singh was hosting a dinner in honor of Charles Lachman, a cofounder of Revlon, and had "spent hours carefully finalizing the list of around fifty celebrities from Indian high society," when the then-defense minister, part of an agrarian elite, decided to call on him.[37] Singh describes the situation: "Since I did not want the defence minister to feel uncomfortable in front of the champagne-and-caviar set, I decided to quickly call up some prominent Jat [local landowning caste of Haryana] leaders."[38] Singh describes his corporate and agrarian worlds and his efforts to balance them, but that evening his agile endeavors failed: the party ended with an unhappy chief minister.[39]

The dinner party story demonstrates the temporality of friendships in the industrial worlds of contemporary India and the agility with kinship they require: Singh deploys his own background to gain affinity with the local Jat leaders who control access and development permissions for land in Gurgaon. At the same time, his familiarity with New Delhi's elite through his family and his military background enable an affinity with global and local corporate heads. Through his dinner parties he works to construct and maintain his real and fictive kin relations. At a Holi party I am invited to on the outskirts of Gurgaon, the ease, affinities, inclusions, and exclusions of soirees become all too apparent.

An industrialist and dominant-caste member of South Delhi elite, Mr. Jeysingh owns a farmhouse in the Aravalli range between New Delhi and Gurgaon. It is Holi, the spring festival of color, and across the manicured lawns sit men and women with well-polished accents and even-better-honed connections across the city. Dressed in impeccable white with hints of pastels, they affectionately smear each other with organic colors to celebrate the arrival of spring. Mr. Jeysingh, our host, is a well-known industrialist who wants to translate his landholdings into a real estate venture. He greets us as I arrive, invited by my friend. "You did not need to wear black, we are not that kind of party," Mr. Jeysingh says as he sees my outfit and oiled hair in anticipation of rowdier celebrations similar to those at my public school of architecture. I realize as much myself, as my friend points out a prominent cabinet minister's child chatting deep within the circle of friends.

It is a beautiful March day, and blue-green tents are spread across the large lawn: one with a bar, one with food stalls and seating. A lone tent in the distance shelters *qawwali* musicians singing praises of the patron saint of Delhi, Nizamuddin Auliya. The Aravalli forest around us radiates with the sheen of filtered light as the *sufi* music intoxicates the air. In a late afternoon haze of color-drenched laziness, drunkenness, and general overindulgence, the host asks a young lady with a sultry voice to perform for us. The sound of her voice moves through the hot and heavy afternoon air, and calls of "wah wah" arise from the small crowd. The *qawwali* musicians approach. "What a wonderful voice, *wah*, if we may also present a *farmaish* (request)." "Please do," the host says, pointing toward the tent where the musicians sit. "Our tent is too far, perhaps we can present here." The musicians are *qawwals*: impoverished, Muslim artisans. "Color me, my lord, color me in your color," they sing, hoping for a generous, drunken tip. The music, the sun, and the alcohol draw the partygoers together, forging friendships and opening doors for more business and real estate deals, as the Muslim men merely sing.

To be comfortable in the intoxicated spaces of capital like those of Jeysingh and Singh is to straddle the worlds of global business and the local landowning elite. Jat political heads and farmers facilitate real estate dealings, as do the friends and kin at Mr. Jeysingh's event. It is to switch forms of money and conduct both formal and informal finance through quiet smiles and backroom chats. Real estate and construction depend on the fluidity between the material-intangible, informal-formal, rural-urban, public-private, farm-firm, and black-white worlds of finance, where the worlds are not oppositional but interreliant and coproduced. These fluidities are made possible through surreptitious and undocumented transactions and facilitations that depend on social networks: Jat farmers, political elites from across India, and Baniya developers in the region. These fluidities and connections extend into global private equity firms who recruit clients across the Global North and South, clients who sit on each other's boards of directors.[40] Fluidities have barriers embedded in their ebbs and flows, barriers constructed and disbanded by networks of real and fictive kin. Some participate in and facilitate the kin relations that enable financial transactions. Others sit at the borders of these soirees, watching and witnessing dealings, like the *qawwal* singers, who will never be let in.

SUBLIME SEDIMENTS

Every day at sunset Mr. Kumar and I drive past the fields into Gurgaon's peculiar urbanscape. Our car passes a higgledy-piggledy mess of factories, shanties, urban farms, skyscrapers, and malls. We turn onto the NH8 leading toward New Delhi. It is lined with alcohol stores and roadside food shacks; the shacks have strings of shiny, neon lights to attract customers. A short cut to avoid traffic takes us through sleepy neighborhoods of two-story bungalows, somewhat kitschy and covered with a layer of dust. We make our way back to the highway. Markets open onto the road with shops that sell a variety of industrial and building equipment. Looking down narrow alleys, I can see villages turned into shanty towns. Brick-lined and yellow-painted government offices whiz by as the car picks up speed. The highway beckons with its strip malls topped by an enclave of swanky office blocks. I see the Mercedes sign glint at me in the now deep-purple sky. Gated communities surround us in their cement splendor, and angular malls line the road. The sail-shaped DLF tower crowns the area. Real estate in Gurgaon grew so fast, it was almost magical. As skyscrapers sprang up in forests and hi-tech highways carved through wheat fields, they created a sense of architectural wonder. The new architectures and infrastructures speak of rising wealth and create an atmosphere of financial gain and strength.

The fluidity of finance fed this particularized urban configuration. Not only does finance move across different social worlds, but it also transforms into different material states in order to produce real estate. This is a form of the ephemeral without which the construction industry would not work. The fluidity and transitional states lend an enchanted quality to financial operations and real estate growth. Rumors and stories of bribes, cash, and political corruption weave into the history and processes of real estate and construction in Gurgaon, giving rise to wonder and horror. These fascinations and terrors obfuscate the social intimacies that construction finance operates through. I move through different stages of construction— from policy and planning decision-making to the everyday of site-based construction—to look at the ways in which finance transformed, the kinship relations formed, and the magical aspects of real estate were experienced. Real estate and real estate finance achieve a magical and sublime quality as stories of profit circulate.

The popular history of urban development in Gurgaon traces urbanism not to the military town or district headquarters but to India's first public car manufacturing company, conceived in the 1970s.[41] Started as a public venture, the company acquired a Japanese collaborator in 1982. Much of Gurgaon's urban and economic growth is attributed to this car plant, a legacy that makes Gurgaon's state of Haryana the car and motorcycle capital of India. It is rumored that the car plant arrived in Gurgaon owing to the close relationship between the chief minister of Haryana and the minister then in charge of urban areas, Sanjay Gandhi, and that it was named after Maruti Mohan, the daughter of the liquor baron Kapil Mohan from adjacent Uttar Pradesh. Sanjay Gandhi was the son of India's prime minister at the time, Indira Gandhi, as well as the brother of former prime minister Rajiv Gandhi, and the uncle of the Congress Party's current leader, Rahul Gandhi. When Sanjay Gandhi died in 1980, Indira Gandhi is rumored to have removed from his wrist a watch engraved with the number of the Swiss bank account that held their laundered money.[42] At that mythical founding moment, a relationship of dynastic politics, political and social nexuses, and appearances-disappearances of money came to be forever linked with the urban growth of Gurgaon.[43]

K. P. Singh's DLF led the first wave of privatized development.[44] In the late 1970s, DLF bought parcels of land from farmers. Singh met Rajiv Gandhi when the soon-to-be prime minister's car overheated in an area where Singh was conducting land acquisitions.[45] The meeting led to future support for development in Gurgaon from the future prime minister of India.[46] DLF began its ventures building real estate in New Delhi and already had governmental connections. Rahul Srivastava, in his book on Delhi, includes a letter, dated 1954, by a resident labeling DLF a "rich party" and accusing the public Delhi Improvement Trust of "forcing the public" to give construction work to DLF.[47]

These assumptions exist today. In 2012, Mr. Kumar and I would hear news of an alleged land deal linking DLF to Robert Vadra, son-in-law of India's political first family (he is married to Rajiv Gandhi and Sonia Gandhi's daughter).[48] Activists claimed that Vadra made US$60 million in 2012 through land deals in Gurgaon, and that he received benefits from DLF. Newspapers reported that the land deals involved creating multiple construction and property development companies that exchanged and escalated land costs, flipping land, changing land uses, and obtaining "interest-free loans" from real estate companies that were never repaid.[49] Both DLF and Vadra denied these charges, but the story nevertheless circulated widely in 2012 and reinforced the belief that secret liaisons drove the speculative real estate economy of Gurgaon.

Real estate and construction in Gurgaon acquire an aura of terror and awe as popular narratives insist on political influences in the sector. When informants named developers, they would often list the politician or political party they were in alliance with; as I drive down Gurgaon's main highway NH8, my companion matches developers to political parties as we pass their buildings. Politicians also publicly become backers of real estate in their respective regions, often privately trading favors for holdings in the company or for property in the projects (often held by extended family members rather than by the politicians themselves), or even financing land purchases through cash reserves. These liaisons, it is rumored, provide steady flows of cash for growth and facilitate the acquisition of land, changes in land use (from agricultural to residential and commercial), and construction permissions. The haphazard state of urban development in the region can be attributed to these liaisons, as planning rules were bent again and again for the sake of unchecked real estate development.[50]

The 2000s saw real estate and construction finance further exceed national boundaries. In 2005 the RBI further relaxed its regulations for FDI in real estate.[51] The RBI later opened 100 percent FDI in NBFCs, many of which finance real estate and infrastructural construction.[52] These moves allowed foreign investors to fund projects in collaboration with local finance and real estate companies but also resulted in accusations of financial mishandling and embezzlement. For example, 2018 saw a $1.6 billion scandal involving the India Real Estate Opportunities (IREO) fund, in which investors filed a lawsuit against cofounder Lalit Goyal. Goyal allegedly moved "capital away from property projects via side dealings with people close to the . . . property developer."[53] IREO and Goyal deny these allegations but are not alone in facing them. A quick Google search on real estate scams in Gurgaon (Gurugram), political connections in real estate, or real estate lawsuits in Gurgaon finds a whole host of organizations, people, and politicians named. The fact that many of these accusations and lawsuits exist substantiates the existence of the financial sublime.

In September 2012 I talk with an investment banker who tells me that the post-2005 years saw a number of offshore hedge funds in tax-free havens such as Singapore and Mauritius invest in Indian real estate. Several of these hedge funds, he explains, are composed of laundered money making its way back to India. "It is common knowledge that most of the FDI in real estate comes through *hawala*," he states matter-of-factly. *Hawala*, a term originating from financial transactions among West African traders, refers to the informal circulation of money across countries. In its simplest form, you hand a certain sum to a local agent in the country where you reside, and your relatives are given money by the agent's network in the country of your choice. In India, *hawala* is connected to the illegal smuggling of drugs and gold bricks, but also to simpler money transfers across the region.

Several contemporary monetary circuits mimic and morph these historical techniques. In banking transactions, a series of shell companies accompany an army of professionals (accountants, lawyers, bankers) who work in tax havens and manipulate international loopholes to transfer cash out of and into the country. Malhotra and Das describe how a "classic black money operator opens many shell companies to route money before it is invested."[54] This process, known as "layering," obfuscates the trail: "Assets are rarely in the beneficiary's name and money is moved through jurisdictions where Indian laws are not respected."[55]

Capital occupies ephemeral material states as it moves between bank accounts and borders. The financial sublime emerges as capital turns into import goods, narcotics, diamonds, gold bricks, carpets, and car rentals and back again into cash, only to melt into the comfort of a legitimized bank account and make its way back to India, where it is embedded in the land.[56] These ephemeral workings are also visible in the 2018 fall of IL&FS, one of India's biggest shadow lenders or NBFCs, with a default of US$12.8 billion (₹91,000 crore) and allegations of fraud.[57] Out of the 11,402 NBFCs registered in 2017, 4,135 entities have violated the Prevention of Money Laundering Act of 2002 through the magic tricks of finance.[58] The Panama Papers, for example, revealed that more than five hundred Indians had shell accounts in the British Virgin Islands, many of them with business stakes in NCR's real estate development.[59]

These financial transformations occur on a smaller scale as well. Shilpa, a young professional, wanted to buy an apartment for her now deceased aunt, who moved from Kolkata to New Delhi. Her aunt sold her old Kolkata apartment to be closer to family, and part of the payment arrived at Shilpa's flat in the form of two young men with a duffel bag. As is often the case with older apartments in Indian cities, Shilpa's aunt received part of the payment in cash transferred across cities through *hawala*. Coming into the living room, the young men opened up the bag and began placing stacks of rupees on the living room table. "I began counting it, I didn't know you are not supposed to count it," Shilpa explained her confusion with informal protocols. Not knowing what to do with so much cash, Shilpa approached Rameshji—a chartered accountant known to convert checks to gold and cash—who, for a small fee, converted the payment to gold. She described the moment to me: standing on a busy NCR street with a small, heavy purse, worried that someone would snatch it from her hands and take her aunt's savings with them. A year later, Rameshji would reconvert the gold into cash, so that Shilpa could pay for her aunt's new apartment.

Shilpa's aunt was an old, small fish in a deep and expansive ocean of money's material magic in real estate. But her example speaks to the convertibility of money and the ephemeral properties of convertibility: money refuses to rest. At times these ephemeral transactions require a locational stability that is brought about through the construction industry itself. Black money is born from the soil and laundered back into new land. Mr. Kumar explains this anchoring in real estate: "Black money and the property industry are co-dependent. Without one the other would collapse." He states matter-of-factly, "Simply put: if my apartment costs

30 lakh and I paid 20 white and 10 black. Tomorrow if I go to sell it in white I can only get the money on the 20 value, not on the 10. Everyone who makes black invests it in the property market." He laughs ironically: "We cannot all afford Swiss bank accounts. Black money picked up by builders too needs to be invested into new places. It is all a continuous cycle." According to him, the property market is so dependent on black money that it would cease to function if black money were eliminated. He speaks of the dilemma of the anti-corruption protests: "If Hazare is successful and the Janlokpal successful too, if we begin to weed corruption out, and with it weed black money out, what becomes of the property market?"[60]

As money—in the form of cash; global, regional, and local capital; materials; property; and gold—circulates through the muddied and muddled streets of NCR, it acquires a magic and life of its own. It weaves a web of spectacular speculations and is discussed on street corners at tea stalls and in five-star restaurants alike. It builds its own hierarchies of power and intertwines all of us within the moral sphere of capitalist desire.[61] Money feeds the growth of surreal real estate worlds. Characteristic of these transactions is the work of social relations and kin. Fathers, brothers, uncles, aunts, and our people become the key mediators in the convertibility of money, the social infrastructures of the ephemeral workings of finance. Together they stabilize money into land, and sediment it into the architectures of the region. This circulation and conversion fortifies an underground terrain of cash, an over-ground material terrain of architecture, and a relational terrain of social networks in Gurgaon.[62]

SUBLIME ATMOSPHERES

The term *black money* brings together a speculative cloud of financial terms and practices from real estate, construction, and beyond. Many material and intangible states of capital—cash, equity, gold, cement, property—as well as a variety of practices—bribes, banking, pilferage, brokering, and legal maneuverings—empower real estate and construction activity in the region. While the previous sections described the fluidity between forms of capital and the social networks through which they further real estate, this section focuses on a specific practice, the bribe and the kinship networks it creates. There are myriad material manifestations of the bribe or kickback: an informal cash or in-kind payment often seen as a primary unit of black money. Black money is involved and generated at every stage in construction and real estate activity. Moving beyond large-scale financing, I look at the ways in which each stage of construction—from land acquisition to construction completion—produces a financial sublime that comprises an obfuscating, magical atmosphere undergirded by the intimate work of kin.

Narendra is a small-scale land broker in Gurgaon. On most days he can be found riding his motorbike through villages and fields, smoking *hukkah* with headmen at *chowpals*, drinking in local bars, or lazing on the *khat* in the shaded courtyard of his house. Narendra is Ahir and a member of Gurgaon's landowning community and seems to know all the landowners in the area. A kinship and social relationship expert, Narendra can name the village and relatives of any person when you mention their name, many of whom are his own kin. As a middleman between the urbanites and villagers, he helped broker land deals, visible in the material wealth of his growing home: in the four years I visited him he added a compound wall and wrought iron gate, built a new room, and bought some heavy wooden furniture, a new motorbike, and a new car.

The construction industry relies on individuals such as Narendra, whose brokering and social connections form the connective thread between local landowners (can be secondary owners as well), individual buyers, and developers. The buying of land to build on is one of the first acts of construction, and as Mr. Reddy implied, often up to two-thirds of the land price is paid in cash. The difference between the circle rates (official registered prices for the area on which property tax is paid) and the market price of land is paid in cash to avoid taxation and launder accumulated reserves.[63] Brokers such as Narendra, too, receive their fees in cash. Cash transactions reduce taxation rates for the sellers and are useful for cash-heavy dealings such as marriages, the purchase of luxury goods, land transactions, and gold sales. The number of luxury car and product showrooms has multiplied in Gurgaon. The shopowners offer heavy discounts for goods paid for in cash; these earnings often make their way back into real estate.

The power of locale and kin relations appears in land transactions, and a payment often indexes local political power. Ram, a young and ambitious site supervisor, learns this the hard way. Ram comes from a land-owning family in Bihar and supervises the Haveli site. On the site one day, he is restless and preoccupied. The problem is with some land he bought on the outskirts of Gurgaon. The previous owner sold Ram the land in a direct transaction and did not "consult" the local gang leader (or *bhai*, lit. brother) when he sold the land. The *bhai* was incensed that he had not gotten a payment from the transaction of the land and began illegally leasing it to a local shopkeeper as revenge. Ram is worried, since occupation of land allows people a claim to it. He could not go to the police, because the *bhai* "drank with the police every night, they were all together [*milein hain*]," and there was no point in getting locked into a court case; he knew that the *bhai* would make trouble for him if he did so. He asked the original owner to pay the *bhai*. "It is not my problem," he tells me, but he still looks anxious. Local alliances and grounded knowledge control financial transactions. Small players and middlemen arise through symbolic and social capital. They form keystones in the arches of land transactions in Gurgaon and demonstrate the intimate interlinkages of social networks and cash exchange in the politics of urban development.

Like Narendra, Maansinghji is a useful man (*kaam ka aadmi*) embroiled in the politics of Haryana's political and landowning caste—Jats—known for their military and agrarian connections. Maansinghji, a Jat himself, acquired his wheeling and dealing skills during college, when he was part of student political groups. More interested in politics than exam papers, Maansinghji repeatedly failed his exams, and it took him almost ten years to finish his undergraduate education. He did not have the capacity to study and asked a local minister friend to demand that the exam papers be brought to his house so that he could write them there. (The minister first suggested that he cheat instead and that he would take care of the plagiarism case against him.) What he lacked in textbook knowledge Maansinghji made up for in political connections through his student activism. He provided students for political rallies at a cost and was once jailed for seventeen days with people who became cabinet ministers. He critiques corruption in the development of Gurgaon: according to him, the chief minister allowed a nearby industrial zone to be extended by India's leading business house and allocated large tracts of land as an SEZ. "With the excuse of the SEZ the chief minister's *aadmis* [men] purchased land cheaply, people sold the land because you cannot do anything with land within an SEZ." While the farmers sold at 60 lakh (US$83,000) per acre, the chief minister and town planners later changed the land use, and the cost of the land became 4 crores (US$550,000) per acre. He gesticulates in anger: "You can say it is a development. . . . You are the private developer, you put the money and got land use changed and made money." According to him this is profiteering of land and not development: "Did they supply water? Did they build a sewer? Did they put a road? Only [demarcating] on the paper [that] this is a 'R' zone or this is an 'industry' zone? Is that development?"

Though vocal on how developer-politicians produce bad urban development, Maansinghji is also known as the one you call when you need "something done" in urban development in Gurgaon. He claims he helped broker an infamous land deal between a minister and a developer. They called him on his phone and inquired about land. "I called and got it done [*karvaya tha*]," he boasts.

The material-intangible scapes of capital transformations in construction define who is a useful person and who is not. Like Maansinghji, politicians have several middlemen (often extended family members or members of the same kin community) who mediate transactions, help move their money, and manage their informal assets. A businessman seeking a No Objection Certificate for his small enterprise describes how he was asked by the local minister in charge to go meet "our/his man" (*apna aadmi*) before he came to him again. The minister's man ran a small empire of real estate and business holdings, and the minister held shares in the company. Holding stakes in a third-party company often indexes money laundering and dealings and supersedes a now-illegal form of property holding known as *benami* property, or property in another's name.

As mentioned previously, urban development politics in India are politicized, and state officials can be primary dispossessors and accumulators.[64] Alliances form between developers and politicians as various permissions and planning initiatives are passed. The locations of rail and road corridors and other forms of infrastructural development are linked to land prices, and real estate and infrastructure developers often pay bribes to state officials to change the location of infrastructural projects. Bureaucrats who refuse to conform to this system are often penalized and thrown out of the *hamara aadmi* circuits. The story of Mr. Das best illustrates this.

I first noticed Mr Das's name on a hot, humid afternoon in July 2012, as I sat drinking syrupy tea with a group of planners on their afternoon break. My eyes ran down the board listing chief planners behind the large desk we sat at, and Mr. Das's name stood out because of the strange dates that followed his name: July 15–19, 2008, the board read. He was chief town planner for four whole days. Upon inquiry, the planners told a most curious tale. It was rumored that on his first day as head of the department, Mr. Das decided to demolish an illegal compound wall. As he filed the necessary paperwork, unbeknownst to him forces were gathering. On the second day of his job, he supervised the demolishing of the wall. A number of police cars arrived and arrested Mr. Das. The illegal construction, it turned out, belonged to a close friend of a political leader. Mr. Das was jailed for unauthorized demolition—an irony, given that it was his job to deem what was and was not authorized. On the fourth day he was released from jail and transferred to a rural area, and a new name was etched under his on the wooden board that encodes the material memory of the incident.

Nexuses of developers, politicians, their kin, and friendships exercise power in construction. The power of privatized capital and the power of the state combine through *apna aadmis* and their transactions of cash.[65] Together they multiply the corporations and companies they maintain stakes in, subdividing and diversifying their fortunes into companies related to real estate. Kin lines are important here, as the people you trust are often from a kin community you are rooted in, indexed by the terms *apna* (mine) and *hamaara* (ours), thus solidifying kin networks through the mutual dependency and trust that informal exchanges demand.

Conversations about kickbacks, bribes, and disappearances of money, however, circulate across all classes, religiosities, and castes and surround all forms of construction work. Subas, a newly married Banjara (Scheduled Castes and Tribes community) from Chirawa, Rajasthan, travelled to Gurgaon with his wife Beena and fifty clan members. He describes road construction schemes in his district that provide laborers with work under the Mahatma Gandhi National Rural Employment Guarantee Act (MGNREGA or NREGA), but also speaks of kickbacks that make it difficult to survive. "The world these days is useless, everyone just makes money off each other." Payments in NREGA are whittled down as each supervisor in the chain takes a cut. Subas explains, "If at the top [₹]300 is given, then the [people in the] middle will only get 100-100 [₹100 each]. Eating, eating [*khatein-khatein*], they eat [the money]." The pilferage results in individuals like Subas, who are below the poverty line (BPL), ending up with miniscule amounts. "We dig up the road under NREGA . . . put mud on the side of the road . . . they give us ₹20-20 a day . . . it is 115 [the official day rate is ₹115]. . . but only ₹20-20 come, everything else is eaten up," he complains.

Subas's use of *khatein-khatein* (eating-eating) references the stage-wise kickback and stake each person in the hierarchy of construction demands, but also the lack of exact knowledge about who takes the money and how much. The bribe gains an omnipresence and scale of its own in construction. Laborers pay bribes to get jobs and small contracts. Contractors make large gifts to secure larger contracts. They pay bribes in order to hire workers, bribes in order to transport material, and bribes to security in order to pilfer materials. When I worked in an architectural office, material suppliers would offer me percentages of products if we recommended them to our clients, begging the question of how much filters down to those who need it—as the case of Subas exemplifies.

Bribes are part of Gurgaon's everyday, so much so that they are referred to as *suvidha sulkh*, or facilitation tax. Other common terms for bribes include spending money (*kharcha paani*), added weight (*wazan*), tea-coffee (*chai-pani*), and sweets for my children (*bacchon ki mithai*). Each term has a specific social or facilitation register, moving the concept of bribery out of the realm of illegality by demonstrating its social value. Bribes tend to be in cash but can also take a variety of other forms. A manager speaks of dropping off a large bronze statue of a god as a Diwali gift at a bureaucrat's house; an official describes receiving an apartment from a developer for his help with a project. Another takes me to a hotel where the manager knows him well, for a free meal; we are treated with respect for an alliance kept.

Cash also transforms into material supplies in construction. After land and labor, cement and steel are the two largest financial investments in construction. In March 2013, I sit on a construction site and chat with

Uttar Pradesh–based site contractors about their experiences in construction; they chuckle with great pride as they narrate how they made money on a former construction site. Arun speaks: "On that site we made sure we got all our money's worth. We brought 125 pieces of scaffolding and while going we took away 150. On that site it was 'take as much as you want.'" He became friends with the site engineer: "Put a pot of clarified butter [a euphemism for a bribe] in front of the engineer and he would say 'let me sign that.'" Shiv pipes in, "I have also taken things. I sent broken pipes to site and took away brand new ones. Yes, when we put up the steel meshes for scaffolding . . . we took away all new ones." The conversation turns into competition as Arun boasts, "We put number two bricks [inferior quality]. They were not going to get passed. They had a material-testing lab. I went and asked them straight—how much do you want? He said 5000 rupees. I told him please adjust that to 100–200 rupees." Shiv laughs in recollection, "Yes, you sent me there—I had to give them 700 rupees out of my own pocket, only then he agreed." Arun nods. "He approved 1.5-lakh bricks. He was one of our men [*apna aadmi*]. He said that he needed to reject at least half a truck [to make it look like he was doing his job]. I said OK. He would send the truck back. I would go to the gate and put some money down [in front of the guard] and say the engineer signed this." Arun smacks his hand on the table for dramatic effect. "The guard used to sign the release sheet [and take the truck in]." Shiv *laughs* again, "Once our truck went in—it never came out."

Arun and Shiv's bragging attests to the pride with which contractors squeeze money and cut costs. Their conversation describes the tip of the iceberg of tactics of generating money in the process of construction. They describe magical acts through which inferior-quality real estate is constructed, and the systematic and casual ways in which bribes produce this inferior construction. Their stories also demonstrate the nonchalance and matter-of-factness that accompany the giving and taking of bribes.

As the bragging contractors illustrate, bribes have a strong social register; you make friends as you give bribes. The people involved in illegal financial transactions become "your people." Bribes, and black money, involve a great deal of trust, as there is no paperwork or legal structure to protect you. You do not see where your money goes. There are no receipts, and no records; giving a bribe is an act of faith. Bribery is a mode of demonstrating your skills and usefulness as an employee. As the case of Shiv shows, juniors are mentored into the system, and mentorship often extended only to those of the same ethnicity, religiosity, or caste. The bragging also demonstrates the male bravado and hypermasculinity that infuses bribe-giving and -taking and is used to exclude women from construction work.

As a project progresses, it is said that systematic bribes are given to government officials within the twenty-odd departments that need to sign off on it from start to finish. Often officials are bribed to overlook building violations and speed up paperwork. Individuals in construction supervision and management are nonchalant about visiting offices for permissions, bargaining with officials, and paying them. One speaks of a building inspection and their interaction with the inspector: "They are asking for 12,00,000 rupees for the No Objection Certificate so that we can continue work." I gasp at the amount, knowing that many certifications exist in building construction.[66] The manager explains, "They will only give the certificate if we meet the standards, of course. They do their job but they also want the money. I bargained them down to 1,00,000 but they cannot do it for any less. The money is going to their HOD [head of department] too."

Systems of bribery, among bureaucrats and government officials, are said to be hyper-organized in Gurgaon. The bribe is distributed across ranks with a percentage designated for everyone, from peon to politician. It is said that you never pay just one person but the entire hierarchy of permission-givers. Gurgaon is the most coveted urban development or town planning position in Haryana, and people often give bribes to get posts there or are given posts as rewards due to the lucrative real estate industry. Bribes extend beyond government positions in construction-related work. Workers on site talk to me about not having enough money to help pay for a position in the police, about giving bribes to get appointed in a government-run crèche that receives food and supplies for the requisite midday meals, and about bribing senior officials for government jobs they are eligible for as part of their Scheduled Castes and Tribes status. The omnipresence of bribing also ensures that those who have less get less, as paying money is seen as a facilitation fee in an overstressed governmental system. This exacerbates income inequality, reproduces class and caste hierarchies, and only furthers bribing practices, as taking bribes is a means of class mobility.

In the final stages of construction, real estate brokers flip property for three to ten times the amount they paid. Property buyers pay large amounts in cash to secure space. A salaried employee for most of his life narrated to me how he created black money when he bought the apartment he lives in: he withdrew money from an ATM every few days for over three months to create three lakh rupees in cash, a large sum for him at the time. And when a consumer moves into their home, a system of bribes often accompanies the buying and registration process, too.[67]

Black money does not circulate in the construction industry alone but moves in and out of this and other industries. A week before I leave New Delhi, Amar, one of the directors at Wandering Woods, describes how developers are now investing in the power industry as a way of securing electricity for their properties. They are developing their stakes in connected industries: natural resources and energy.[68] Ponty Chadha serves as an example of these networks. Known as the liquor baron of North India for his monopoly on alcohol outlets in the tristate area, Ponty moved into property development in the early 2000s but also owned assets in film production and sugar. Ponty's empire shows how money, alcohol, and real estate transform into each other to expand and multiply capital. Known for his ability to create alliances with the government in power, Chadha was not a man to contend with. In 2012 income tax raids were conducted at his many properties, only to find large, nearly empty safes and office computers that had been reformatted. The income tax official who ordered the raid was transferred from his position soon after, while rumors circulated about 100 crores of rupees in cash being found.[69] In October 2012 Chadha and his brother shot at each other in a dispute over their multi-million-dollar farmhouse property on the outskirts of Gurgaon. They both died in hospital, and the government officials present during the shoot-out absconded. The encounter, and the strange presence of state officials, is a harsh reminder of the violence and dangerous liaisons omnipresent in property and black money exchanges. This violence, combined with stories of ill-gotten wealth, exemplifies the awe and terror of the financial sublime in NCR.

The multiple interpretations of bribes also challenge the nature of corruption itself as corruption mixes with spirituality, friendships, good work practices, and proper forms of masculinity. Bribery is also about challenging class and caste hierarchy. Maansinghji, our middleman bureaucrat, very matter-of-factly says, "You think corruption is wrong ... corruption is not wrong. Look at this phone." He holds up his fancy smartphone. "Where will all this come from? All these big-big people keep eating all the money and we should do nothing? All the money in this country has gone into the pockets of the rich." He speaks charismatically, taking dramatic pauses and manipulating vocal tones and volumes to highlight his point, betraying his political roots. "How will my children go anywhere in life? The children of lesser people, how will they move ahead in life? Through corruption." The staff around us agree, nodding enthusiastically.

For individuals such as Maansinghji, taking bribes is not negative and illegal but a correction to the corruption of the elite. It is an equalizer of fortune. He recognizes the extreme disparity of economic growth in India and acknowledges the plunder and exploitation through which this growth occurred. What is evident in these interactions is the shift in the moral valence of corruption. It is no longer bad to be corrupt; rather, it is a basic right, an act of trust, a service fee, an incentive to do your job well, or a means of class critique and ascendancy.[70] It is a way of protecting family. At the same time, Maansinghji and the staff who agree with him are lower middle-class or working-class people with connections, indicating the improbability of those with no money and no connections moving ahead.

If the social life of money (its ability to be moved into property, architecture, gold, or energy) articulates the "regimes of value" money is embedded in, then the social life of bribes in real estate and construction reveals the way value discombobulates.[71] Value is not only economic but is a complex form; it can be also understood as heterogeneous ("economic, ritual, aesthetic, ethical"), "enmeshed," "entangled," and multiscalar.[72] The ephemeral atmospheres of capital and finance in Gurgaon produce a multiplicity of economic, moral, and social values; these values that do not exist in separate spheres.[73] Instead, "multiple or hybrid forms of value occur simultaneously" where individuals hold several oppositional values together or exercise a "provisional agency" or contextual orientation of values depending on the situation.[74] This give rises to a plethora of entangled values in relation to money that transform according to context, people, and time. These shifting, often antagonistic, and enmeshed values contribute to the construction of the financial sublime. Value proliferates in the expansive atmospheres of the financial sublime.

THE FINANCIAL SUBLIME

The three contractors, after jostling over who made the most money from the last project they worked on, begin to tell me ghost stories. I am enthralled as they compete with each other to entertain me. The sun sets on the construction site, and the only light is from a naked bulb behind Bholeji. I see outlines of trees and steel bars in the dimness of twilight and I am more than a little frightened as they narrate their tales. Bholeji begins: "There was this holy man in this village. He used to walk on water, on the Ganges. His home was by the water. People used to see him walking on water. It was like there was no water, but it was a road." Arun scoffs: "That is nothing. There was this man in our village. He went to the village temple and prayed for six years." He drops his voice. "If you saw him at night, you would see that his limbs are in different pieces, all apart, and hanging on the tree. If anyone saw him, they would faint." It is already dark on the construction site, and strange shadows fall across the unfinished architectures. Bholeji continues his story: "That man, we could see his head and his hands, but his torso, we could never see that. Here"—he points at his torso with his hands—"there was only a cloth tied here. We used to see him on the shore of the Ganges."

Several stories of ghosts or supernatural beings such as the ones told by the contractors emerged during my fieldwork on construction sites. Ghosts are part of construction histories. There is a belief among many workers that human sacrifices are made at the commencement of large-scale construction work, a belief that also reflects the number of worker deaths connected to construction. Land is associated with the ancestors of families who own it and is often inalienable in the sense that the ghosts of family will haunt it long after it is bought or sold.[75] What is striking in these stories is not only the discombobulations and disorientations that relate to the piecemeal nature of financial transaction in the region but also the omnipresence and accepted nature of supernatural activity. Experiences of witchcraft, ghosts, disconnected limbs, zombies, and disassociated bodies are often spoken of as forms of reckoning or markers of economic transitions that reveal the anxiety of these transitions.[76] For me, these stories are not seen as uncanny or as diagnostics of economic change but are feared and respected as part of a copresent spiritual unknown world.[77] The stories mirror the ephemeral materialities of money, the magic through which money appears and disappears, and the discombobulated knowledge that surrounds it. Like finance, they represent the unknown, yet accepted, workings of Gurgaon worlds.

In aesthetic theory the sublime refers to that which is imagined and perceived as beyond and bigger than us. A dominant thread of the sublime is associated with the natural world and with a sense of both wonder and terror, which exist in dialectical relation within the sublime.[78] "The size, the intensity, the extension, and the sheer power of the modern capitalist (. . . postmodern, late capitalist) economy" can be understood as sublime.[79] But the sublime is a distinct experience as well as a quality of phenomena (like the economy), begging the question of who experiences it and how. It is often accompanied by colonization (in the case of the American landscape or early political economy) and occurs at the cost of those who have a variant relationship with the landscape (e.g., Indigenous Americans) or economy (South Asians). The sublime works on the erasure and denial of the accumulations and appropriations that occur as it is experienced. The financial sublime in Gurgaon operates on a similar yet different trajectory. It emphasizes the material and is produced, I argue, through the shifting and circulating materialities of money.[80] Like the natural sublime, the financial sublime here is a social and kin-based provincial production that enables accumulations and appropriations. Like the natural sublime, the financial sublime produces a discourse of magical and ethereal atmospherics that shock, awe, and mask accumulative political economies, but the accumulations are known to those exploited.

Financial processes are a key force behind the rapid urbanization of Gurgaon, NCR. The speed at which finance circulates and the magical, social, and moral states it occupies are mirrored in the story of limbs appearing and disappearing. The amount of wealth the elite accrue becomes wondrous.[81] It is impossible to trace the cycles and states of money as it moves from property to drugs to alcohol to doctored account books, and from politicians to industrialists to middlemen to mafia. Finance emerges as a cloud of small practices, rumors, and gossip whose total working and organization is speculated on. The continuous shifting states and valences money occupies; the solid forms it takes as land, bills, and gold; and the lightness of its numerical and accounted side all serve to construct a financial sublime. Just like the limbs moving around the tree, money too appears in new configurations every day. It is magical. At times it is solid—then, just like that, it disappears into air.[82] The many materialities of money manifest at times in parts, sometimes in the whole, changing places and spaces, to nestle into the distinct built landscapes of Gurgaon. The construction-scapes of Gurgaon, the vacant plots of land awaiting speculative booms, the apartments, the glittering malls, the overflowing excess of urban villages, and the luxury cars on the road radiate with the accumulations and movements of capital.

Construction and real estate industries generate a *financial sublime* for the people of the urban region, where money appears bigger than us all, moving and melding through accounts and infrastructures to become a known-unknown. This form of the ephemeral is bred through the deliberate intimacies of caste- and class-based kinships, both real and fictive. Financial knowledge and profits are shared within select class-caste and -ethnic communities, excluding access to outsiders. The sublime feeds the power of kin; it mixes awe, anxiety, intimacy, and exclusion to propel the real estate and construction industry of Gurgaon. Maansinghji, Subas, and Jeysingh all know the reality of the workings of the financial sublime, but each participates differently within it. It is the very construction of the financial sublime that generates the greed and need for more bribes, more hoarding, and more real estate. The financial sublime produces the want to be part of it. The terror and wonder and the intimacies and exclusions of development are inscribed into the reassuring stack of rupee bills that are stuffed into mattresses at night.

3 Drawing Fantasies

"Where is your home?" I ask Bala in awkward Bengali. Bala, a lean and chatty Malda worker, has approached me to ask if I spoke Bengali. I respond to his question with my own. He laughs at my linguistic awkwardness but replies, telling me where he has been. He knows a lot of India, he says in Hindi, and has traveled all over the country: Bombay, Tamil Nadu, and Gujarat. He has constructed electrical lines in Tamil Nadu, packaged soap in Gujarat, and worked as a *beldar* (laborer) in Bombay, but he is from West Bengal. "It is beyond Kolkata," he replies as he describes his home. Bending over, he swishes his index finger along the ground. He traces a winding path, draws a circle, and places a stone. "Over here is my *jhilla* [district], you cross a mountain pass and you get to my village."

The geography of West Bengal comes alive through Bala's tracings on the ground; I imagine the winding road past the narrow *ghat* (mountain pass) that he describes. The road moves into green forests, the village, and the hills. We are transported out of the space of the busy construction site and into the imagined and remembered geographies he draws. The imagined spaces dissipate as thumps and thuds around us draw us back

85

Figure 7. Bala draws a map to his village in West Bengal, 2012. Photo by author.

into our construction world. Wandering Woods, the real estate construction project on the urban periphery of Gurgaon, thrums with construction activity, but it too was once a mere drawing. The site and its surrounding region were formed through the commingled plans, images, and etchings that engineers, architects, planners, developers, brokers, farmers, and laborers drew and continue to draw.

City plans, building renderings, maps, and architectural drawings are often understood as concrete, permanent artifacts inscribed with bureaucratic finitude, but many scholars argue that plans are lively, dreamlike, and phantasmagorical devices of social and political struggle.[1] Building on their stances, I argue that the ephemeral nature of plans and drawings in the construction industry produces not fear and awe (like construction finance) but fantasy and desire. Drawings in the construction industry are ephemeral in the fact that they change continuously: they exchange hands and are erased, manipulated, redrawn, reimagined, and circulated by those across the class and caste spectrum, giving rise to mobilities and power on the one hand and erasures and silences on the other. Acts of drawing and the fantasies these acts create are active, aesthetic sites of political-economic control and struggle; the transmutability of drawings and their circulation produces desires for and dreams of alternate worlds.

Turn a corner in Gurgaon and you will find a drawing, from planning offices and architecture studios to developers' cabins and construction sites. Drawings present themselves in small government (*tehsil*) offices, in schools, colonies, and parks. Plans, drawings, diagrams, and maps of the areas under construction loom larger than life on the billboards above roads and leap from the fences that cordon off private plots. Drawings are painted onto road signs, drafted on computers, printed into brochures, and even inscribed onto the earth. Here I focus on drawing not as a product but as a process that involves the ephemeral understood as erasures and transformations of lines and drawings in construction. The production and inscription of fantasy and desire, in and through acts of drawing, fuel urban development, accumulation, social mobility, and class-caste struggle in NCR.[2] The ability of the ephemeral to evoke the fantastical demonstrates that contemporary construction industries harness human psyche and subjectivity in order to further production-consumption.

I switch between formal archives of large-scale masterplans of the region, marketing drawings, architectural drawings, and informal archives of drawing (sketches in the sand, rough sketches on notepads, and dreams for homes). I demonstrate how the malleability of formal and informal master plans produces pathways of profit in NCR. Marketing plans and drawings through their relentless circulation in urban areas produce middle-class homeownership fantasies while eliminating the contribution of laborers. Technical drawings for construction and the constant back and forth that reshapes them highlight the battle over power and mobility in the production chain. In the shifting sands of Gurgaon, drawing becomes not only a creative and generative act but also one that challenges the ideological control of urban planning and development. It forms a realm wherein the fantastical, as tied to social desires, is deployed as a vector of power and class and caste struggle.

REGIONAL MASTER PLANS

The National Capital Region Planning Board (NCRPB) sits inside the India Habitat Center (IHC), a monolithic brick structure located in the Lodi

Garden area in New Delhi. The Lodi Garden institutional and government zone exemplifies New Delhi's architectural splendor. A series of monumental buildings—the World Wildlife Fund, Max Mueller Headquarters, the India International Center—flank tree-lined roads. Peacocks coo within the large rain trees of this majestic neighborhood as Neelkanth Sir and I walk toward the NCRPB office one summer afternoon. A dust storm (*aandhi*) arises. The trees above us rustle, and we can hear windows and doors slam. These violent thuds are accompanied by the rattle of sands shifting and a gaggle of people yelling. My heartbeat rises in response to the urgent sounds of an NCR summer.

Sir and I are heading to NCRPB to find information on the regional plan for NCR. A retired planner and geographer, he learned to decipher the city and urban regions he grew up in from the contour lines on the maps that his staff planned with. He often speaks of the translation of statistical information into lines on a plan and a plan's ability to enact real-world change. My architecture and urban design days left my lower back strained from bending over a drawing board but inculcated in me a respect for the amount of labor and time drawings demand. Neelkanth Sir and I share a love of seeking out plans.

A number of beautiful ruins surround us as we walk through the Lodi Garden area. Named after the parks surrounding the tombs of kings of the Lodi dynasty, Lodi Garden commemorates the last of the five Islamic dynasties that formed the Delhi Sultanate in the thirteenth through sixteenth centuries. The lush, green gardens, full of swallows on trees and intricately carved tombs, are located adjacent to the center of Delhi. To the north sits the Capitol complex of India. Envisioned and completed by architects Lutyens and Baker in the 1930s, the area has a baroque plan, similar to Washington, DC. A neoclassical-meets-Indian (Indo-Saracenic) architectural style represents the last days of British rule in India. North of the Capitol extend old-style government housing and elegant bungalows, white with fluted Ionic columns and green lawns overflowing with bougainvillea and birds. These monumental structures give way to narrow trade areas. Dense and populated old Delhi sits in the North: built in the Mughal era after the fall of the Delhi Sultanate, the area stands apart for its historic architecture, mosques, temples, and gurudwaras. More commercial areas with narrow streets that overflow with shops and stalls, billboards, and boxes stand in the former location of ancient markets. Sprawling university grounds surrounded by middle-class housing and commercial areas built in the early 1900s sit even farther north. To the west we see three-storied apartment blocks, sardined together around small colony gardens, in lanes full of parked cars, crisscrossed by telephone, television, and electric cables. It is here that many Sikh and Punjabi refugees settled in the postpartition years. In contradistinction, to the south of Lodi Gardens sit a ring of upper-middle-class housing and affluent bungalow plots. To the west of these bungalows extends the diplomatic enclave. The sub-city of Rohini, developed by the Delhi Development Authority, lies at its northern edge. Pockets of informal settlements, or *bastis*, such as those in Shakur Basti, Indira Camp, Kathputli Colony, and Seemapuri, occupy the interstitial spaces between the affluent neighborhoods in the city-region, many of whom are in a constant battle to survive.[3]

When the NCRPB was established in 1985, the area I am describing housed the majority of the region's urban residents.[4] The Delhi Development Authority's severe restrictions within city limits, however, prompted development beyond these bounds. On the east of Lodi Gardens runs the river Yamuna. Close to its winding path lies the boundary between the NCT and the city-suburb NOIDA (New Okhla Industrial Development Authority). Vegetable fields and rushes intertwine with *bastis* and temples on the Yamuna floodplain and lead you into the state of Uttar Pradesh and NOIDA. In NOIDA gridded roads, already overloaded with traffic, form the boundaries for large-scale housing complexes and commercial districts. A sleek new expressway leads us to Greater NOIDA, a green, golf course–centered suburb built as an investment opportunity. In the north sits Ghaziabad, once an industrial hub, now lined with residential gated complexes. South of Delhi nestles the state of Haryana, in which Bala and I stand. Haryana houses the NCR city-suburbs of Faridabad and Gurgaon. NCR forms a 55,083-square-kilometer urban region.[5] It is an urban footprint that would not have been dreamt of thirty years ago; the fantastical speeds at which the region grew exceed our imaginations.

Fantasies of speed and growth evaporate in the NCRPB office. A dingy staircase leads us to a dull maze of off-white wood and glass-partitioned walls. The NCRPB is a special planning body created in 1985 in response to concerns over unchecked urban growth in the Delhi metropolitan area. The capital's urban region now encompasses multiple cities, three states, and the NCT.[6] The relentless pace of construction and real estate speculation promised to push its boundaries even further in the coming years to include large tracts of land in the state of Rajasthan just a few miles away from Gurgaon. The NCRPB was founded as a central governing body that would create a master plan for the entire region and ensure coordinated growth.

At the entrance of the office an attendant rests on a chair, drowsy and drugged by the heat of the day. Neelkanth Sir rouses him to make inquiries, and we are shown to a master planner's cabin, Mr. Sahani's. Mr. Sahani does not look too pleased to see us but welcomes us anyway. He offers cups of tea. As we make small talk, and Sir and he exchange information about mutual acquaintances, my attention is drawn to the large splotches of color and the tangle of lines on the wall to my left. This is the transportation master plan for NCR.[7] The plan weaves a detailed and intricate future for NCR through spiderweb train tracks, bus routes, roads, and rapid rail. Printed on shiny card stock and framed in cheap plastic, the plan glistens with the promise of an urban utopia. A geographic information system (GIS) map forms the base; amoebic red areas mark current urban land; land that could be converted from agricultural to urban is yellow. I marvel at the fact that almost 60 percent of the land on the map is slotted for urbanization, hence development and construction.

The plan exudes an innate charisma. It glows with technocratic authority. The suburban areas around Delhi are red dots. Dashed lines, representing a nonexistent regional rapid transport system, extend from each suburb center to merge into a rapid transportation ring around Delhi's central business district. An orbital road corridor runs around the entire city and shoots bold, sunray-like highways down into all the suburbs. Fingers of protected forest areas and agricultural lands wind gingerly around the corridors in two shades of green. A verdant, well-functioning, and efficient megalopolis thrums through the delicate veins of the plan. I am mesmerized by its intricacies.

Mr. Sahni describes the plan in a practiced manner. "This regional master plan for 2021 was notified in 2005. It encompasses over 33,000 square kilometers of the tri-state National Capital Region." He barely pauses for a breath. "It has an inner road corridor, [and] an outer corridor, its trade complexes are integrated with the suburban railways system, and [it] has eight rail corridors feeding the city." He drones on about the visions and arrangements of the NCRPB in what seems to be an oft-repeated speech.

In the two-hour meeting, Mr. Sahani narrates the trials and tribulations involved in putting together the plan. What is unsaid but understood by the three of us is that this plan will never come to fruition; unlike the elements on Bala's map all the infrastructure on this plan does not and most likely will not exist.[8] Many of the lines on this plan will be morphed, as the region does not have the money to construct the infrastructure the plan promises, nor do the various stakeholders agree upon it. High levels of corruption also ensure that it is impossible to match the vision of the plan to the realities on the ground. The NCRPB transportation plan is as fleeting and temporary as Bala's drawing in the mud.

This plan and the figure of the man who drew it—the planner—dominate academic discussions on urban development. The power that plans wield and the authoritarian vision they have of the world, their ability to discipline and shape us and to erase life as we know it, are knowledge that most dispossessed hold.[9] Neelkanth Sir and Mr. Sahani feel otherwise. They share a frustrated conversation and a lackluster attitude toward the plan they should be proud to have made. They talk about planners leaving the public sector to join the private sector. Constant reshuffles and the exercise of political authority on their work and lives have left them both feeling frustrated and incapacitated. Planners are the figural heads of the urban world, as the chief town planner (CTP), Mr. Gupta, explains: "We do not plan. The plan is sent to us, already made. We just outline it. All we do is patch-up work. Fix this thing, fix that thing." Mr. Gupta rubs his fingers together in the air to indicate money. "The politicians do what they want. Every day I wait for a phone call." A phone call that will order him to move to another district. "Look at the Delhi-Mumbai Industrial Corridor plan. The plan has not been passed yet and already politicians own all the property on all its sides!"

Regional and city master plans in NCR wield incredible power and promise. As Mr. Gupta describes, however, they tend to be figural, utopian, and born through collective deceptions. Master plans, planners explain, contain an inherent fallacy: they are produced through a collective knowledge that they will never be realized as planned. The plans may be false representations and fantasies, but they allow agency and accumulations.

They form an important site of power, "claims making," and "subaltern politics."[10] Plans determine which land grows in value and which tracts lie underdeveloped and barren. They create space for individual manipulations.

In the past twenty years there have been seven master plans for Gurgaon and NCR, each drawn up by successive governments and each opening up new parcels of undeveloped land for development. In 2007, 2011, and 2012 about 22,000 hectares of land were added to each plan (see the appendix).[11] Twenty-two thousand hectares is a little more than one-third of Mumbai's land mass, or about four times the size of Manhattan. Every plan, as Neelkanth Sir often decries, was really about control over land conversion and development, as land prices doubled, quadrupled, and more. Mr. Gupta describes how planning offices are bombarded with requests for land conversion, new roads and underpasses, and development of amenities that would raise the value of the land around them. As drawings are made, Mr. Gupta narrates, lines come to be bent, erased, and redrawn so as to pass through territories of political interest, revealing the contestations and collaborations of political and capitalist power. In the ephemeral nature of the drawing's aesthetic transformations lie clues to the region's pathways of power and to its fantasies of control and development. The yellow, urbanizable area on the map beams down upon the three of us in the NCRPB office. It shines the color of gold.

Some of my favorite parts of the Gurgaon region lie just adjacent to the yellow "urbanizable" area on the NCRPB regional master plan. These are the existing agricultural lands. Fields of millet and wheat sit at the edge of the Thar Desert; come monsoon, the fertile fields turn a photosynthetic green.[12] Fruit trees, ornamented with the nests of weaverbirds, demarcate one field from the next. Small brick rooms—*dhaanis*—for caretakers of crops are interspersed among them.

It is here that older generations of women farm in their vibrant *theels* (*thel*), comprising large skirts, well-fitting blouses, and dupattas, worn in the colors of the desert. Some sit at the thresholds of homes smoking hookah from mirror- and bead-embellished pipes. Neelkanth Sir's wife and sister-in-law dress me in a *theel* one day and shriek with laughter as I struggle to hide my exposed midriff. They advise me on how to coordinate the outfit. Pair a pink petticoat with light green *dupatta* or a red with

Figure 8. Women farm at agrarian peripheries of Gurgaon, 2013. Photo by author.

a deep blue. Contrast the colors, they explain to me, and "the colors will bloom." The handcrafted, embroidered *dupatta* (*odhni*/long scarf) drapes over my head and down my back as they pleat and tuck it into my waist.

Neelkanth Sir and I drive through these fields one afternoon to meet his friend's son, Narendra. "There are your friends," he comments. Two younger women in more modern *salwar kameez* outfits (pajamas and long tunics) wave to me. The two women turn their backs to us; they cover their heads and faces with *dupattas* to acknowledge Neelkanth Sir's presence as an elder. I recognize them as the two sisters-in-law—Medha and Charu—who live next to Narendra's house.

Narendra's house sits in the middle of fields, on a road so sandy that it has dunes. The regional master plan paints the area we sit in an agricultural green; rail and road routes zigzag around it, in the hope that the produce and grain from this region will be trucked to Delhi at high speed to feed the city's masses. A giant buffalo guards the courtyard of Narendra's house, and his four-year-old son often runs out to help guide me past it. There are *khats* (beds made of coir) in the sand-filled courtyard. Sir

Figure 9. Buffalo at rural home in Gurgaon district, 2012. Photo by author.

and Narendra sit on a *khat* and adjacent plastic chairs as Narendra's wife makes some tea in the shade of their two-room house. Protocol requires that she never show her face to Neelkanth Sir, so I go inside to greet her. Her two-year-old crawls around us and gives me a naughty grin.

I head out with some chai for Sir to find him and Narendra in deep conversation. "If you know anyone for this let me know," Narendra tells Sir. He picks up a twig and starts drawing lines in the sand. I realize they are talking about property Narendra intends to sell. He etches a neat L-shaped block as he speaks. "This is near the school. This is the road. This piece is on the road. Then the rest is at the back." He points at sides with the twig. "There is a seven-meter road here." He draws two lines to depict the road along the plot. "They are asking for one-twenty-five [1.25 crores, about US$200,000]." Neelkanth Sir looks at me and raises his eyebrows: "This is for one acre; there are ten!" He turns to Narendra: "Is this a second sale?" Narendra nods, tells us that this land belongs to three different people. "The farmers sold these [fields] a long time ago," he says, indicating the timeline of sales.

Narendra points the twig to the far right and draws slow strokes through the sand. "If you cut ten farmhouses of one-one acre each, even then the land will give you a bounty [*faad ke degi*]." He asks Sir if he knows anyone who wants to buy and looks at me as well. "On which side of the highway is this?" I ask, knowing well that land on this side of the highway is marked as agricultural and land on the other side of the highway is slotted for urban development. "This side," says Narendra, "but not to worry, that is not a problem."

"They call [Narendra] *patwari*," Sir jokes later, "because he wanders here and there [dealing in land].[13] Since he was a kid he buys from someone, sells to another." A *patwari* is the local authority on land revenue and records and is a coveted local government post. As official documents are often in disarray or literally in tatters, subdivided among many ancestral stakeholders, the post holder acts as a broker in the sale of land in the region. According to a popular joke, "May you be a *patwari* in your next life" is a common blessing local mothers give their sons.

I often suspect that Narendra's ambitions are driven by his wife. A determined woman, Janaki grew up in an informal settlement in the west of New Delhi and is not very fond of agrarian life. Narendra left his ancestral home to move them into this house in the fields, in part due to Janaki's insistence on autonomy from Narendra's mother and brother.[14] There is talk about her: Sir tells me that Narendra loves his wife very much and is "under her influence." Narendra's mother, Janaki complains to me, is accusing the couple of moving here and neglecting her. Janaki does not enjoy these aspects of rural life.

Janaki's elder son runs in, demanding tea, and she pours him some in a delicate ceramic teacup. He drinks it, holding the cup with both hands. She looks wistful as she tells me that he will soon be sent away. The schools here are no good, so they plan to send him to a good boarding school. "At least I will have this younger one for a few more years," she tells me, picking up her younger son. She draws the *dupatta* over her head as she walks me out into the courtyard. As we pass Narendra's scooter, she tilts her head and whispers that he is planning to buy a car.

The lines of the NCRPB plan descend onto the farmlands around us. It is through their movement from planning offices to fields that the lines conjure alternative worlds. The production and circulation of master plans lead to property speculation across the region and open space for entrepreneurial individuals like Narendra, Janaki, Medha, and Charu. We realize that the vast terrains of yellow urbanizable land, and the intricate road networks that produce them, are a contested and murky territory, full of brokers and opportunity. Several locals, like Narendra, make a good living consolidating, flipping, and brokering land deals. They act as middlemen for developers scouring the region, each one capturing and brokering space: wedging, shifting, and molding the lines of the NCRPB to claim their own small stakes. The imagined and unattainable plans of NCR comprise ephemeral lines; redrawn and reworked by many, these figural manipulations of property generate fantasies of power and mobility. The ephemeral sits at the heart of both formal and informal drawings; it builds collective and individual fantasies of gaining power and capital, through drawing plans, in the land economies of Gurgaon.

MARKETING DRAWINGS

The area around Narendra's village and the property he trades in fall under the territory of "New Gurgaon." This area is thirty minutes away from Gurgaon and separated from it by a tollbooth. Virgaon village, and the developments that grow on its agricultural lands, are also in New Gurgaon, the construction of which is transforming Virgaon. A number of older homes have been demolished and rebuilt as dormitory buildings to house migrant workers by the dozens; six men often sleep side by side in a room twenty-seven feet square. The growth in population is attributed to these dormitories. The migrants work in the factories and construction sites in and around Virgaon, drive rickshaws, work as service staff in restaurants, and work as part of cleaning crews in malls.

The number of residents and the demands of the surrounding urban development overwhelm Virgaon. The narrow village lanes are dwarfed by the ornate mansions and dormitory blocks that flank them. Waste from the neighboring real estate developments piles up on Virgaon's streets. The area lies outside the jurisdiction of the municipal council, falling instead under the control of Virgaon's village governing council (*gram panchayat*). The village heads are said not to care either. Their farmlands were sold years ago, and they now sit on cash and new landholdings as they await the next land rush. They build lavish bungalows where their ancestral homes used to be. New Gurgaon too grows outside the boundary of the village settlement (*lal dora*), its mega-structures towering over the village space.[15] Billboards depicting majestic apartment buildings, sunset-washed skies, modular kitchens, and shiny marble floor slabs traverse the region. The promised architecture constructed by workers living in Virgaon, workers like Nazeem.

Nazeem is a young laborer on the Haveli site from Malda district. He lives in a dormitory in an urban village in Gurgaon. An outgoing young man who picked up Hindi faster than his Malda friends, Nazeem chats with the staff at Haveli. He becomes good friends with Maheshji, the Rajasthani tile mason who waterproofs areas with *kota* tiles. Nazeem's cell phone plays Bollywood and Bhojpuri songs as they work. His cell phone, Nazeem tells me, has all kinds of videos. At night he watches movies on it. As Veer, the young mason (see chapter 1), says, "We [workers] know how to live a life of *aish* [pleasure]."

Unlike Veer's family poverty, which brought him into construction, Nazeem says that he didn't have to come to work on construction sites. He wanted to see *Dilli* (Delhi) and came to NCR for a summer adventure. Nazeem's father has 13 *bhigas* of land (a measure that varies, but can correspond to about 4.3 acres), and for Nazeem that land provides financial stability (although he says they have a below poverty line card for food subsidies and admits that the *jhuggi* [shack settlement] he is housed in is better than his family's home). Both Veer and Nazeem are young men who revel in pleasure; they both want to wander and roam. As they work on construction sites, their ambitions and dreams alter with the conjurations of property around them.

Marketing drawings and plans that proliferate across the region conjure up fantastical lifestyles. The circulation and omnipresence of master plans in NCR is not just a tool of middle-class desire but moves across the class spectrum to evoke a desire for property and home.[16] Veer too dreams of buying some *zameen* (land), and Nazeem wants to make improvements to his own *kothi* (hut) to match the one he lives in here. Bhojpuri cinema and Bollywood imagery, the bungalows, skyscrapers, and lifestyles within them, infiltrate their imaginations. They too want to settle, set up shop, and find their slice of paradise. At the same time, both men know their place; they acknowledge the reality that they are unwanted and erased from the marketing documents and final architecture that they help concretize. Nevertheless, they fantasize.

The images and discourses that feed Veer and Nazeem are part of NCR's urban imaginaries. I visit a real estate fair that celebrates the paradisal promises of New Gurgaon. It is held in a giant exhibition center in New Delhi. A large parking lot holds a surprising number of white compact cars, icons of India's growing lower middle class. The exhibition center is an exposed concrete, brutalist structure with a shadow-filled and musty interior. Large metal freestanding fans try to propel the fast-failing and leaky air-conditioning into the expansive depths of the building. A frayed red carpet frolics under our feet and hides an uneven cement floor, and a number of partitions divide the open space into small booths. Women and men in polyester trousers and yellowing collared shirts set up brochures, stack questionnaires, and pin up large-scale printouts. The advertisements glisten with beautiful skyscrapers that soar in front of crepuscular skies that Michelangelo would be proud of.

I meander through the stalls, staring at the images, only to be lured in by a "consultant" determined to land a new client. I tell him I was interested in Gurgaon and he pulls a plan out. I would soon see this plan at all the stalls whenever I referenced Gurgaon. A beige color fills most of the city of Gurgaon, depicting its urban areas. Darker beige gridlines demarcate the urban areas into sectors. Neat numbers name the plotted sectors. A series of thick, dark-gray lines depict existing roads and highways, and black lettering locates the railway station, town center, and major highways. Red dots depict proposed metro stations that will take years to be built, if they ever are; red lines hold the promise of new roads to come. A green patch stands out, proclaiming the building site. The consultant explains to me that there are three areas in Gurgaon: the old town of Gurgaon, the area between the two highways, and New Gurgaon. If you want to buy property, it is New Gurgaon where all the construction is happening, the consultant says. "The apartments are only three kilometers from Gurgaon, there is a new bypass being built from sector 70A. The boundary of Gurgaon is shifting to include this."

Figure 10. Example of an architectural rendering of a building project. Image courtesy JDAP, India.

The consultant suggests that I look at a housing complex known as Beautiful Sunrise. He opens a printed brochure and points to some glowing, tall white buildings. "Each is oriented differently so that no building looks into the other," he says. "They are each named after a different natural concept. There is a lot of green space around." When I inquire about the construction phase, he says that Beautiful Sunrise already has a ground-floor slab, while the other project—Gurgaon VV—has eight floor slabs built already. He insists that the way to go is new construction, as the already built ones are old already. "New Gurgaon is a good place for you, ma'am. You can get a flat now for 70 lakhs [approximately US$115,000], but if you invest in new development you can have it at 69 lakhs [approximately US$113,500], with a car park."

The car park and the brand-new apartment fulfill my hard-earned, middle-class life. The images from the brochures gleam in glory. They lift me away from the musty surroundings and carry me to an alternate India with no rural migrants, no sewage, and no waste—only delightful sunsets, tall palm trees, fountains, pools, and chirping birds! The musty smell of the dripping air-conditioning breaks my daydreams to remind me that modern fantasies are not and have never been real. Real estate fairs like this are a common occurrence in NCR and other metropolitan areas in India. Throngs of people, young and old, circulate among these spaces looking for first homes, retirement homes, or investment properties. While the rising property prices in the region please investors, a large number of scams, delays in construction, and badly constructed buildings also frustrate buyers, and there is much discontent.

As I visit this real estate fair, a battle takes place over farmlands in Greater NOIDA. Various groups of farmers, including the Bharitya Kisan Union (Indian Farmer's Union), conduct sit-ins and block highways. They are protesting unfair compensation for the government-led acquisition of farmlands. NOIDA, unlike Gurgaon, is known for its state-led development: the local government acquires land at low rates, through eminent domain, and then sells it at higher rates to create industrial and real estate properties. Several real estate projects in Greater NOIDA had been halted or declared illegal, leaving buyers furious at the money they had lost or the interruptions to work. Gautam is one of these buyers.

Gautam is a determined young architect. For ten years he watched friends join the real estate rush and move from smaller architectural firms into developer-led ones. He chose to stick to the small, well-known, craft-focused practice he worked with. For this choice, he earns less money than his contemporaries. Gautam grew up in different parts of India and finally came to live in Delhi fifteen years ago. When I first meet him, he talks about a property he has bought in Greater NOIDA. Gautam saved money and obtained a loan, alongside his father, to invest in a three-bedroom house. This was to be the family's permanent home. He chose it because he trusted the developer and the apartments were well designed. The apartment was a two-hour commute from his current office but was affordable.

We visit the house of Gautam's friend, an architect who now works for a multinational company. He has bought a house in Ghaziabad and is showing Gautam the new property. The friend's three-year-old daughter runs around the house, and his wife proudly moves through the two-bedroom apartment on the first floor of a three-storied bungalow in a small, plotted neighborhood. Gautam's friend bought this property by leveraging a loan and flipping a small investment he had made on an unbuilt flat in Virgaon area.

Later, Gautam drives me up to the property he has invested in. An empty plot sits where his apartment should be; there is a "stay order" against construction in the region following farmer protests.[17] In the meantime, his family squeezes into a small apartment in Delhi. We sometimes drive by to check on the status of the building, only to see an empty plot of land waiting for the courts, farmers, and builders to agree. It will be years until the building comes to be.

In 2016 the government of India introduced the Real Estate (Regulation and Development) Act, which added protections for consumers. The inability of developers to deliver on their property due to stay orders, insufficient funds, or outright fraud resulted in several lawsuits against real estate developers. By 2018 almost all of the major developers in the region, including Jaypee, Unitech, Amrapali, Emaar, DSK Group, PACL, Supertech, Ultratech, Ats Infrastructure, Omaxe, DLF, M3M, Vatika, and Logix Groups were involved in litigation.[18] The 2018 bailout plan proposed for infrastructure financing giant Infrastructure Leasing & Financing Services (IL&FS) demonstrates the overextension of the construction sector in general, as well-laid-out drawings and plans are dissolved through insolvency. Fantasies of real estate crumble one by one; the intricate drawings and the geographies and lifestyles they promise dissipate in court battles and decaying real estate.

Marketing plans, like the ones the consultant showed me, are mirages: documents designed to both seduce and deceive. They promise an oasis of happy living in the sand dunes of Gurgaon, an escape from the harsh lifestyle of Delhi streets. Unlike master plans, they are not set up to fail and do not morph or transform as they are constructed. Rather, they are designed to lure and then evaporate (like several developers and funding agencies themselves). Their relation to reality is siren-like, yet the desires they evoke disseminate and make their way onto construction sites and into the dreams of Nazeem and Veer.

Drawings are illusory, fantastical, and promissory devices that construct powerful potential energies. The mirages and illusions they weave in their circulations move across classes and spaces. They conjure slices of paradise and moments of pleasure. They rebel against the dust and dirt of the street and transport us to a different space and scene. Their collective fantasies prompt accumulation through the conscription of the

dreams and desires of workers. The fantasies spur home loans and speculative real estate. At the same time, many of these fantasies evaporate in
financial dysfunction and scams. In NCR, fantasies are attainable only
for a select few.

CONSTRUCTION DRAWINGS

Row upon row of mega-construction sites occupy the fields of Virgaon.
Images of future towers, fountains, and golf courses sprawl across corrugated metal fences that block worksites from curious eyes.[19] The names
and logos of developers festoon the perimeters of the property, announc-
ing their presence and advertising their product. Each gate is protected by
small guardhouses and uniformed security personnel. Behind them, tower
cranes meticulously build stories of middle-class stability.

Gopal, a Bengali architect, works on building plans in the site office
of Wandering Woods. He sits in one corner of the shared site office, from
which he coordinates the drawings for the entire site. The staff in the office
do not like Gopal because he acts as if he is too good for the construction
site. He thinks so, too. He tells me that he does not want to be here, but
they made him an offer he could not refuse. Mr. Kumar tells me Gopal is
paid more money than he is. The company hired a private car for Gopal to
be brought to work.

I watch Gopal work on a slow afternoon. A flat-screen computer is
mounted at his workstation. The screen is dark black, crisscrossed by
red, blue, green, and yellow neon lines that array parallel to each other
in L-shaped outlines. Buttons line the right-hand side of the screen, their
function indicated by a series of icons: curve, straight line, fillet, angle,
circle, rectangle, and arch. Gopal zooms in and out, focusing on a micro-
detail of a wall; he carefully selects a cluster of lines, symbols, and text,
then zooms back out as he pastes the micro-detail along the wall. Select-
ing all, he mirrors the entire detail, and a clone is born. The fluorescent
lines glow. The detail Gopal works is ten times bigger on-screen than in
reality. He fusses over the edges and corners as he cleans and neatens the
diagram and zooms out to see the whole. The filigreed fluorescent lines
spread like a delicate lattice across the black screen. Woven delicately

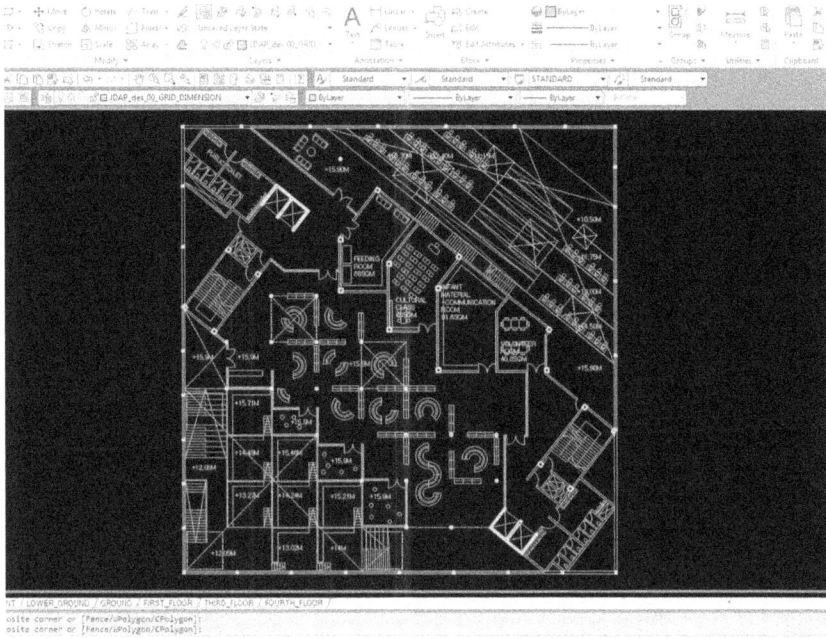

Figure 11. Computer drawing of a building floor plan. Image courtesy JDAP, India.

through Gopal's hands, they glow with the complexity and refinement of detailed craftwork.

Digital drawing technology such as AutoCAD and Revit creates an alternate world within which to dwell, an escape from concrete realities into fluorescent filigrees of lines that you create and control. Gopal talks about the endless design possibilities, the curvatures and angles, the strange footprints and fantastical forms that digital design makes possible. "Technology has made new kinds of designs possible. Before we were limited by what we could draw—now look at all the forms," he says with great passion. Though drawings are perhaps Gopal's escape from a construction site he does not want to be on, they are also convenient and practical. Every day, construction drawings stream into Gopal's mailbox from architects' and consultants' offices. He combines and checks them, asking for clarifications or details. The drawings he produces are collective documents that transform and transmit at great speed. "Before we had to hand-deliver drawings to site. Now if I need a correction I just call and they send it via email," Gopal explains. The service consultant for Wandering Woods further details the opportunities of digital drawings: "Before you were restricted to working within your city limits in order to get [the] best pool of services within capable distance," he says, sitting in his small, well-designed office in New Delhi. "But now, for example, we are doing a project . . . in Manali: the lead architects are BHB [name changed] based out of the US—they have a coordinating architect based out of Bangalore, the services consultant [is] based out of Delhi, the project is in Manali, we are based in Delhi." The networks of people and locations that are formed through digital drawings have been a "sea change," he explains, "by virtue of the fact that we can reach out to a larger pool of talent both on the creative and services side."

Construction drawings—the digital ones that circulate between offices and physical ones that circulate at sites—are ephemeral in the sense that they are remade again and again through the back and forth of a number of workers. Similar to the kinship networks that are constantly reworked to further real estate growth, drawings transform through consultant, foreman, supervisor, and laborer inputs. Wandering Woods has construction teams spread across the globe: architects in Southeast Asia, consultants in New York, and engineers across NCR. Drawings zoom across the internet and shuffle between various parties. Consultants, engineers, and contractors comment on and reshape them. They move back and forth between site and office as construction activity commences. Gopal gathers them all.

Unlike master plans and marketing documents that make money off the land and further a desire for property and home, technical drawings do not enter the public realm; they do, however, bear the promise of skilling and social mobility. Since construction drawings circulate among individuals of all hierarchies in the production chain, they also form an active site of social struggle. A range of drawings fall under the umbrella of construction drawings. Conceptual design drawings are the first. Simplistic and imagistic, these are placed on a site plan of the proposed property and pitched to the client through a series of three-dimensional rendered images, which often make their way into promotional brochures. Next, municipal drawings derived from the conceptual drawings are used for development permission. Here, lines respond to the bureaucratic necessities of building bylaws and developmental plans. As two young architects joke, it is like pressing the "Indianize" button, to make the fantastical curves conform.[20] Next come design development drawings. Drawings nest and grow dense as exact sizes of rooms, heights, and other spatial requirements are calculated. Rooms and façades increase in sophistication as the functions of rooms are fixed and designs are detailed. These development drawings move to the structural consultants, whose lines embed calculations of where and how building loads will transfer, the kinds of structural elements required, and their sizes. The engineers evoke the forces that will move through the structures—weights, footsteps, earthquakes, wind—and plot their paths into the ground. Architects redraw building plans according to the specified structural plan and send the drawings to various service consultants. Each consultant supplies information and drawings, which the architect coordinates and compiles, ensuring that there is no conflict and that requirements are met within each construction phase.

As the construction industry formalizes, the emphasis on drawings increases. Design practices move away from immediate on-site supervision and guidance and instead place a strong reliance on drawings. They are stamped with instructions: "for construction," "not for construction," "revision number xx," "service plan." Lists of dimensions, labels, details of materials to be used, quality and quantity of materials, service conduits, grid lines, and other information appear on them. The information recorded makes drawings units of the production of the urban environment, but the sheer volume of drawings becomes inversely proportional to their value and permanency. "Clients are only interested in getting stacks of drawings—you know, 4-inch *ka set chaihye* [they want sets of drawings four inches thick]," Anish, the architect at Haveli, tells me. His client demanded a *thappi*, or stack of drawings. "So I printed out the drawings on 200 gsm [thick card stock] and gave it to him. They want 4-inch, 2.5-inch reports, that is all."

Drawings become quickly discarded construction industry currency. They propagate as they are drawn and revised; new drawings arise on the discarded mass of the old. According to Anish, even the tiniest changes need to be recorded in drawing form: "You know *aaj kal* [these days] these young architects in offices, they do not think, they just keep producing drawings one after the other. No one takes accountability. Only the people who do the checking . . . end up taking accountability." Changes in drawing are recorded, per good bureaucratic practice. The drawings create the illusion of coordination, organization, and control.

The processes of construction involve several parties: service consultants, structural engineers, landscape architects, clients, architects, on-site teams, civil work contractors, special-work contractors, service contractors, master builders, and helpers. The team collaborates to produce drawings at every stage of construction. In reality the production of drawings follows no fixed path. They ricochet back and forth according to the whims and fancies of clients, at the mercy of surprises on site, the ineffectiveness of various parties, and errors. An architect describes how a client decided to change the function of the building while it was being constructed. "All the plans had to be redrawn and everything recalculated. It was a nightmare." Another describes discovering an incorrect site plan after the design development phase. "Half our buildings were in water [the location of a pond was marked incorrectly]—we had to redesign everything."

As brokers like Narendra trade and flip land, developers try to acquire and consolidate property. Plotlines shift with political processes, and site drawings are at their mercy. The lines of building are erased and redrawn on the basis of government permissions, new laws and regulations, changing markets, demands of developers, a lack of consumers, the skills of contractors, new land acquisitions, changes in materials, and the whims of architects. These whims, fancies, politics, and dramas, the service consultant says, transform the projects in such a significant way that you have no idea how it came about. Drawings move from person to person, warping, winding, bending, and breaking until you cannot recognize them anymore. The process, as the consultant describes it, is just like the game of Telephone.[21] What was once drawn is not what will be built. The drawing, like the initial utterance in the childhood game, unfolds in the processes of construction into a scrambled reality far different from its original.

To draw is not only to create and to escape into fantasy but also to enter into a collective. It is to collectively fantasize but also to collectively struggle to realize those fantasies within the networks of power that structure drawing worlds. It is to be part of a web that actively negotiates its social standing and power. At a moment of anger with two architects, Ram (the site supervisor of Haveli) vents to me, "These two girls! The work has stopped at site and their drawings are just not finishing up! . . . The drawings have so many mistakes." He is referring to two young women architects who visited the site the previous day. "Shreelal shows them the mistakes, because he is a nice contractor. If I were the contractor instead of him, I would just go ahead and construct as per drawings. Then I would see what they would do!" He ridicules the women for thinking the construction site was a "picnic" day for them, as the two women came to the site dressed in jeans and carrying a pizza box. "They are the type to suck the blood out of contractors. This design here, add bamboo there. Increasing costs everywhere. Because this takes a lot more time, no?"

The two women appeared incongruous among the contractors and workers, but they issued changes and instructions with a commanding air. Middle-class women are less frequent presences on construction sites in North India, unlike in Mumbai where I practiced architecture. I was reminded of a moment during my first days as a practicing architect and the lone woman on site when, frustrated that I was not being listened to, I was instructed by a senior architect to demand minor tweaks to projects in order to demonstrate authority over contractors and mark my social positionality. Drawing, not drawing, withholding, detailing, complaining, and issuing instructions for changes are all power struggles in construction. A struggle over drawings is a mode of incorporation into the classed field of construction, and in this case a site of class, caste, and gender struggle.

On the Wandering Woods site, plans are printed in a large paper format and come neatly folded in an accordion-like manner. Key individuals at the site will be seen clutching them to their chests. Alibhai is one such individual. He is a civil engineer in charge of "lay-outing." Along with Veer, he is part of the first wave of people on site. Together they "mark" lines and place what is known as a "starter" (a low mortar boundary) to define the shape and location of columns, walls, elevator shafts, and floors to be built. The two make a distinctive team. Alibhai is slim and always seems to have a slight hunch. It is as though he is constantly poring over a drawing. He is a self-defined, lower-middle-class Muslim man from the neighboring state of Uttar Pradesh. His two children and wife still live in his childhood village home with his parents. Whenever I meet him, he quizzes me on geometry and chuckles to himself when I cannot answer his puzzle.

He and Veer work on the site the entire day and "mark out" the architect's drawing.

Of all the masons on site, Veer is the most charming. Short and speedy, he endears himself to women and men alike as he strolls through the site in a macho way. "You, you, I saw you eating that mango yesterday, hun. Don't lie, hun," he teases a woman laborer, and she hides her face and giggles. Another time he grabs my voice recorder and heads to his contractor. "Yes, yes, tell us how do you do shuttering for a footing?" he asks him, holding up the voice recorder and chuckling as he mimics me.

Alibhai and Veer's conversations usually consist of a series of numbers, and the two of them pore over plans at regular intervals. Alibhai carries a calculator in his hand and Veer a *karni*, an almond-shaped scraper used to mix concrete. Alibhai opens up the plan, and Veer stares at it. The two of them point at numbers, rushing to calculate angles and lengths from the existing markers on site. Veer stands at a distance holding a white pole. Alibhai looks through the Total Station machine, asking him to move a little left and a little more until he obtains the right angles. Veer draws an x at the point. As Alibhai calls out numbers, Veer runs a tape across the concrete floor and draws a white line along it with lime powder. He marks the measurement—4.75 meters—along the line. He then moves to another column and waits for Alibhai's calculations. Alibhai explains, "I am in charge of the right position of the building." They are marking the layout. "Layout means drawing marks. . . . The drawing and the measurements in it, that drawing is marked on the ground, on a plane, either using Total Station, or tape, or red string." Alibhai and Veer are a team, but Alibhai is the educated civil engineer with a degree in surveying. Veer occupies the highest ranks of masons, the layout mason, a master craftsman or *raj mistri* (king mason), and is the highest paid but also reputed to be the most intelligent and trusted. A layout mason's daily access to and interaction with drawings enables him to eventually master the art of deciphering them. The layout for the building we stand in front of was drawn wrong: the entire building is tilted slightly, it is not in plumb, and the columns are not exactly over each other. The windows cannot hang straight. The architect is livid. Only time will tell how Veer and Alibhai's shaky efforts unfold.

"It is the construction industry's dirty little secret: most laborers are illiterate. Can they read your drawings? Drawings are just to cover your butt!" An irate foreign architect lashes out at the Indian construction industry at a conference. His words ring true. To be able to read a drawing you need to be able to read English, and most laborers can barely read Hindi. The gap between offices and construction sites is a social divide. It is through this gap that lines and drawings leap, in giant acts of faith; through this gap whispers distort in the gaggle of languages that forms society in India.

On site, to teach a laborer how to decipher the lines on drawings is to give them a leg up into contracting work and a better future. Reading numbers and instructions in English is a pathway into better work. Veer comes from a family of metal workers, but he is tired of masonry work; he would love to quit the industry and open a shop. Veer's dream is unlikely to come true, as construction work often traps workers for life. Interpreting drawings with Alibhai, however, is very likely to take Veer into small-scale contracting work and to give him the ability to lead his own team.

The circulating whispers of drawing production remind us of their liveliness. The ephemeral circulations of drawings create social groups. The interpretive gap between drawings the ability to decipher and participate in the acts of drawing are sites of social fantasy and struggle in construction. The lines of construction drawings generate the promise of mobility, money, power, and authority. They construct illusions of better futures for those who master them and anger against those who cannot. To draw is not merely a creative act but a political-economic one; it is to conjure a set of fantasies that, through the act of drawing itself, produce differential political-economic realities.

DRAWING DREAMS ON SHIFTING SANDS

Prakashji is a soft-spoken, older mason working with the architects of Haveli; he specializes in waterproofing floors with broken pieces of tiles known as China Mosaic. I spend time by him as he lays China Mosaic on the terrace floor in a pattern set by the architects. He takes a rejected ceramic tile and a pair of pliers. He breaks the tile with a swift tap, shattering it into shards that he arranges in a puzzle-like manner on a thin slurry of cement. He rotates and chooses tiles, making sure that the gaps between them are kept to a minimum. A sea of mosaic unfolds as he works. His thumb and index finger are covered with plastic fingers cut from a yellow glove; the yellow plastic prevents the sharp edges of the tile from cutting him. He clips a tile from time to time to match the edges with the shards laid on the ground. I watch him as he adds specks of yellow every few centimeters. They feel like speckles of sunlight in the gleaming white mosaic.

I squat beside Prakashji to learn how tiling works. Prakashji is a long-term migrant to NCR. He came here almost twelve years ago and lives in an informal settlement on the outskirts of New Delhi (from where he commutes every day). His wife moved in with him after they got married, but they do not have any children. On days when he is not around, his companions tell me it is because he is taking his wife to the doctor. A large amount of his income is spent on doctor's visits to diagnose the cause of their infertility, they report; the rest he is saving up for a house.

As he lays mosaic, Prakashji likes to talk about his village. The white spaces of the tile fill with the landscapes of his home: the fields with water pumps for irrigation, the eighteen acres of land they used to own, the pond where he once saw a ghost, and the routes he used to move along when he was a boy. His sisters-in-law, he says, insisted on dividing the ancestral lands and home. One day, he tells me that he will go home in March. This time he wants to stay longer. He wants to build a permanent home on his share of ancestral land. He takes his *karni* and scrapes at the cement-sand mixture upon which he lays his tiles. He explains the plan of the house to me. He draws a rectangle; this is the plot. He draws another rectangle. "There is a courtyard (*aangan*), and a kitchen at the back. I will make two rooms." He draws a square in one corner and two rectangular rooms facing it. He is going to make it of brick, cement, and steel. I ask him how he knows how to bind steel. "I learnt by staying here. What is he doing? How is he doing it?" He describes the learning curve: "I understood a little, then I would go and ask the doer. If the mason is nice then he will tell me this is why we do this. Some do not want to tell." Prakashji describes how he learned by looking and asking: "This is the way the plinth gets done, then the steel, [and] then the roof," gradually developing a confident working knowledge of building construction. He reminds me that he uses the same tools in his own trade.

Prakashji confirms what other masons on site have already told me. He tells me his wife and he are having trouble conceiving. He keeps taking leave to go see the doctor with her. Meanwhile he wants to finish the house. As we sit, an architect comes in and screams. "Who told you to put yellow? Take out all the yellow. I am not paying you to use your mind." Prakashji hastens to remove the yellow. He pours cement slurry across the diagram he has just drawn. He covers it with broken tile.

Prakashji reminds us that lines and drawings not only occupy and circulate in professional circles but also saturate the texture of people's lives. These fantastical imaginaries empower individuals with new tasks and visions. They come to inhabit impromptu sketches of plot sizes and gnarled visions of future homes. They infiltrate into the everyday. There are drawings made on walls and drawings scribbled on notepad paper. Some, like Prakashji's sketch in the slurry, are quickly destroyed, but others linger and mature through the process of time. Drawings are the shapes of a better life, mixing wants and needs into the churning sands of NCR.

A few months later, Neelkanth Sir and I meet again to continue our pursuit of master plans. This time we hunt for the older master plans of Gurgaon. I tell him I do not have the 1991 and 2001 master plans, and he decides to rectify the situation; he and I head to the planning office to look for them. As we walk into the drawing division, a woman greets Sir. She is a junior of his. Sir, in his blunt, sarcastic style, quips, "oh, you are here now." The new appointee responds, "Yes sir, I am posted here now—in the drawing wing." Sir nods, "OK—that is good." A group of men come to greet him. "Namaste, Sir, how are you?" They bend to touch his feet. "Is Mr. Chowdhary here?" "No, Sir, he is on holiday." Sir turns to the woman. "OK, you are in the drawing department, you give us some drawings." The woman looks mortified. "Sir, come, come please sit down." Neelkanth Sir and I walk toward the room she points at. We enter an empty conference room and turn around to speak with her, only to realize that all the planners are gone. He goes back into the earlier room and returns. "They all disappeared!" he laughs. We go back looking for the planners and find them all sitting in a different room. We ask them if they have the master plans, but they hem and haw. "We are also looking for them, Sir. We have put in a request at the headquarters in Chandigarh but no one can find them." The plans, it seems, are gone.[22]

Aandhi (a summer dust storm) in NCR turns the atmosphere murky. We cover our faces and squint our eyes. Sand moves quickly onto pavements and properties, blurring the lines demarcated by construction, shifting, erasing, and evaporating the boundaries of the built environment we try so hard to define. The sand mingles with construction debris and dust. It sings as it sifts through the atmosphere. It remakes geography. The shifting sands index the fluidity and transmutability of plans, drawings, diagrams, and lines in Gurgaon. The undoing and unmaking of drawings mirror how individuals make and unmake their futures in the struggle to survive at the edge of this desert. The heightened atmospherics resonate with the very fantasies of making drawings, the powerful circulations of image forms, and the wants and dreams they conjure through their lines and circulations.

What does it mean not only to experience the fantasies conjured by drawings but also to produce them by drawing lines? Drawing is considered a creative, generative, tactile, and relational act, but it is also an act of power and control.[23] As individuals in the construction industry demonstrate, to interact with drawings, to draw itself, is to construct fantasies. As forms of conjuring, capturing, and manipulation of desires and dreams, drawings have political-economic weight and act as sites of class struggle and aspiration. They become about not only individual desire and longing but also economic struggle.

In the construction industry in Gurgaon, drawings become more than creative and technical tools; through their circulations and material transmutations, they serve as vital socioeconomic and political forms of life. The ephemeral qualities of drawings—their ability to morph, change hands, move from paper to the ground, and be erased—further agency, mobility, and ambition on the one hand and perpetuate silences and erasures on the other.[24] Like the restless desert winds of Gurgaon, drawings dance between the ephemeral realms of the material and intangible and the imagined and the constructed. The permanence of paper and record too become fantasies as drawings evaporate off papers and mutate. The accumulations and erasures, agencies and action, despair and desire in construction economies are all spurred by the fantastical world of drawings.

4 The Industry of Sound

THE CALL OF THE MACHINES

The whistle to commence construction work at Wandering Woods blows at 8:00 a.m. The simultaneously shrill yet dull sound echoes through the ten-acre project. It bounces off the almost complete building block that forms the first phase, winds through the tall tower that constitutes phase two, and falls deep into the large basement pit that is the third phase of construction. The diesel generators are turned on. Acidic, black fumes and steady, steam-engine-like *chuga chuga* sounds infuse the construction site. Machines begin to switch on as workers begin work at their individual stations: the periodic screeches of the drill, the thumps of the concrete pump, the braking and reversing of hydraulic lifts as they drag and drop stones from spot to spot, and the gentle rumble of the cement mixer join the steady beats of the diesel generator. The sounds spread through the site. They percolate into concrete slabs and columns. The golden-hued earth thrums, and our bodies tingle. Land, body, and building pulsate with mechanical beats. Construction sites across the neighborhood join the jam, the air saturating with collective rhythms. The sounds herald the transformation of farms and fallow lands into office blocks and homes.

They herald the retreat of the forest and the upward and outward growth of Gurgaon's urban jungle.

Thrrrrrr, thump, thwaak. The inside of the jewel-hued basement pit trembles with sound. Loud resounding *whirrrrrrrrs* are all Santoshji and I hear. The compactor claims its sound-space. Hammers on steel join its *purrrs*. The machine stops, and the noise breaks. My body shudders and my skin prickles. "This compaction machine makes so much noise [*awaj/awaaz*]!" I exclaim. *"Awaaz nahi karega to yeh bethega kaise?* [How will it compact if there is no noise?]" Santoshji laughs, and remarks, "I can't even hear my own cell phone!"

The compactor vibrates. The sound is dull, gut-wrenching, and all-encompassing. "This line [the construction industry.] . . . [I]t is the kind of line where you have to either hear a few things from somebody or be heard saying a few things to somebody [*sunna padta hai . . . sunnana padta hai*, either you get told off or you tell people off]."

Santoshji—the marijuana smuggler turned dairy farmer turned site foreman—raises the importance of sound and hearing in construction: mechanical noise is fundamental to work on a construction site. Sound indicates a steady pace of work on a construction site. To labor on a construction site is to listen and be listened to. It involves orienting yourself to the sound of machines and people and learning to respond to sound. To work in construction is to be attuned to the atmospheres of mechanical sound, for there would be no construction without sound.

What relevance do these symphonic surroundings have to practices of work? How do the presence and sound of machines structure industry politics? How does aurality, as both aesthetics and metaphor in construction, push us to rethink a political economy of labor? While sound infiltrates the construction sites in many ways—from the act of listening to steel and concrete to understand stresses, to the angry tirades of supervisors and laborers fighting with each other—I focus on the most dominant soundscape of construction—the mechanical—and tie these to metaphors of sound: noise, beats, and rhythms of work and life mobilized by those in construction in NCR. Machines mark a particular dimension of industrial political economy, known to speed up and divide processes of production. Read most commonly as forms of noise, I argue that the ephemeral sounds produced by machines—such as the excavator, concrete mixer, concrete pump, and tower crane—generate an innate set of sounds and rhythms, and thus life potentialities. Each machine, in its unique working, bears its own creative potential. Sound's ability to reference a particular task and to be felt at a visceral level, as well as the sheer force with which a machine overtakes your senses on site, make it a disciplinary device of industrial economy. Sound is part of the industrial ephemeral complex as it saturates the senses, disciplines and deteriorates workers, and then dissipates; it is an ephemeral æsthetic but also produces ephemeral workers by shortening their life spans. Paying attention to sound demonstrates the multisensorial forms of industrial power and labor struggle; it makes us attentive to the multiplicity of life rhythms workers navigate and the improvisations through which they manipulate and mediate them. We would not understand the visceral workings of industrial political economy without an attention to sound.

Sound as an aesthetic device often gets less attention than its more glamorous cousin of vision and visuality, yet there is no ignoring industrial sound. The roar of the furnace, the whistle of steam, the steady beat of weaving machines, and the trundles and synchronies of the assembly line have accompanied us from the rolling mills that Karl Marx writes about to the factories of Henry Ford. The aural phenomenology of industrial spaces surrounds laboring experience, and debates around the effects of industrial noise go back as far as the Industrial Revolution in late nineteenth-century Europe to problematize the interactions of humans and machines.[1] Even today, as digital technologies overtake heavy industries, the steady swooshes of production lines and the regularized taps of keyboards inculcate a sound and a work ethic of their own. The sounds, beats, and rhythms of machines form the elemental atmospherics of industries, yet these techno-aesthetics are often considered by-products of work and not formative to working processes.

Scholars of sound agree that sound is an intimate and affective way of knowing and being in the world.[2] Sound is spatial in that people are immersed and absorbed in it.[3] This immersive quality of sound in construction allows it to shape behavior and practice: sound is deployed as a device to get workers to work faster and enables efficiency and speed on construction sites.[4] Attention to the production of sounds, the forces of sound, and aesthetic and compositional qualities themselves allows insight into labor politics in construction.[5]

The affective sensorium conjured through the noise and rhythms of machines enables entrepreneurialism, disciplining, and even physical destruction on construction sites. Machines on Wandering Woods strive toward an atmosphere of "acoustic rationalization," in which the primary demand is for machine-like efficiency and lithe speed.[6] This techno-acoustic atmosphere sets working standards on construction sites, but its rhythms and beats act as spaces of opportunity for some workers and can cause the marginalization of others. Acoustic rationalization inter-sects with a multiplicity of urban and national rhythms. These rhythms complicate and contest acoustic rationalization. I listen to backhoes, RMC mixers, and tower cranes to render audible the power of the ephemeral rhythms of machines in construction.

BACKHOES AND THE RHYTHMS OF HISTORY

Mud and stone poured onto the back of a truck sound like an earthy rain-fall. *Thump, thump, thump, swoosh, swoosh, pitter-patter,* and then the silken silence of still, wet mud. The weight of stone and the lightness of dust as it rises from a fall. A louder thump and a deep metallic scratch-ing sound. The regularized beep of a machine backing up. The Komatsu excavator and its operator are hard at work.[7] Together they expand a basement pit. Two metallic belts with horizontal treads rotate parallel to each other. The belts and their rotors allow the Komatsu to climb near-vertical surfaces and to navigate uneven terrain. Perched on top of the platform is the dusty ochre operator's box. An extra-long arm emerges out of this enclosure: it is thrice the length of the base and has a claw-like scoop at the end. The box and arm rotate 360 degrees, allowing the driver to move sideways, forward, backward, or in any direction they want, in arachnid fashion. The word *KOMATSU* is emblazoned on the arm. It is owned by a local Haryanvi contractor.[8] I move closer to strike up a con-versation: "This digging work—are you the one getting it done?" Chan-dubhai shakes his head as he continues to observe the machine. "No, the site needs to be finished up fast so I gave it to a friend. We do that. If I have extra work, I give it to him and if he has extra work he gives it to me." Silence. I try to strike up a conversation again: "The Komatsu is a fun machine to watch?" Chandubhai replies, with pride in his voice: "It does the work of twenty men, that machine. . . . The JCB cost 25 lakhs, the Komastsu 35 lakh.[9] Nowadays you can buy them all on installment."[10] The Komatsu digs diligently as Chandubhai chats. "Look at that. The work she is doing. Twenty men will take seven days to do that. . . . Nowadays whoever has a little money, he buys a machine, and becomes a contractor"; he is describing his own career path. "Competition has increased so much."

Machines take over the construction-scapes of peri-urban India. Where once stood hand-cranked cement mixers, women *coolies* and *beldars*, and rope-and-pulley systems, now appear sophisticated machines. Dhiren, the mechanical engineer in charge of maintenance at Wandering Woods, explains the change. In a dust-covered office adjacent to the basement pit, in a conversation punctuated by an occasional *craassshhh* of metal or materials hitting the floor, Dhiren praises the power of machines. "Technology changed everything. The buildings that took four or five years to build . . . we finish them in one year. The biggest difference is this."

A mechanical aesthetic prevails in his office: cement-coated walls; rusting grey metal desks; corrugated iron sheets that form makeshift office walls; and a large, gray fan that cools us. Even the tube lights spread a gray light that glistens off the gray rings our chai cups left behind. The only colorful punctuation is a large psychedelic poster of Lord Shiva—Hindu God of destruction—on the wall. Angry Shiva glints in technicolor as Dhiren explains the machines on site and their use: "We have batching plant, the mixers, that is [for] concrete. . . . We have pump that discharges [the concrete] from one place to [another], say from down level to top level. That is, it is [a] totally mechanized form . . . what [the] labor used to do first." Dhiren explains that the new machines mean "less manpower and less time. There is more efficiency." He goes on, "We have [the] tower crane for lifting purpose. All the work used to be manual; there was a chance for accidents. One man would lift 50 kilos. He would take ten to twenty minutes. That a tower crane lifts now within seconds." Machines have sped up construction, according to Dhiren. "The building is completed very fast. . . . [I]t is safe, there is a lot of efficiency and also accuracy."

The tower crane, the RMC mixer, the concrete pump, the elevator, the JCB and Komatsu excavators, the compactor, electric drills, rollers, cutters, welding machines—the list goes on and on. Turn them on, and the

Figure 12. A backhoe at work on a Gurgaon construction site, 2012. Photo by author.

construction site reverberates with sound. The day is punctuated by the harsh rapping sounds of pneumatic drills, the boom of falling steel bars, and the swooshing-sizzle of blowtorches as they weld steel to steel. Efficiency and speed are the name of the game. Each machine also opens up the potential for a different form of listening and being, a different way of understanding bodies, buildings, and space. Let us explore the Komatsu's way.

Long *beep*, *beep*, *beeeeeps* surround Chandubhai and me as we watch the Komatsu back up and move forward in repeated patterns. The machine *thumps* and *grrrs* as it lifts and drops its scooped arm. All day long the Komatsu meticulously digs this massive block that will be a basement car park. The machine and its operator fill almost twenty trucks with mud. The walls of the pit are scarred with the machine's tooth marks, evoking Van Gogh's brushstrokes. The freshly dug walls expose the consolidated layers of soil that comprise the land: each stratum gleams in a different hue of yellow and brown in the evening light.

Excavation is an activity that roots you into the soil. It forces a confrontation with locale and history through the *mitti* or soil of the land. The Komatsu encourages us to look at the layers it uncovers, a reminder that these armies of machines did not converge onto construction overnight but congregated through historical aggregations. Through this the excavator not only makes literal sounds but also unearths the historic rhythms that produce contemporary construction practices. A history of agrarian and infrastructural development led to atmospheres of privatized, mechanical rhythms, the Komatsu encourages us to look at the industrial and agrarian histories of India that fed the rise of machines.

Independent India's first prime minister, Jawaharlal Nehru, was committed to industrial development as he strove to reduce import dependency and promote manufacturing. Of primary importance was reinforced cement concrete (RCC) technology, supported by the steel and cement industries, to build national infrastructure. The early 1900s had already seen British engineers in India experimenting with RCC. By the 1930s, both infrastructure and buildings in cities such as Mumbai, Kolkata, and Delhi were built from the material, and the construction of the new city of Chandigarh in the 1950s popularized and commercialized RCC technology. Iron and steel began production in 1907 with the Tata Iron and Steel Company in Mumbai.[11] The first five-year plan allotted 76 crores to the iron and steel industries, and the second gave them the highest priority.[12] New steel plants took root in the 1950s. The deregulation of controls in cement industries in the early 1980s saw the rise of cement conglomerates with foreign collaborators. Increased deregulation in the early 1990s saw steel withdrawn from public sector production, the removal of price controls, and opening of the market to 100 percent foreign direct investment.[13]

Cement too was decontrolled in 1989 and delicensed in 1991, opening doors for private-public partnerships.[14] The working group on cement pushed for more housing development, infrastructural projects, and ready mix concrete.[15] The number of machines for construction multiplied as steady supplies of cement and steel demanded speedy construction techniques. The first commercial ready-mix concrete (RMC) plant opened in Mumbai in 1994.[16] In 2018, India became the second largest producer of raw steel and cement in the world.[17]

The government of India's infrastructural development agenda gathered speed in tandem. The scale, modular construction, and costs of infrastructural development paved the road for technological development. Every year since independence, India's annual budget earmarked a growing amount of funds for infrastructure. Each budget plan brought a demand for more machines. In the 1970s, Haryana's chief minister Bansi Lal introduced ambitious roadway plans, and Prime Minister Vajpayee initiated a national highway-development project in 1998.[18] Infrastructural development saw an increase in public-private partnerships as well as build-operate-transfer (BOT) schemes as new expressways, irrigation projects, and bridges were proposed. Allocations for infrastructural development in annual budgets climbed steadily between 2002 and 2012, and the twelfth five-year plan (2012–17) included an infrastructure allocation of US$1 trillion.[19] The pressing need for infrastructure meant increased privatization. The large operating budgets and fairly modular nature of infrastructure prompted an increase in production of construction machines, whose ready availability then filtered into private real estate construction.[20]

The changed rhythms of an agrarian revolution supplemented these mechanical intensities. India's Green Revolution took place in the states of Punjab and Haryana (Gurgaon's home state) in the 1970s.[21] A Ford Foundation–aided agricultural yield program—the Green Revolution—gave rise to larger landholdings as well as a strong farming lobby in Haryana. The Green Revolution targeted agricultural practices in the region and aimed to enhance food and grain production. Combined with a parallel rise in the mining industry, the Green Revolution increased the use of mechanical equipment, bringing tractors, earthmovers, and excavators. India set up its own equipment manufacturers in 1949, further consolidating them in the 1980s.[22] The late 1960s saw the advent of private machine manufacturers.[23]

J. C. Bamford (JCB), a well-known manufacturer of backhoes and excavators, set up its largest manufacturing plant in Haryana in 1979.

By the early 2000s, most of the large construction companies (such as L&T, Skanska, and PCL) had established a presence in India, imported or bought construction equipment, and acted as contractors for major construction projects. As Euro-American construction markets collapsed in 2008, machine manufacturers expanded into the Indian market. This move was supported by Indian banks, which allowed financing for machine purchases. "In 2008, JCB Heavy Products opens a new £43 million factory, followed in 2009 . . . to create the world's biggest backhoe loader factory." In 2014, JCB was leading India's construction equipment manufacturing boom, with "one in every two construction machines sold in the country made by JCB."[24] A year earlier, India had become a center for construction equipment manufacture and was exporting equipment to Africa and Asia.[25] Construction sites reverberated with a new kind of sound.

Wandering Woods was well underway in 2012 when I reached Delhi. As Dhiren described, it thrived on machines. The 2000s acted as watershed years for cost-effective use of big machines in NCR: construction for the Delhi Metro began in 1998, and in 2003 Delhi won the bid to host the 2010 Commonwealth games. Dhiren reminisces about the atmospheres of the Commonwealth Games: "One thing is that they [the Delhi government] only had four years. Companies in India, they cannot work with that speed. That is why they hired foreign companies." Foreign multinational construction companies brought a sea change: "They had big machines and different technologies. Indian firms looked at this and they also learnt."

As Dhiren describes, the preparations for the 2010 Commonwealth games saw an influx of multinational construction and material supply companies, which catalyzed construction skills and real estate in the region. While global markets registered a dip in the growth rate of construction equipment, India saw an increase.[26] Both exports in and manufacturing of construction equipment in India stepped up in the early 2000s.[27]

As the powerful Komatsu works, it unearths the combined rhythms of economic and developmental histories. Affluent agrarian communities and their bartering of land, steel and cement industrial expansion, infrastructural and industrial development, and foreign direct investment—the rhythms of national development and international economies echo into the rhythms of working machines in Gurgaon.

The cacophonous crescendo of construction testifies to the fact that machines set up rhythms and tempos. The whirs and stirs, the thumps and thuds, the beats and bangs are a battle cry for faster rhythms of work. Each machine, space, and phase within a construction site has its own rhythms, be they the scooping and carting of excavation or the twisting and shaping of steel rebar work. The mechanical and human worlds synchronize as humans match the sensorial cues of their machines, and the ephemeral beats of machines force bodies and behaviors to rationalize. The fleeting quality of sounds create an accelerated rush, a "volatility and ephemerality" that reshapes our "thinking, feeling, and doing."[28] The pulsating rhythms push bodies in a dromological, militarized fashion to organize, be deployed, and deploy; they act "as a motor and producer of speed."[29] The sound dissipates from sites but nevertheless enters dreams, seizes limbs, and reverberates in bodies—*chuga-chuga-chuga*—as one sleeps at night.

THE RIGHT MIX

The pride and joy of the Wandering Woods site is the RMC batching plant. Dhiren calls the three engineers who run it and tells them to expect me, and so after lunch I walk to the edge of the site. The sight of the RMC batching plant takes my breath away. It stands majestically between the project and the plains. The plant is a mountain, fronted by a giant tricolor mound of sand and gravel in a pleasing palate of grey, brown, and yellow shades. A funnel-shaped tank of water and a control cabin sit above it.

The three foremen are waiting to mix a batch of concrete. They want to show me how the machine works. We climb up the metal ladder into the control cabin. The engineers yell down to the group of Adivasi brothers who work in the cement store. Sundar, the eldest, responds with a nod. He and his two brothers run back and forth from the cement store, emptying bags of cement into the trough below with a steady thump, keeping time with the machine as it scoops sand and gravel. The mechanical scoop scrapes as it gathers gravel. The cement reaches its inputted weight, and a—*grrrrrrrrr*—ensues as the container lifts to empty it into the circular

Figure 13. A ready-mix concrete machine on a Gurgaon construction site, 2012. Photo by author.

drum. Next, a rain of gravel descends. The materials are weighed at each stage, the target weights calculated according to the strength of cement required, the humidity, and the temperature of the air. When everything is in the circular drum, the engineers press a number of buttons, and loud rumbling noises ensue. In a precise five minutes, the drum mixes together the cement, sand, gravel, and water to produce concrete. It pours the mix out into the waiting truck in a smooth flow. A perfect ready-mix is born.

Buildstrong, the development company for Wandering Woods, also formed from a fortuitous mix. Managing director Mohan had been running a midsize architectural firm; his relative, an investment banker, had started an investment fund for construction and invested in Mohan's company. Mohan scooped up people he knew: his juniors, colleagues from his partner's firm, his former boss, and his friends from allied industries. In 2008 the firm's office was in a small basement, and the team comprised eight men. They had several million dollars and "a dream." Construction work for their first project—Wandering Woods, a 1.6-million-square-foot commercial complex—commenced in 2008. The company and their lives gained momentum. Four years later, in 2012, Buildstrong was running six mega-projects and had an in-house staff of eighty. The team bought new cars, took trips to Europe, and moved into a swanky new office space. "So many people made a lot of money. Real estate was doubling money in three to four years," Amar (the sales director) reminisces. "We entered [the market] with a lot of noise . . . we increased the level of noise. In my mind we were the loudest ones and took other investments as competition. Boom—what an appetite!"

"Noise," in Amar's sales language, stands for business pomp and aplomb. It is the sound of financial might and promise. This form of noise does different work than the compacting machine in Santoshji's description of it: Amar's noise spurs construction through its speculative promises. In the early 2000s, real estate in NCR was booming. The noise of its economic success and promise thrummed through urban India. Entrepreneurs had to work fast.[30] Ready-mixes of development firms emerged in those years: contractors and architects turned developers (e.g., Omaxe), cement and steel companies that moved into real estate (e.g., Jaypee, Tata), and existing corporations that expanded their firms and holdings. Unitech Developers, for example, now comprise Unitech Realty Pvt. Ltd., Unitech Hi Tech Developers Ltd., Unitech Residential Resorts Ltd., Unitech Builders Ltd., Unitech Reliable Projects Pvt. Ltd., Unitech Infra Ltd., and Unitech Global Pvt. Ltd.

Developers multiplied and increased construction speeds. They sold property before it was built, expanded constructions sites, and moved their people and machines in, creating millions of acres of construction sites like the one the engineers and I stand in. Noise here seduced and heralded success; noise was speculative and enhanced the real estate market. The noise of developers generated more and more projects. It drew workers and machines to the site. It created specific regimes and rationalities of sound that sought to discipline workers.

The three foremen from the RMC plant and I chat in the shade of the mountain-like machine. Kishwar, a mechanical foreman, is the most talkative. Having studied only to the tenth grade, Kishwar does not have a formal degree but learned on the job. His childhood friend's uncle was a laborer who learned how to use an RMC mixer in Libya; he took Kishwar to a site in Delhi. He initially proposed that Kishwar become a crane operator, but the tower crane frightened Kishwar. All the machines looked strange (*ajeeb*) to me, he narrates. Three years later, he is used to the machines.

In fact, the cycles and speeds of construction are now part and parcel of who he is: "If the building is a two- to three-year project, if it does not get done in two to three years, then we begin to feel strange." The acoustic rationalizations of construction, its repeat cycles, its beats, and its everyday rhythms are well inculcated in Kishwar: "We don't feel good when the plant is just standing. If the plant is just standing then our minds start feeling strange, we don't like it at all, because it is about our bread and butter [*rozi-roti*]—if the plant works we will get fed [*pet ko dana milega*]." A transplant from the state of Orissa, Kishwar feels a great sense of loss from his migration experience. He was unable to go back home for either his father's or his mother's deaths, and the cycles of construction have inevitably taken over the cycles of his familial life. "I lost the happiness of my life in Delhi [*zindagi ka sukh kho diya*]," he says.

The RMC does not care for Kishwar's emotions. The mixer is at work, and everyone must match its motions. Bodies tense. *Chuga chuga chuga*: I hear the cement mixer kick-start. *Thrrrr*: a cascade of gravel. A quick press of switches. *Thumpa thump*: the trough drops. The rhythms of mechanical time set the groove. The trough rises when the weight is met. The cement drops and the machine emanates the swishing sounds of mechanical pleasure and efficiency—of a job speedily done.

If national development rhythms enabled the rise of mechanical armies in construction, then the noise of speculative real estate furthered the speeds of mixing and production. The speeds are felt by those such as Kishwar in rhythms and cycles. Their lives are intimately connected to machines, their working tied to the working of mechanical beasts. The workings of machines produce a *chaal*, a gait, a clear line of work. It forces workers to fall into the rhythms of acoustic rationalizations. The machines enable and define this rhythmic gait. If it weren't for these acoustics, to paraphrase Santoshji, there would be no construction work.

MATCHING THE SPEEDS OF THE TOWER CRANE

The iconic machine for building at speed is undoubtedly the tower crane. It extends high above our heads against the brilliant blue summer sky. The terrace is its realm, and it governs all who stand below it. A giant

Figure 14. A tower crane lifts material onto a terrace at a Gurgaon construction site, 2012. Photo by author.

girded arm and control room perch atop the lithe and narrow girded yellow shaft. The crane works through counterweights and balance. All day long it cuts imaginary arcs in the sky. The gentle whir of its movement demonstrates its sophistication. Wires slither down to the ground, and the counterweights move back and forth to pulley materials into the sky.

Several young men work under the shadow of this crane, pitching their bodies as they tie steel, cut plywood, and distribute concrete. Their work is about counterweights and balance, too. These men will move up the ranks. Some will learn how to read drawings and work their way to foreman positions. Laborers will learn masonry or electrical work and strive to be skilled professionals. The civil engineers who supervise them hope to be area supervisors, block supervisors, and "site-in-charges." Some may even start contracting on their own.

I repeatedly ask supervisors, foremen, and workers on site about who advances in hierarchy and who does not. Sharifbhai, a steel foreman working in the basement pit, describes the dominant narrative, the story of the

Figure 15. Workers balance on bars as they bind steel on a Gurgaon construction site, 2012. Photo by author.

tez (quick, smart) *ladka* (boy). While he explains, his men are busy around us cajoling steel bars into the angularities of a staircase. "The person who is a *tez* worker, everybody wants that boy.[31] The boys who are working with me, the one who is *tez*, the engineer sees him—that this boy is *tez*." The *clang, clang, clang* of steel against steel melds with our conversation as Sharifbhai speaks. "Imagine that the foremen is not there: if I am gone, the engineer has an estimate that this boy is *tez*—even if the foremen is not around he will get the work done."

"How can we recognize a *tez* boy?" I ask, and he explains, "There is one boy, a worker. It is like this. We have to explain things to him again and again. We get fed up. Amongst them, I see that this boy is educated. He is *tez*. We only train him." He pauses to give instructions on the number of bars on the final landing before emphasizing his point. "No matter how much you train an illiterate, we will have to break our heads over him again the next day. We do not have to waste our heads over the *tez* boys." He finishes with a flourish: "In one line we explain to them and they quickly understand."

Tez is derived from *tezi*, the Hindi word for speed. It often stands for bright, intelligent, and means shining like the sun. It can also refer to craftiness and can be used to describe crazy winds. The word is versatile, but it encodes a dynamism and quickness of mind-body.[32] On site, I see several young men who epitomize this *tezi*. They effortlessly charm supervisors and women laborers alike, are called upon to work, and then supervise. An engineer will be found teaching them a thing or two in their free time. The boys are ambitious and smart.

It is *tez* boys who learn the ways of machines—though Kishwar the RMC engineer argues that it is working with machines that keeps the mind *tez*. According to Kishwar, a worker who is tuned to machines will be *tez*. He describes how he will choose his successor: "We will tell him *do this work, do that work.*" Kishwar often give trainees work that is below their job position in order to test their willingness. "If he does that then the man [*banda*] can learn." It is about how fast a worker picks up the work. "Like our helper, we tell him *do this work*. After he does it, the next time if we do not have to tell him and he does it on his own, then he can learn." According to Kishwar, this display of initiative and eagerness registers with the person in charge, who then decides to train the boy. "As they get experienced, then it comes into the guru's mind that I can train my man. . . . [T]hey [the gurus] will train their own men, not outside men." The term "my man" here is important, since often these affiliations fall along caste and religious lines. It also embeds gender discrimination: it never enters the foreman's mind that women can be skilled as well.

For Kishwar, workers' speed and commitment come not only from talent but also from poverty and need. "If they have any *majboori* [binding necessity] then they will do the work. . . . [T]he ones who have come to roam or earn money [extra cash] will run off," he says. *Tezi* is an act of culling, of separating the quick-witted from the dull, the fast from the slow, the needy from the nonchalant. It is a recognition of those who are willing to inculcate the rhythms of work into their sensibilities and those who without complaint meet the beats and demands of the machines. It creates a body of workers who adhere to rationalized, mechanical rhythms, whose *dimag* (mind) and body are as *tez* as the machines.

Munnalal, a contractor on the Haveli site, is a *tez ladka*. He and his cousin Sahil are from rural Uttar Pradesh and come from a family of steelworkers. They work together on site, where Munnalal has an item-work contract.[33] The contractors love Munnalal because he is incredibly fast. I can see his *tezi* in his approach to work and the faith people put in him. I am surprised to learn that his brothers are well-educated and own property in Delhi. He tells me they refused to pay for his education after his father died; that is why he still works in steel. He describes to me how hard it was to set up on his own, but he still managed to become a small-scale contractor, having had some initial help from his maternal uncle.

Sahil started the same way but had a different trajectory. He traveled with contracting companies and worked in Dubai, Russia, and Bahrain (Munnalal often boasts that Sahil worked in Dubai). Sahil, however, tells me that Munnalal ridicules him, sneering "Dubai return" as he points out Sahil's mistakes. Nevertheless, both agree that Dubai was a better place to work.[34] "In Dubai we saved a lot of money. They kept us well. We did not have to pick up the steel ourselves and they did a lot for safety," Sahil says of his time there. "They do not make you work as much through the day. Everything was great." He tells me technology was better in Dubai, as was safety equipment.

The two brothers work efficiently together. They move in synchrony between the *clangs* and *cracks* of the rebar bending and cutting machine. The rhythmic taps and twists testify to the expertise and skill gained from working with machines. Knowledge of machines organizes workers into groups: skilled, unskilled, experienced, quick, manual, technical, pipers, shovelers, fitters, and benders. Machines hierarchize and differentiate; they create the benchmarks of efficiency and accuracy and force *majboor* (needy) individuals to meet them. The mechanical beasts pick out the *tez* boys and teach them to be more *tez*.

No one represents *tezi* better than Bijli (a name that means electricity or lightning). Bijli is the only female *thekedar* (contractor) on the Wandering Woods site. Wanting to choose a name everyone in the business would remember, she was dubbed *Bijli* by her youngest daughter. She became a *thekadarin* (contractor f.) through an improvised life rhythm: she skillfully turned her family from laborers into contractors by meeting the rhythms of construction work. She found out that Jitendraji (the site supervisor) was looking for contractors to do piecework. With a husband and brother-in-law in the trade, Bijli jumped at the chance and asked to meet Jitendraji to show him her husband's and brother-in-law's skills. "I took the *theka*. . . . I ran it for a year. . . . [T]here was a *beldar* from here . . . who did not have masons or labor. . . . [W]e, husband and wife, were drinking chai in a shop. . . . [W]e said we do contract work." Bijli is strong and outspoken about her initiative. "What is the name of the *thekedar* [he asked]. I said it is a *thekedarin*, ladies *thekedar*." Bijli describes the moment she became Bijli and chuckles. "No one remembers my real name—even if I tell they forget it." Bijli's speed and street smarts paid off. Four years later, her family has *theka* work on the Wandering Woods construction site. She even found work on site for her son-in-law, but did hand off the contracting to her brother-in-law. The *tezi* of Bijli nevertheless manages to improve the lives of her family by meeting the speed of construction rhythms.

Standing on a construction site, buried in the timed beats of the machines, I think of rhythm and its connection to speed. If speed governs the aesthetic regime of our times, then rhythm is its accomplice.[35] Speed is the product of an accelerated rhythm. It is only when Bijli accelerates her own life rhythms to meet those of construction opportunities in NCR that construction achieves speed. It is only when Munnalal and Sahil join the beats of the machines that construction progresses. Together they produce sound and speed: "All the modalities sing a part in this chorus, changing from step to step, stepping in through proportions, sequences, and intensities which vary according to time."[36] It is, however, the gaps in these changing rhythms that hold importance here, as the gap between beats, or the "milieu," is a creative, prolific space of economic and political opportunities.[37] Such a space for individuals like Bijli and Munnalal opens the possibility of improvised, agentive action; they seize the opportunity, take the job, move to the beat, and match the mechanical rhythms.

Musical improvisation is about capturing a rhythm, but it is also about mastering the gap between.[38] Machines, while they govern and hierarchize bodies, also create this prolific space, saturated with the potential of skill building, the dignity of labor practices, and the chance for upward mobility. Indeed, it is within the beats of machines that Bijli, Munnalal, and Sahil improvise, grab, and transform the ways their lives unfold and the ways forward for those they love. To work and improvise within these rhythms is to live a life infused with potential and to be part of the chorus of everyday life. It is to find and maintain your own life's *chaal* (gaits).

SNAP GOES THE MACHINE

A bizarre silence occupies the terrace of the Wandering Woods tower block. The usually bustling space is eerily empty. A few workers mull about, but there are no supervising staff. Rajesh, a young laborer, greets me and tells me the crane is broken. I climb up on the plywood platform to investigate. He leads me to the spot where the large hook fell from the sky. The strong plywood is torn apart by the impact. The broken hook, hoist, and wires of the crane are lying nearby.

I stare up at the still crane. It is a significant break. "Good fortune it fell here [on the roof]. If it had fallen down [to the ground level] it would have taken someone with it." I remember the women in the camp telling me that somebody had a near miss today; they were probably referring to this incident. "Work will be stopped for at least three or four days—if the crane does not work no steel can be brought up, no work can be done." There is no *chaal* (gait, movement forward, steady line of work). Rajesh speaks to me as I register the profound silence around me: "The crane is shut so all the work is going slow. . . . [I]f work does not move [*kaam nahi chal raha*] then my mind is not occupied [*man nahi lagta*]." He is used to the rhythms of construction life. "This life is about standing on site for twelve hours, If I go anywhere else I do not feel at ease."

Mechanical silence is uncanny on a construction site—it creates an ominous feeling that the silence means economic decline. Slowness takes over when both machines and bodies snap. Slowness takes over when *chaal* is lost. Slowness is considered the enemy of a healthy economy and is punished on construction sites.

Sharifbhai, as he continues his description of the *tez ladka*, points to a man dragging large steel bars across the site. The man's back is hunched, and his torn green shirt is muddy and red from the rust on the steel bars he carries back and forth. "Look at him, his whole life he will only do *helperi* [be a helper]." Salim the eternal helper does not look up at Sharif-bhai. The man—only a few years younger than Sharifbhai—is destined to labor in the lowest ranks for the rest of his working life as he carries the weight of steel on his back.

Salim greets me a few days later. He is accompanied by a well-dressed young man carrying, to my surprise, the tool of the steelworkers' trade, a steel bar with a tiny hook at the end that helps tie steel wires. "Madam, do you have a job for my nephew, some factory job? This line of work sucks your blood. He can learn how to operate a machine," asks Salim, hoping his nephew's youth and *tezi* will buy him a chance.

What happens when rhythms accelerate so much that bodies cannot keep pace? What happens when you slowly grow old and can no longer be *tez*? When muscles and limbs snap like the overworked tower crane? When *chaal* reduces and dissipates? Munnalal disappears from the site one day and does not pick up his cell phone. Workers tell me that he is likely drunk somewhere. Two days later they find him, and he is brought to the site looking hungover. A screaming match ensues as the site contractor chastises Munnalal for the stoppage. Workers gossip that Munnalal is very good at his job but likes alcohol too much. They describe Munnalal falling into a pit because he was drunk one night. There are whispers everywhere on site.

I sit beside Munnalal during a lunch break several days later, when he is back on the job. He brags to me about how he bought fifty bottles of beer at the last festival. I mention to him how alcohol catches up with your body when you are older. He looks repentant as he tells me, "I do not drink alcohol anymore. Just beer." He pauses to explain: "But this work . . . you work so hard that you cannot keep your senses. I was awake for thirty-six hours that day. I just needed the drink."

The distribution of alcohol as an incentive to finish work faster has links to rewarding migrant labor in colonial plantations and is common on construction sites. So is alcohol addiction. Often it is so cold that laborers drink to be able to work and sleep. The construction site and labor camp are littered with chewing tobacco packets, *beedi* (local cigarettes) packets, and bottles of local brew. Machine-like efficiency makes demands on humans.

Technology is changing in Gurgaon. A new project by a famous developer brings a Malaysian construction company that uses Mivan technology. Monty, an architect friend from my undergraduate days, is their architect. He explains the technology to me: "The entire structure is cast in concrete. They make aluminum shuttering for all the walls. They cast it [an entire floor] and move upward." The construction technology pours entire walls in one block, with inbuilt frames and doors. "It builds fast and quickly upward. We will need less and less labor. Technologies such as these will weed labor out," Monty says.[39]

Who will go? All the non-*tez* people, most likely, the ones who inconvenience employers the most. Already so many are gone, most often the women. When I was growing up, sites were full of women, carrying mud and mortar on their heads; several of their children played in the gravel next to them.[40] Now the number of women on large-scale construction sites is negligible: a mere 10 percent, if that. I ask the chief site engineer why. They used to do all the lifting and carrying: mud, bricks, and plywood. Pulleys, elevators, and cranes replaced them, he explains. Older rhythms of carting and carrying replaced with newer beats of pulleys and cranes.

Silence spreads on the floor slab as the machines shut down. The mechanical beasts cool and come to a standstill with sultry *hisses* and *pops*. A gentle heat radiates off them, their bodies standing as proud warriors against the masses they replaced. The human machines of construction, the laborers who supported these new rhythms, have paid for construction speeds through their health. Addictions, ailments, and accidents—sleepless nights, alcohol and tobacco use, overexposure to dust-filled environments, and a willingness to work in suboptimal conditions—wear at them. Workers strive to keep up, to move on, to maintain a rhythm that is not their own. Many lag behind, fall, deteriorate, or get churned out as they try to match a rhythm that seems to accelerate endlessly as they grow old.[41]

ALL THIS RHYTHM MAKES SO MUCH NOISE

In 2013 the *Economic Times* publishes an article about India's real estate slowdown.[42] It is no longer the decade of exponential price increases. Developers are unable to sell or lease property. The rupee does a free fall. This downtrend makes me think of the tempos that govern the spaces of NCR, of the different lives that mingle across class lines in India's construction industry and the rhythms that they produce and negotiate.

After six months of delay, the first phase of Wandering Woods reaches completion: the building is ready to be handed over to its occupants. The site engineers celebrate. Before they head for the dinner hosted by the developers as a reward, Mr. Kumar the engineer tells me that the leasing team has been walking around looking incredibly stressed. Nobody wants to lease the property. If they cannot find someone to lease the office space, they will have to start paying the investors out of their own pocket. There is unrest. Amar, the head of the leasing and sales team, quits; rumor has it he got into a fight with the director. He leaves hoping to do consultancy work. When I meet him, he tells me that there is a lot of work in the pipeline—left unsaid is that there is not much ready to go at the moment.

The noise of the political economy of real estate and construction differentially accelerates and slows down lives. Sahil, the "Dubai return," references the 2008-real-estate-crash-led downfall of Dubai's construction boom. Locals like Chandubhai speak of changed village lifestyles. Bijli slows her speed as she hands her business to her brother-in-law. Monty too moves to other cities to partake in a new urban rhythm. I move from Bombay to Boston and fall into an academic one. As the tempos at which we live our lives switch back and forth, we renegotiate ourselves into different rhythms.

On construction sites, the introduction of new machines, the transformation of everyday technologies, and the economies these new technologies herald produce a political economy of sound. The temporalities expressed by this speed and rhythm are likely to be juxtaposed with a number of other senses of time in the everyday lives of individuals: familial, geographic, bodily, and social. Negotiating these various rhythms within the forces of rationalization that machines evoke can be read as an act of violence.[43] Often it is the intermixing of these rhythms, the dissonances and differentiations between them, that gives rise to discontents and produces an atmosphere of noise.

An altogether different noise was in the Dilli air. In the far distance, next to Jantar Mantar, groups of people sat in protest. "Did you visit the rally on Sunday?" Mr. Kumar asks. "I took my children there to protest, to understand what the independence struggle felt like," he says. "My friends and I went there this weekend. We North Indians know how to fight," claims Gopal, the electrical work supervisor. Anna Hazare and his anti-corruption protests were the talk of the Wandering Woods site.

On the day of Raksha Bandhan I decide to visit the ongoing protests. Jantar Mantar, an ancient astronomical laboratory, is now a site of public protest in independent India; it is here that Hazare sat on a hunger strike to enact changes to an anti-corruption bill.[44] I walk past swarms of young men from rural and small-town India, all wearing Anna's distinctive white cap. I pass through several metal detectors to get to the main arena. Anna Hazare presides on the stage as people give speeches beside him. One by one, women come up and tie a *rakhi* (protective band tied by a sister on her brother's wrist) on his wrist. Team Anna's protests evoke different sounds, for there is anger over unemployment in the air.

The demographic that swarms around Hazare is angry: young, educated men, from small towns and rural areas. Their bachelor's and engineering degrees have left them unwilling to do *labori* but unable to get white-collar work. Their frustrations echo with those of workers on site, who often talk of agrarian decline: increased land parceling as families expand and dependence on high-yielding grain varieties, pesticides, and mechanical devices bringing increased production costs that farmers cannot meet. "It is a loss to farm [*ghata*]," Mamun, a mason from West Bengal explains. "Look, for example I plant tobacco in one *bhiga*, in that one *bhiga* at the least I have to spend 5,000 rupees. For fertilizer . . . we need five, six quintals. Then the tractor, it takes 1,000 rupees [to rent]." After all the accounts, he states, "[I]t is a loss." The noise of unemployment, the opportunities denied by corruption, and the frustration of being exploited fills the air.

Kiran Bedi—India's most famous female police officer—takes the stage and screams into the microphone. Her speech is punctuated by whistles, claps, and an audience proclaiming "*nahin*" (no).

> Will we keep being the partners of corruption? Nooo!
>
> Will we keep being a part of lies, harassment, and betrayal? Noooooo!
>
> Will we keep witnessing women being unsafe? Noooo!
>
> Will we raise our voices against this behavior? Yesss!

The predominantly male audience yells and screams. The police whistle at no one in particular, and the auto-rickshaws outside the complex honk; the musicians on stage launch into a song as the speech ends. Men and women line up to greet Anna and argue as they jostle for space. The space is permeated with noise.

Noise is an irrational sound. Understood as interference or pollution, it stands in contrast to clear signals and the individual voice. It connotes distortion, chaos, impurity, illegitimacy, parasitism, or mutation.[45] Noise, however, can also be political, clear, and rational. It can be an oppositional cultural form, it can support civil democratic processes, or it can be politically critical.[46] "'Bringing the noise' is not accidental . . . but an expressive practice and a deliberate act of subversion."[47] Like rhythm, noise is affective and can raise fears and discontents.[48]

The political economy of sounds in construction is marked by acoustic rationalization, discipline, and rhythm on the one hand, and noise, entrepreneurism, and anger on the other. It comprises the *chaals* of acoustic rationalization, efficiency, and the speed that machines strive to create. At the same time, it is also the noise and anger of people tired of matching or molding to set rhythms. Noise is the unrest of those who must manipulate small gaps of opportunity to survive and the discontent of those who lag behind. As life speeds up and a variety of life rhythms interact and transform, a cacophony, a gaggle, a crescendo of noise fills the air in NCR. Noise highlights the ragged and raging discontents and desires through which workers attempt to survive in a fast-narrowing, competitive, machine-led economy. Noise indexes political economic struggles within the un-synced rhythms of economy, society, and politics. Noise embeds the intimacies and affects of labor struggles in construction and real estate in NCR. It is the force against the dominance of acoustic rationalizations; it is the sound of seeking alternate life rhythms.

5 Inside the Pit

Over three hundred workers walk, drive, and run through the white and blue gates of Wandering Woods every day, as the timekeeper stands at the gate, taking attendance. Hard hats, gloves, and boots are picked up from the shed, and workers commence their tasks. Some drag earth to and fro, heaving their bodies into ploughs and shovels. Others control machines, shifting gears, driving rollers, and channeling pipes from floor to floor. Floor managers stand and supervise to maintain order and pace. Many do rounds across the three phases, inspecting, instructing, tackling issues, and chiding workers with expletives. Specific sounds, smells, and substances emanate from the working groups as a collective of human-nonhuman sounds reverberates across the punctures and pits on site.

Work at Wandering Woods is divided into several areas known as "working points." Jitendraji, the chief site contractor, explains this organization: "We have 300 labor[ers] and . . . we have about twenty to thirty working points: for example the first basement, the third basement, the thirteenth floor." He speaks of the different micro zones in construction and how he supervises them. "We also have a chain. We have a supervisor and a foreman. Then tower-wise we have an engineer. Then we have a manager. . . . Someone is in this corner, somebody in the other corner. . . . [I]n one tower, we have fifty laborers and there are only two staff members." Each working point tackles a different task depending on the needs of the day. Jitendraji keeps track of progress. "So, every day I make one or two rounds to the towers. And we discuss what do we have to do tomorrow morning. We do the planning in the evening. . . . [T]he labor gathers at one point in the morning, and . . . they divide the work." Jitendraji's meticulous planning ensures that construction at Wandering Woods condenses into distinct working atmospheres. As the architecture grows, the atmospheres of the spaces shift matching the nature of construction work: excavation, tamping, formwork, carpentry, concreting, curing, chipping, electricity, plumbing, tiling, plastering, and painting produce their own atmospheric zones. Working points are spaces with amplified sensoriums and activity. As Jitendraji described, several of them exist at Wandering Woods.

On the terrace of the tower under construction sit a team of carpenters, steel binders, and specialized fabrication workers supervised by the tower engineer and foremen. This team is governed by the wind. They swing, high above the ground, perched atop bars of steel, and embrace the open air. They bend and hammer, and tie together and wedge apart plywood and steel to form the shells of new floor slabs. Their work is framed by the incredible vistas of the mottled landscape around them.

A very different atmosphere prevails in the basement of the same concrete shells. Teams of electricians and air-conditioning specialists weld ducts and run wires through concrete cores. Here the sparks from welding torches fly through the darkness, lit in spots by the strong orange haze of halogen lamps. Water drips from the freshly cast concrete slabs above, and metal dust from cut ducts covers the ground. The smells of earth, fire, and water mingle in unsettled ways. The terrace of one of the structures is a different atmosphere: a number of plumbers wrestle with a giant leak on the flooded terrace. They wade in knee-deep water, tools and surfaces slippery. Water soaks their clothes, and dampness lingers in the air as they struggle to prevent a deluge. The immersive atmospheres of construction, as with most industrial work, are aesthetic, sensory, and affective environments generated through labor. The shared atmospheric experience and the social relations these atmospheres engender tie to laboring experience in construction.

Atmospheres in anthropology are understood as an entanglement of emotion, substance, materials, existence, and practice.[1] Comprising the space that surrounds us, atmospheres communicate knowledge through sensory and material cues as well as through affects. Construction work lends a particularized insight into this understanding of atmospheres, because it is an active site of their production: a focus on construction presents the relations between production of atmospheres and the subjectivities they produce. An attention to atmospheres in construction demonstrates how atmospheres are charged with caste, gender, and class hierarchies. This attention to inequity is inspired by authors who critique the whiteness of affect and by extension atmospheres, and like them it emphasizes how embodiment and affect theory derive from the lived experience of marginalization.[2]

To be attuned to atmospheres is to dwell in the ephemeral dimensions of spaces as they shift and transform. The ephemeral manifests as the continuous displacement and movement of workers from one construction site to the next as well as in the atmospheres that emerge during specific kinds of work on construction sites. These atmospheres are temporary in nature, but their specific atmospheric conditions are linked to the class and caste solidarities and struggles that take place on site. Dwelling in and analyzing ephemeral atmospheres allows us to understand class consciousness and a politics of labor on construction sites. Atmospheres and their aesthetics, I argue, participate in creating precarity and dislocation for workers and create class, and caste, difference and anger.[3] I make this case by considering three key forms of life interlinked with the production of atmospheres in construction work: *mazdoori*, *majboori*, and *jugaad*, that is, the politics of labor, necessity, and precarity on construction sites.

MAZDOORI

Not too far away from Wandering Woods, in a smaller construction site closer to downtown Gurgaon, workers build the scaffolding for the columns and slabs of a palatial bungalow: Haveli. The small plot, in comparison to Wandering Woods, fronts a large, gated-community park. The clear sightline from the park allows an outsider the view of various teams at work. All is calm upon the site as workers commence their working rhythms on a cold January day. The tender morning light of an NCR winter washes over the concrete and columnar structure, filtering through its slabs and openings, casting light in hazy patterns across surfaces. The small cement mixer is cranked on. Workers commence the construction of new columns. The sounds of their working rhythms permeate the site: plywood falls on plywood in loud *thud-thuds*, and the rasp of cement as it mixes bristles my skin.

Mahaab and Mohamed are creating starters for new columns in the left basement. Mohamed—or Lambu (tall), as they call him on site for his lanky frame—folds his wiry body to scrape cement onto the ground. Mahaab stands beside him, feet apart, one hand at her waist, staring into the distance and looking mildly bored (as she often does) with the goings-on on site. Bittu Chacha, their neighbor and the eldest member on site, is starting some carpentry work on the second floor. His youngest son Teju is with him. Father and son look similar but bear different mannerisms: the younger defiant and diffident, working reluctantly and slowly, and the elder soft-spoken, riling up only to cuss his son and remind him of who feeds and clothes him. The easygoing, white-mustached Rajasthani waterproofer, Maheshji, inhabits the lower basement, laying stone slabs on the floor. Nazeem, a young laborer from Malda district, assists him. Munnalal, MD, and their teams work on steel and carpentry on the first level. The two subcontractors are the fastest and most aggressive workers on site but have an affable roughness to their mannerisms that allows them to set up a steady banter among themselves and with the site supervisors. Munnalal has his cousin Sahil with him, and MD has his son Nazarul as a helper. Ram and Jai, the two youngest supervisors on site, representing the project management and contracting teams respectively, sit atop the roof on plastic chairs drinking small cups of tea made by Mahaab and warm themselves in the morning light. Shreelal, the supervisor in charge of the site, isn't here yet, but the small troupe of Malda boys have already spread across the site to do their chores. They haul cement bags and gravel for the small portable mixer that churns cement-concrete.

When asked who they are and what they do, these individuals would each reply differently. Some might say "painter" and others *mistri* (mason).

Those who deal with steel might say *lohar-chaal* (steel-lines), others might use the more generic *bandh-kaam* (building work in general), and still others might modify the English term "helper" to describe their work as *helperi*. In describing their work, many would trace the hierarchies of labor and skills that they passed through. MD, for example, traces the arc of a standard laboring career as a movement from *beldari* (carrying things), to *mistri* (mason), to *raj mistri* (master mason), to *karigar* (skilled worker or craftsman), up to *thekedar* (contractor, or in most cases a subcontractor). When describing their day-to-day actions, however, most would identify their work as *mazdoori* (*majdoori*).

Originating in agricultural work, *mazdoori* refers to working in fields for a day wage. In NCR, it is tied to the seasonal but sometimes permanent migration of agrarian day-wage workers into an urban area to labor on construction sites. The term indexes an alienated labor that extends the fruits of one person's labor for the benefit of another, and it often has an urban-rural connection (for example, the movement from harvesting another's field to building someone else's home). *Mazdoori* can describe labor in farming, forestry, construction, rickshaw-pulling, recycling, or other kinds of contract work.[4] In many cases *mazdoori* is also ephemeral labor, as it is seasonal and shifting and takes workers back and forth from the village or from site to site. *Mazdoori* can mean unskilled and physical labor, as opposed to *karigiri* (literally artisanship or craftsmanship, but also describes skilled work such as masonry or steelwork, which are often also referred to as *kala*, or craft). Important to an understanding of *mazdoori*, though often neglected in discussions of labor, are the atmospheres and aesthetics of work: the sawdust, the heat, the sweat, and the sensibilities that form an understanding of how much one works and for what. The atmospheres—the materials handled, smells and toxins released, temperatures and treatments of work—inform workers where they stand in the hierarchy of laborers and help them calculate what they are due. In construction, many use the word *mazdoori* because it connects to their mode of payment, the day wage, known as *dihadi*. Dues or *dihadi* are counted through hours of *mazdoori* and help individuals build a relationality among themselves.

Over the course of my fieldwork and the years that followed it, the word *mazdoori* would be evoked repeatedly to speak of work and laboring populations on construction sites. As Bilal, a young steel worker, puts it, "Each and every person is compelled to labor [*mazdoori*] all his or her lives—you study, you have to labor [*mazdoori*] to survive, and so does that man there. We all have to labor [*mazdoori*] in order to survive." Though the term is attached to physical labor, Bilal's use of it moves across classes, religions, and genders, challenging the distinction between physical and other forms of work and constructing a relationality based on economic survival—a relationality recognized on construction sites.

"*Yahaan dihadi jyada milta hain na* [*sic*; we get more day wage here]," says Mahaab to me when I ask her why she and her husband work in Delhi and not closer to their Bengali home. Nava Raipur, the soon-to-be capital of Chhattisgarh, sees a high demand for construction labor and is much closer to West Bengal, but Mohamed and Mahaab prefer NCR. They have worked in the region for almost ten years; Mahaab's parents work in Dwarka near the airport, plus, as Mahaab points out, the money is good here.

Lambu, as Mohamed is known, is one of three brothers from a financially stable family in rural West Bengal (Malda district). His father is part of the local village governing council, giving him access to favors and finance, which he extends to his sons. Mohamed, however, is far less educated and entrepreneurial than his brothers. Mahaab says this is because he is "quiet" or does not speak much. Mohamed's shy, gentle, and genuinely quiet manner may not help him in school but does make him the ideal *mazdoor*. He never says no to anything, nor does he raise his voice. When yelled at, he tilts his head slightly, eyes down, to listen as the supervisor screams at him for his mistakes. This earns Mohamed favor in the eyes of his supervisors, and it shows in the tasks and social positionality the couple enjoy. Together, they make about 24,000 rupees plus overtime a month. The pay, Mahaab states matter-of-factly, is the only reason they are here.

Mahaab and Mohamed moved through several construction sites before arriving at Haveli. While construction sites embed in the context of a neighborhood, those who build them are always in a state of motion and experience constant displacement. Hustling, leveraging social capital, and creating favor are part and parcel of laboring action as workers move from site to site. Social infrastructure forms a primary component of these mediations and constructs networks of *mazdoori*. Individuals from different regions meet on construction sites; Haveli itself has workers from West Bengal, Rajasthan, Uttar Pradesh, Bihar, Orissa, and Haryana. They are a mix of religions and a mix of dominant and nondominant castes and Adivasi (Indigenous) workers.

I watch Nazeem and Maheshji work. As they hold the large slabs together and set them out gently on the bed of cement, they share information: how to determine the required thickness of the *ghol* (cement slurry) by observing the viscosity with which it drips, the source of the Bhojpuri songs Nazeem plays, and the location of nearby construction sites. Construction sites form synaptic nodes of knowledge exchange and resource sharing.[5] *Pehchaan* (literally to recognize someone, but understood as social network) is created by dwelling and working in the atmospheres of construction sites.[6] The mundanity and collective rhythms of construction, the slowness of some days, and the camaraderie established through the shared experience of heat, moisture, and cold, as well as the enjoyment of syrupy cups of chai during tea breaks, enable a laboring affinity and the exchange of information.

As I sit, stand, or awkwardly squat with workers, they give me tips on jobs. Mumbai pays more than Delhi but is farther from home. Kashmir and hilly regions (*pahari* areas) have the best *dihadi*, but the cold is intolerable, and you have to work in icy conditions. Chhattisgarh has a lot of building work, but they do not hire locals and do not pay as well as Dilli (Delhi). That contractor does not pay on time; the other site has a crèche and running water. There is work on the site in Dwarka. You work in America; is there work in America? Will you take me there?

Mohamed's friend Mamun often inquires about work in America (usually indicating the United States), and I tell him that it is very difficult to get into the country. Mamun, who accompanied Mahaab and Mohamed to Haveli, is often seen roaming around and chatting with neighborhood watchmen and workers. Unlike most of the other workers, Mamun is accompanied by his wife and their four-year-old son. The four-year-old spends his time by the construction site, where various adults holler to him and hand him a little *kishmish* (mixture of dry fruit), biscuits, or a small glass of *cha* (chai). He often plays with the two older boys who belong to a third Bengali couple, and sometimes a young woman from a local NGO visits to teach the children. Mamun is much louder and more outspoken than Mohamed. His wife too speaks much more publicly than Mahaab, who only speaks to me when we are alone. While the three Bengali couples come from the same region, it is obvious that Mohamed and Mahaab enjoy more privileges. Mohamed may be more skilled than Mamun, but this only partially accounts for the fact that he is given highly skilled work, such as "lay-outing." He is also paid more, a fact that Mamun is aware of and resents. Mohamed's quiet demeanor and Mahaab's subtle maneuverings secure a higher status and *dihadi* for the young couple.

These differences in *dihadis* articulate themselves in the performances of labor on site: Mahaab works more slowly than Mohamed (she is paid 9,000 rupees to his 15,000), and Mamun is less attentive to his work than Mohamed. MD and Munnalal work at high speeds, as they are paid not in day wage but via a *theka* (contract) for the work done and not time spent. The quicker they move, the faster they finish the job and get paid. Calculative logics and their accompanying labor performances structure the forms of *mazdoori* on site: slowing down work, doing half-hearted work, and pilfering materials are all ways of responding to unequal pay. The calculative logic between *mazdoori* done and *dihadi* paid feeds the atmospheres of work.

It is noon, and Bittu Chacha has worked for about five hours now. The sun has grown stronger, and Chacha's clothes are already laden with sawdust. Squatting on the wooden battens rising over the scaffolding, Bittu Chacha spent the morning repeating the same actions, sawing and laying down plywood for a new floor slab. His is a workday measured in the square feet of plywood he sets, a day where the material manifestations of Chacha's labor form the supporting structure of another man's house. It is no surprise, then, that the sun, sawdust, and opulent structure feed Chacha's experience of injustice and exploitation and add salt to the violation and nonrecognition of his *mazdoori*.

Bittu Chacha migrated to NCR from Bihar in his youth. He had "no one in the city" and was fearful that people would cheat him or trap him (*fasayenge*). "When I first came [to the city] many people cheated me. One of the *thekedars* [contractors], he did not give me fifteen days of *mazdoori*," Chacha says of his initial years in NCR. "The first [*pehela*] *thekedar* used to give us money after three-three months. . . . Now you tell me, I have a loan on my head [*sar pe karz chadha hain*], how do I tell them that you do not give me money?" Chacha's usual calm demeanor is broken by his anger at the memory of the event.

His words evoke a lineage of *mazdoori*. The term recognizes a history of exploitation that can be traced to India's landlord-tenant (*zamindari*) system. *Mazdoori*, in the Indian context, can be seen as a dependent relationship between landowner and worker and is often used to distinguish day labor done for a wage from farming your own land (*kheti*).[7] While the *zamindari* system saw differences in experience across regions and groups, the collective sensibility of alienated labor and accumulative capital in the *zamindari* system still structures construction work today.[8] This sensibility is carried from village to site and even represented in Bollywood narratives and is very much encoded into the word *mazdoori*. It is also connoted by words such as *malik* (owner), *sahib* (sir), *amir* (wealthy), and *angrezi* (English, English-speaking) when speaking of contractors, landowners, and developers. This historiography and these systems of connections lend workers the language of exploitation and rights: the right not only to payment and but also to criticize those who control wages. *Mazdoori* involves a "meticulous calculation of services and compensation."[9] It is also accompanied by "a feeling of dignity" and a sense of ownership; *mazdoori* is not labor that a worker is "embarrassed of" but money hard earned.[10]

Bittu Chacha takes these arguments a step further: he presents *mazdoori* as a way to gain a foothold in and a right to the urban area he works in. His years of *mazdoori* give him a connection to the region. His experience provides him with a knowledge of people and space. *Mazdoori*, then, also speaks to the making and marking of place and claims: it ties the production of the urban built environment to class identities and working-class rights to income, equality, and space.

Mazdoori creates an ever-changing world at Wandering Woods. The surrounding landscape transforms as I walk through the construction site. This is an ephemeral world where new staircases arise suddenly, a plywood piece eliminates an entry, and a few bent bars form ladders onto a new floor. Stones and slabs are laid down in flooded areas, and steps are constructed out of planks and chemical drums. New passageways are continually forged in keeping with the changing architecture as workers produce the quickest paths to work. Social pathways and connection emerge in similar, piecemeal, and innovative ways.

Bittu Chacha lives next to Mahaab and Mohamed: his tin-walled hut is separated from theirs by a giant mulberry tree. Like Mahaab and Mohamed, Chacha's housing is indicative of his social positionality on the site. In his late forties, he is the eldest member of the working team and a long-term employee with Sharanji, the construction contractor. Mahaab and Bittu call each other *chacha* (uncle) and *beti* (daughter). I too use *Chacha* in recognition of his age. For Mahaab, Bittu Chacha brings an added sense of security as he sits around while she cooks and takes care of the house (unlike the other men, who spend their free time in the park opposite the site or taking a stroll in the neighborhood). He often eats with Mahaab and Mohamed. His wife never comes to the site; it is forbidden for women in his village to mix with outsiders, and she rarely ventures far from their family home, but Bittu Chacha's younger son—Teju—works with him. "One is studying, the other said 'I will not study'—he has studied till matric [matriculation, tenth grade], what will he do?" says Chacha, as an explanation of Teju's presence.

As they work together, Chacha gives Teju regular instructions. Teju does not take to them; instead he seems resentful, works furiously for a while, and then disappears for long periods. He makes friends with Nazarul, MD's son. They seem to be the same age, but Nazarul, unlike Teju, works diligently all day. I see him banging at boards and carting things, and he often looks up at me and smiles. One day he climbs the scaffolding at the back of the construction site and hoists himself up onto the branches of the mulberry tree that spreads across the corner. He picks some of the ripe fruit and offers some to me. As I eat in delight, he climbs up again to pick more of the delicious fruit for me, handing it to me before going back to work. He is quiet, shy, and doesn't speak much when I attempt conversation with him, only giving me brief replies. The two boys hang out with the Malda boys.

I see Nazarul and Teju sitting in the large park after lunch one day; they are holding hands and leaning on each other's shoulders in affection.[11] Together they approach the Malda laborers. Nazarul pushes one of the boys in play. Another pushes back. Suddenly they all turn into warring toddlers, pushing and wrestling with each other. One boy hits the other with his construction helmet. A bunch of them tussle with each other. I laugh to myself at their silliness, but the hypermasculinities of the industry under construction are not lost on me. "Such a man's world," I write in my field notes that night.

The temporalities of work—the rhythms of the day, the commencements and halts, the working hours—build social relationalities on construction sites. These movements and rhythms, in interaction with the materials and architecture under construction, give rise to distinct sensoriums that structure the experience of labor and the working day. It is within these atmospheres of heat and dust that *mazdoori* creates the solidarities of *pehchaan* among coworkers, the hard work and harsh conditions allowing calculations of the amount of *dihadi* they each deserve. In writing of the phosphorous factories of nineteenth-century England, Marx describes factory floors as surpassing the worst horrors of Dante's inferno.[12] Profit is produced by subjecting workers to harsh conditions, longer hours, and faster production. In the descriptions of environment and space juxtaposed against his calculations, Marx, like Mahaab and Mamun, connects the atmospheres of labor to wages. The incomplete architectures and the social proximities they bring, the changing pathways and personal interconnections, the labor and sun all radiate into the understanding of *mazdoori* on construction sites. The atmospheres of *mazdoori* help form networks and enable connections across ethnic, religious, caste, and gender divides. The atmospheres infuse into the class consciousness of *mazdoori*, combine with a historiography both real and imagined, and form pathways to claims and rights among the iron cages of construction.

IRON CAGES

An iron maze exists on the ninth floor of the Wandering Woods tower. The semirusted scaffolding creates a dystopic array of bars in every direction. The columns extend infinitely to mimic a hall of mirrors. The rusty poles support a wooden mold with recently cast concrete. Cement water drips through the gaps in the planks and puddles along the floor. Exposed lightbulbs glow like beacons trapped within the cubic dissonance of the iron cage.

A group of carpenters work amid this electric blaze. Part of the floor slab above gains enough strength to support itself, and the crew disassembles

the scaffolding. The clanging of metal reverberates. It shakes the floor slab
we stand upon with the might of youthful labor as the men fling iron poles
onto the floor. The strange light, the grating sounds, the heavy lifting and
hauling, the movements of the men, and the gridded aesthetic of the scaffolding resonate with Weber's iron cage, seemingly trapping workers in an
endless and eternal maze: the steel maze of binding necessity.[13]

Jitendraji calls for me to come see some new iron work on site, and
I run to the steelyard to meet him. It is the middle of the afternoon in
summer, and the steelyard is ablaze. I hope not to burn my feet: already
my tennis shoes have holes, and my feet have cuts from the binding wires
and stray bars that jut out across the site. I hop from heated bar to heated
bar, over to where the men are finishing up some formwork.

The hardest job on site is that of a steel work *mistri* (mason). Who
wants to work, the other masons say, with steel bars that are heavy and
rusted? Harsh steel bars tear clothes and stain what they do not tear.
Your hands turn black holding bar after bar. Calluses develop on your
skin as you twist bars together with the might of the last meal you had.
"You do not last beyond forty doing steel work," Sharifbhai the steel foreman proclaims.

Jitendraji stands around observing the site, as he often does, and I see
one of the steelworkers bring a young man to meet him. Fair and light-
eyed, the visitor does not look like he has stood in the sun for even a day.
Construction work, Veer says, "draws the best of the best and the worst of
the worst. Here a man works in the sun, your face must be black. A person
becomes dark, the shine on your face reduces." Construction is often a last
resort: "If they do not get any work anywhere else, if they have had a hard
time in some other work or [have] been thrown out of it, then they will
get work here," Veer says.

Well-dressed in a shirt, jeans, and sneakers, this young man does not fit
into Veer's assessment of someone who does construction work. He looks
incongruous on a site where everyone is covered by dust. I eavesdrop,
with the other workers around them, as they converse. "You have one-
year experience?" The young man seems to want a job. "What is the thickness of that wall?" Jitendraji asks in his slow, dry drawl. The young man
mumbles in response. "And this steel bar, what is its width?" Seeing me
eavesdropping, Jitendraji hollers to me, saying "Madam, you always ask

us how you entered this line [of work]?" He repeats my opening question when conducting formal interviews on site to demonstrate his knowledge of my conduct on his site. "Look at this gentleman, he works in exports and wants to come into construction." He says this more for his own benefit than mine. I ask, "What is his answer?" Jitendraji looks at the young man and decides to speak both for and to him. "In this line, we have to stand in the hot sun [*dhoop*], we have to work so hard. Stay in exports," he advises. Then he continues, turning to me, "Everyone in this industry comes into it for one reason only, call it by any other name [*ussein joh bhi naam do*], but it is *majboori*."

I nod. This too is a word I hear all too often. When I ask workers how they began in the industry, they often bring up the situational context of *majboori*. *Majboori*, translated as need or obligation, is a term used to refer to binding circumstances, often related to poverty. It indexes a combination of unforeseen events: alcoholic or dead fathers, sisters to marry, illness, sudden financial loss (say, due to crop failure), and forms of discrimination and violence. It compels workers to work and often traps workers in construction work. *Majboori* feeds this industry; as Jitendraji says, construction feels like a trap.

Bittu Chacha began his construction life doing steel work. A trusted long-term relationship with the contractor allows Chacha to work into his forties, despite his slowing down and aging by industry standards. Bittu Chacha comes from a large village on the banks of the Ganges where a bomb blast took place during elections one year. In the slowness of the afternoon, at the door of his hut, he traces the forms of *majboori* that brought him to site. "*Samay ek aisi cheez hai* [time is such a thing], I used to do agricultural work [*kheti-baadi-dhaan*], then a son was born and a cow died, then [a few months later] another cow died." Debts accumulated as Chacha's financial responsibilities grew, but the final straw was when his father fell ill. "I spent one to one and a half lakhs (rupees). We went to Patna to get treatment [*ilaaj karvaya*]. Then I came to the city to make money and got into this work."

Chacha worked across NCR for over twenty-five years. He has spent the last seven years with this *thekedar*. Bittu Chacha is well respected on site as the recognized elder—not only by age, but also for the amount of time he has spent working with Sharanji. Most of the supervisors are significantly younger than Bittu Chacha and have less experience. The notion of *majboori*, like *mazdoori*, also resonates among them.

Nazarul is hard at work on the formwork when a new supervisor, Keshav, comes to the site. He straddles the corner of the pit to observe Nazarul, taking up a hypermasculine stance as though he intends to urinate inside the pit. Hollering for me, he quizzes me on my work and I tell him about myself but also appease him by asking him to give me a formal interview. He smiles and says, "yes certainly, certainly," turning again to observe the work. After a while, he turns to ask me, "Why does a man work? [*aadmi kaam kyun karta hain?*]" Not waiting for an answer, he continues: "Everyone has some or other *majboori*—look at that boy"—he gestures toward Nazarul—"it is his age to study, not to work."

Nazarul is silent as he works, and I observe him in the winter morning's pale light. His face is youthful and innocent, but his hands are rough and hardened. His red and black sweater has a layer of dust, as does his sun-darkened neck. He looks disheveled. Every time I look at Nazarul, my heart breaks; instinct tells me he is probably young enough to be my son, and part of me wants to clean him up and feed him (his father, MD, loves him and looks after him well). Keshav breaks my train of thought as he continues imparting wisdom. "Look at those women, they are working on site, with all these men. Women belong at home, they were built to make *rotis* and look after the home, not to work on site, but they came here because of *majboori*." My skin bristles, annoyed. I try to change the subject. "How long have you been working in construction?" I ask. "It's been thirty years—I was fifteen when I first started to work, my father died and I had to come here," replies Keshav. I am shocked and humbled at the answer and ask more gently, "What happened to him?" "Just poverty [*bas gareebi*]" is Keshav's matter-of-fact reply.

Though people repeatedly tell me that construction work is not for those beyond forty or forty-five, what they never directly say is that it is the work of the very young. The labor of construction often requires the strength and energy that only youth provides. Construction draws seasonal labor from nearby rural regions but often also creates labor supply chains that extend nationally and transnationally. The lack of identity cards, combined with the informality of hiring practices, allows for knowing or unknowing underage labor hires. In narrations of their lives, thirty-something-year-olds would tell me about working in the industry for twenty-odd years, estimating that many young men enter the industry a little past puberty.[14] As Veer, the charismatic young layout mason, once told me, "This is my age to have fun, to roam," and indeed this is the age for play for so many youth. Many, however, are compelled to work by *majboori*.[15]

Majboori (*majburi*) can mean many things. It denotes an economy of rural subsistence farming, where labor on the land does not yield enough to feed a family for a year, much less pay for other life necessities. It also speaks to the weight of this poverty being born differentially according to gender: young boys begin labor before finishing school, and girls are married off early, often making their way into construction, domestic, or other forms of work after marriage.

As Keshav suggested, *majboori* also speaks to a cyclicality of circumstance, a generational trap for workers whose bodies decay and degenerate through the work of urban construction and whose early illness or demise sends their sons and daughters to sites. It manifests the worst form of the ephemeral: that of a shortened life span or premature death. *Majboori*, then, expands to encompass a structural condition of life, not understood as a sudden event but as structural violence—a violence exerted systematically (that is, indirectly by everyone who belongs to a certain social order).[16] It describes the conditions of living produced through slow violence and merely articulated in the suddenness of events such as death. Given that a bulk of workers in construction come from Adivasi, Dalit, or non-dominant-caste backgrounds, *majboori* also embeds a history of exploitation.

Scholars of South Asia use the term *majboori* to refer to poverty or economic pressure, seeing it as a set of structural constraints rather than an instance of individuals exercising force.[17] While *majboori* can be seen as a form of helplessness that forces women into work, authors engaging with studies of commercial surrogacy argue that *majboori* can help formulate a strategy, forge new alliances, and construct new social relationships.[18] This perspective offers a more agentive reading that links *majboori* to *mazdoori* in an actionable way. Poverty and vulnerability are negotiated through acts of labor and through the networks of information and solidarity produced on construction sites. *Majboori and* its navigations are structured by social and economic capital, as it takes both to leave a village and arrive on site. *Mazdoori* mediates *majboori* through individual initiative and enterprise but also produces a way of recognizing and helping fellow marginalized folk.

The heightened atmospherics in construction, the harsh material worlds, and the knowledge of the *majbooris* that bring you into them lend empathy and understanding to the person beside you. The iron scaffolding burns hot in the sun and freezes cold in the winter; it scorches or numbs hands according to the vagaries of the weather. To work within these cages of iron is to understand the hardship that comes from cut hands and lacerated arms, from torn clothes and shoes, from work that can be merciless. "My brother," "my uncle," and "my friend" are enunciations that index affection and intimacy. Workers see their younger selves in the faces of new arrivals and watch over their kin in their struggles. The pairing of the solidarities of *majboori* with the proximities of *mazdoori* allows collective energies to consolidate on site. The changing material and sensory scapes of architecture are tools of survival and solidarity, creating forms of political recognition as you balance on the intricate meshwork of steel bars.

BALANCING ON THE BARS

It is a seething June afternoon. Jitendraji and I stand atop a smoldering heap of red mud, deep in the recesses of the construction pit. The pit hums with construction activity, stepped up in intensity due to Jitendraji's authoritative presence. Workers set the wooden scaffolding on a column behind us. "Ay! Keep it straight," Santoshji the foreman yells. Veer, the layout mason, ruffles his hair in agitation as he holds a plumb line next to the column. The large, uneven gap between the string and column line gleefully betrays their construction error. Santoshji screams to Chaurasiya and Imran, who grip the angled plywood from opposite sides. They pull and push in unison. Nandu works to tighten the various *ghuggis* (screws in the scaffolding). They all move up and down the scaffolding surrounding the column and leverage their body weight in order to bring the column into plumb. Jitendraji surveys their enterprise, and quips to me, "In construction you have 5 percent engineering, 95 percent *jugaad*."

For those of us who live and do research in North India, *jugaad* is a word dropped into conversation so often that we barely notice its use. Individuals use the term to speak of a variety of practices including finding a job, solving a problem, or helping someone. It refers to an ethic of sorts through which individuals mediate everyday life. In 2011, Kanu Agrawal brought *jugaad* into academic circles through an architectural exhibition entitled "*Jugaad* Urbanism."[19] Here he celebrated *jugaad* as an entrepreneurial and creative practice that produced innovative, architectural solutions in informal settlements, and gave rise to the distinct informal urbanism that we identify with Indian cities.

The deliciously emic nature of *jugaad* became a popular way for elite Indians to celebrate poverty. Books such as *Jugaad Innovation: A Frugal and Flexible Approach to Innovation in the 21st Century* and news articles such as "Jugaad: The Art of Converting Adversity into Opportunity" and "Getting to Mars Through 'Jugaad,'" celebrated the ability of India's lower classes to innovate frugally.[20] Taking a more critical stance on these practices, scholars of South Asia presented *jugaad* as embedding a "provisional agency" or marking a set of differential, "shrewd improvisations."[21] *Jugaad*, scholars argue, "is excoriated as incorrigibly premodern," accepted as the "law of precarity," and thought not to "evidence . . . free will."[22]

Jugaad connects to *majboori*, as both offer varying forms of exploitation and agency. *Jugaad* works differently across different communities and class categories. Like the act of balancing on the shifting scaffoldings, *jugaad* is an act of constant adjustment in order to survive. In its essence it is also a practice upon which construction atmospheres rely. Construction cannot occur without *jugaad*. I demonstrate how differential forms of *jugaad* distribute risk unequally and increase physical and economic precarity for workers on construction sites.

There is much commotion in the basement pit. A large concrete beam more than ten feet wide, cast to hold back the earth three stories above at ground level, is threatening to fall into the pit. Mr. Kumar, the chief engineer, tells me he is going to do a *jugaad* to take it out. This is a day-long exercise, and I am told to stand far away lest I get hurt by the falling beam. The work unfolds slowly. Two young men slide down the mud slope to the slipping beam and dig holes along its side and bottom so as to draw ropes around it. Groups of men stand atop the slope holding the ropes and pull once they are secured. As the afternoon progresses, they attempt to dislodge the beam. Three men climb the slope to dig under the beam and loosen the soil underneath it; the groups above pull at the ropes to prevent the beam from sliding onto them. We watch for signs of the beam slipping. Mr. Kumar yells tense instructions. Workers around us pause to watch the event: everyone keeps a watchful eye out, and our shared knowledge of the beam's ability to kill and maim hangs over us. Hours later, the beam slides safety to the bottom of the pit, and the team celebrates the *jugaad* of having dislodged the beam without hiring an expensive crane. The concrete beam is slowly broken into pieces by a team of chippers.

"We people are good at *jugaad*," Shailendraji says, as he compares construction work in India and the United States. He boldly claims *jugaad* for India, as he and I walk across the construction site. Shailendraji is a site supervisor and only studied to the tenth grade. He reminds me that he has no official training in construction except for his thirty-four years working and supervising construction sites. He gives me a guided tour of the site, and I ask him the meaning of the term. *"Jugaad* means—who does *jugaad*, what he means by that is, that given the conditions at that time, the conditions at the place, keeping those in mind, keeping those conditions in front of you, and considering them." Shailendraji embeds *jugaad* in context as he explains, "Whatever thing we have available to us, with those things, you achieve the purpose [the solution]. That is what we call *jugaad*." He gives an example. "For example, you need to lift some goods on site. There are two or three pieces of wood around and some rope, there is no scaffolding, or the scaffolding is a hundred, two hundred kilometers away, or the costing [price] is too much. What do people do here? They will apply their mind, take four pieces of wood, tie them together, get another person. They attach the wood, climb it, and drop the goods up." He signals at the fluid boundary between exploitation and agency in *jugaad* practices: "They will not *deny* you. The Indian worker will not *deny* you. He will not say . . . bring me some scaffolding or I will fall and hurt myself. He will do it."

Shailendraji's descriptions raise several interpretations of *jugaad*. It represents a set of constraints and often characterizes circumstances such as economic limitations and the unavailability of resources. Like those celebratory authors, he depicts *jugaad's* inventiveness and creative problem-solving capacity. Indeed, for those working in construction, *jugaad* is often a way to problem solve in order to keep construction work moving, but it is also understood as a personality trait. To be *jugaadu* is to be able to do *jugaad* quickly and hence to be a tactical and smart person. *Jugaad* allows you to learn quickly, make contacts, and move up the construction work ladder. *Jugaad*, most workers agree, defines the nature of construction. But for some, it defines the nature of their lives.[23]

The ad hoc nature of construction activity at Wandering Woods—the shoving of columns and chipping away at beams, the quick fixes—speaks to *jugaad* as an entrepreneurial ethic in construction worlds. Several interlocutors believed that my presence on site was my *jugaad*. Rumors spread on the site that I would get a big government job and come back in a car with a *lal bati* (a red light on top, signifying a dignitary), or that I would get four lakh rupees (US$5,000) for my book. In many ways, I got to this site through a social networking *jugaad*, asking friends and mentors for leads, who then referred me to friends of friends, a few of whom enabled access to various sites. When dealing with the juxtaposition of different social and class positionalities, however, the nature of *jugaad* emerges as highly differential and uneven, as Nazeem's story demonstrates.

Nazeem came to the Haveli site with the group of Malda men. At both Wandering Woods and Haveli, there is much talk of the comings and goings of the large groups of Malda workers who do the heavy lifting on sites and form the bulk of construction labor. Malda workers are the largest and least skilled of contract communities in construction in North India, but they are in demand because they do all forms of labor. Malda is a district in the bottleneck of West Bengal famous for the sweet mangoes it produces but also for its unique geography. Its narrow width and position creates borders with both Bangladesh and the Indian states of Jharkhand and Bihar. One of the biggest open secrets in the construction industry is that Malda workers are not all from Malda: "Malda" acts as a catchall for people from northeastern India, Bangladeshi workers, and other workers from poverty-stricken areas of Bengal, Bihar, Jharkhand, and Orissa. Malda laborers are brought to NCR by a subcontractor on a fifty- or ninety-day contract, with a cook and mate appointed to look after every group. Compared to other groups, they tend to have a greater percentage of women. Due to the strong linguistic divide, the fact that they work and travel in groups, and the fact that several have Indigenous (Adivasi) features, they are often treated with less dignity than the other workers on site.

I ask Shreelal about Malda district and its workers, and Shreelal tells me they are identified by the Malda identity cards they carry. Shreelal hollers to Nazeem, who is walking by. "Hey, you, come here, do you have an identity card [*pehchaan patra*]?" Shreelal demands. Nazeem walks over, looking anxious, and hesitates as he opens up a scruffy wallet. I try to reassure him that I am just looking at it because I do not know what it is. He pulls out a folded piece of paper. "Where did you get it from?" I ask, and Nazeem tells me the village panchayat in Malda. I look at the dust-covered identity card and see that it bears the signature of an official at Kali Chowk in Malda, recognizing the name of the place from other Malda workers telling me where they are from.

Nazeem relaxes a little and tells us that their identity cards are often checked on the train when they travel to NCR. Shreelal pipes up, informing me that Malda workers do not have election cards—that is why they make this identity card; otherwise they are assumed to be terrorists. I stare at Shreelal skeptically, but Nazeem backs him up, saying that his older brother was in jail for four years because he does not have one. Nazeem's friend, who has crept up to our little group, chimes in, saying he does not have one. "How did you get this?" I ask. "I gave them money—the card cost[s] ninety rupees." Nazeem has an uncle (he uses the English word) in the office who got him the card. He needs the card at the India-Bangladesh border because he has land in Bangladesh.

Abdul is a labor contractor who brings individuals like Nazeem from Malda to NCR. A young man from Malda himself, he turned from a laborer into a labor contractor a few years ago, taking help from his wife's family and drawing on his *pehchaan* with contractors in NCR. Largely uneducated and living in one of the dormitories in an urban village in Delhi, he says, he runs his entire operation by cell phone. His father-in-law helps him by gathering workers together at Kali Chowk, and Abdul wanders construction sites offering labor. For both Abdul and Nazeem, *jugaad* describes a mode of entrepreneurialism that allows unemployed youth entry into India's neoliberal economies. Youth on site often speak about *jugaads* to move up in life—buying machines, switching sites, getting *thekas* (contracts), and the largest aspiration of all: starting a business or shop in their hometown.

Several entrepreneurial *jugaads* make Nazeem's journey possible: the *jugaad* enacted by Abdul, who cobbles together some chutzpah and cash, recruiting workers from Malda, and Nazeem's *jugaad* of finding a relative who had undertaken the journey, as well as finding the uncle who gave him the card. *Jugaad* here becomes the mobilization of network and contacts (*pehchaan*) to find a job, and it is a constant condition for both Abdul and Nazeem. The failure of one aspect might send both their lives into a condition of *majboori*. Abdul and Nazeem's *jugaads* bear unequal risks and embed a precarity that requires them to be constantly *jugaadu*. *Jugaad* represents the ephemeral, a temporary occupation, and precariousness, where the constant shuffles of *jugaad* deny workers economic and social stability, in contrast to the durable architectures they create. This connection becomes even more apparent through Shailendraji's category of corporate *jugaad*.

As we walk through Wandering Woods, Shailendraji continues my lesson in *jugaad*. He gives me examples. As we climb to the first floor of the building, he points at a grating. "Look at this, this is *jugaad*." I ask why. "There should be a scaffolding here on all sides. Instead"—he pauses dramatically—"they have made a *grate* with [metal] scraps. That is what we call *jugaaad*." He stretches out the syllable in a dramatic fashion: "*jugaaaaaad*." As we head to the upper story, Shailendraji takes me to the edge of the building and points to an array of trucks loaded with cars. "Look at that, corporate *jugaad*, the trucks should have two more tires [to support the weight of cars], they should be fined—*that* is corporate *jugaad*."

The celebratory discussions of *jugaad* ignore more often than not its acute risks. *Jugaad* practices entail the circumvention of proper protocol, illegality, danger, coercive tactics, and an unequal value placed on human life. All of Shailendraji's examples were embedded with risk: of men falling from a height, toxic poisoning, or a truck collapsing on passersby. *Jugaad* seems creative and celebratory when the risk of one's actions is tied to the furtherance of one's own future, but more often than not, as in the marked case of corporate *jugaad*, it implies a transfer of value of human mental and physical well-being into the accumulative futures of others. Like the cars that threaten to fall on pedestrians, the might of corporate *jugaad* transfers risk onto the poor while pocketing the profit. The scales of corporate and Nazeem's *jugaad* are not equal.

The processes and practices of *jugaad* hierarchize people, determining who will stand precariously up on the top and who will supervise in safety, who will stick their hand into a stalled machine and who owns the machine. While the creativity and entrepreneurialism of *jugaad* extend across ranks and lend opportunity to individuals across classes, the risks embedded into *jugaad* create inequity for the laboring classes. Jitendraji's estimate that construction is 95 percent *jugaad* underlines the degree to which risk falls uneasily and unequally on low-income workers. Abdul himself expresses conceptions of risk in terms of financial and physical loss. He describes his crew: "These boys they come here because they want to move ahead in life [*zindagi mein badhnein*]. If you do not take a risk in life, then how will you move ahead?" He uses the English word *risk* but pronounces it *ricks*. "You will have to take a *ricks*. Now these Malda have been working for five, six months without a *dihadi*, that is a *ricks*, isn't it?"

The atmospheres of construction are infused with risk that must be managed in order to spur speculative real estate.[24] The uncertainty of risk, however, is borne differentially. Those whose lives are an endless series of *jugaads* grow the accumulative potentials of others' property. While the properties of developers multiply and prices rise, risk falls disproportionately upon minority class and caste workers in the industry. The risks of *jugaad* produces income loss, illness, injury, and death in those who bear it; it constructs the *majbooris* of *mazdoori*.

MELTING POINTS

It is noon in the middle of summer, and the construction site radiates with heat. The official temperature hangs at a merciless 49°C (120°F). The long stretch of road along the construction site does not have a single shadow. My hard hat protects me from the direct heat of the sun, but I can feel my head burn inside it. I tighten the voluminous cotton scarf around my neck and walk into the sun-drenched steelyard. Rust-brown steel bars stretch across the yard in straight lines, stacked upon each other and extending the length of the whitened concrete building. The steel cutting machine is on, and three men work in the yard cutting steel bars to size. I recognize one of them as Salim the helper. He pulls at the steel along with another helper, bent over as if hiking a football. I notice that only his partner is wearing gloves and wonder how Salim manages to touch the scorching bars. A hot wind blows across the yard, and I brace myself so as not to get dizzy on the uneven stacks of steel. The men continue to work, dragging the steel and placing it on the machine that snaps it in two. I hear the loud *cracks* behind me as I walk on.

The heat of the day, the scorching steel, and the hot winds create an intense experience of labor. The scalding temperatures feed into *majboori* and the consciousness of *mazdoori* on construction sites. Like other harsh conditions—the bitter winter, where the water and wet concrete creates broken ridges in your skin, and the unceasing cold prevents workers from meeting sleep other than through deep drunkenness—translate into emotional heat or anger and intensify experiences of class inequality. The working environments and body politics—skin burned, clothes torn, throat dry and raspy—constitute the angers and resentments of those who work. The environment evinces inequality and channels the inequalities felt through *mazdoori, majboori*, and *jugaad* into tensions on construction sites.

I watch MD and Nazarul build shuttering. They pry old boards off the already set concrete, forcing the two surfaces apart with a steel rod. *"Arre arre ply gaya* [the plywood goes]," shouts Jai as we hear the wood splinter badly and crack in half, nullifying its resale value. MD keeps prying gently and manages to get it out. Nazarul comes up behind me and begins swinging his hammer at a plywood board. His usually sweet and smiling face is loaded with anger. He swings the steel hammer and hits the plywood, concrete flying all over from underneath; he hurls it at another spot with all his might. The entire day he bangs at nails and boards in an uncharacteristic anger. MD gives him instructions from time to time, but they do not talk much. MD complains to me, "They are not paying us anything for this, they had said they would give us money but nothing has been given for so many days."

Aggressive speculative economies mean that developers invest in kickstarting new projects. They offer buyers staged payment plans and divert the payments into acquiring new land. This dries up the pipeline for work on existing projects and creates a house of cards of projects across the region. A dip in the market and developers run out of money to complete any of them, leaving buyers, contractors, and workers high and dry. Payments for contractors, consultants, and workers are held back as developers juggle their funds. One of the reasons this site has longer term employees is that Sharanji is known to make payments on time, but from MD and Nazarul's faces it is clear that Sharanji too withholds daily wages. For a week or so now, workers have been complaining to me that they have not received their pay.

"I have heard that this *kothi* [house] is for only one man? Is that true?" Nazeem asks me; I am sitting by him as he works. I nod as I confirm the news. This eight-bedroom home with a swimming pool on the roof will all be for one family. As buildings grow across the construction sites, material inequalities confront those who build them. Jai swears that he will spend time in the finished architecture before he leaves the site. He wants his moment of luxury in the building he helped build. "They are not going to even let us into this place once it is built," sneers the ever pragmatic and cynical MD. The material differences in architecture feed the recognition of inequity and inequality and seep into the politics of work.

Shreelal strides into the park as a few of the workers and I sit on the lawns during lunch break and begins to yell at everyone. Some of the workers glance at their phones to make sure they are not being cheated out of a lunch break. He screams, "*Arre*, don't look at the time, come on, come on, get up, come on *bhai* [brother], get to work. You slept enough. You don't get a *dihadi* to sleep." He turns to MD and yells, "MD, you have become very *dhilla* [loose, that is, lax or lazy] nowadays, you are only working to eat your *roti*. If you get even more *dhilla* than this, then even the *roti* will not be left." MD glares at Shreelal. "Bastard, work a little," Shreelal continues. I see the workers bristle; everyone stays put for a while, refusing to cave to Shreelal's yelling. Only I get up, worried that I caused this chiding. Gradually they all go back to work, but the tensions only settle for a while.

In the late afternoon the entire site is alerted to a commotion. I look up from the corner I am standing in to see Mamun yelling at Jai on the other side of the basement pit. Mamun is standing on top of the ramp that leads into the pit; his back is straight, and he glares at Jai, who stands two stories below. He yells and then holds his ground, not backing down. Jai holds his small frame upright and stares Mamun down as he yells, "If you want to do that, just go ahead!" Mamun is screaming about his pay: "They don't even give us any *dihadi*! Do you know they give Lamboo 500 and us only 240 [US$8 vs. US$4 per day]?" The Malda laborers are standing at the bottom and staring at the commotion. Mamun shouts, "I will leave work and go! This is one site, there are thousands!"

Mamun glares at Jai. His friend joins him, as do their wives. The two women descend the slope and begin to scream at Jai alongside Mamun. The whole thing makes quite a composition: the two men and women are at various points on the makeshift steps. Mamun's wife yells at Jai. He cuts a thin and weak figure; he has just recovered from malaria. Jai stares and yells again; Ram comes over and joins him. The whole site has frozen; everyone is watching them scream. Sharanji had at first moved away toward one end of the site. Now he chooses to stand at the center of the small site. As the workers descend, still fighting, he begins to shout— "*mistry—ay mistry*"—in a commanding voice (this is deliberate; his voice is quite squeaky). The *mistrys* (masons) and all the laborers look up at him. Mamun puts his helmet on. "I know exactly who gets what." Mamun responds in a softer tone: "Sir [*saab*], I know you see everything." Sharanji yells again, "Get back to work." Everyone disperses, still grumbling. As I am sitting on the side of the pit in the evening, Mamun comes up to me and complains. "There are masons on site who get ₹500 [US$8] *dihadi*. Why do we get ₹240? We are working too, why do they give them so much and not us? This is not right." He shakes his head in anger.

Later, I ask Ram what happened. He says that the workers were watching television in one of the worker's huts. There were eight minutes left until the end of lunch break, but Jai went and drove them out. Jai said he would cut the electricity because they watched too much television. The masons got angry. "Now you tell me, first they ate lunch during work hours, they should go for twenty minutes [for lunch] and get back to work. No, they don't understand, instead they take an hour, and just stand here all day. Look at those women, they are banging at the *tasla*." I look over: the women are trying to get hardened cement out of the saucer-like metal *taslas* in which they mix concrete. "When you put concrete in it then wash it [immediately afterward], they will save all this hard work, *bas*, they do not pay attention to work." He continues: "They burnt the machine [tile-cutting saw]. They do not think that it is getting hot, it will burn out. It is not our property [*maal*]. . . . It is not their own, *na*, they just burn the thing. They were seeing it get hot, bastards."

I talk to Mamun later, and he too expresses his frustration. Shaking his head, he tells me things are not good. "How can they be good? They haven't given us money for two months." Expenses rise, and he struggles to survive. "I have a child in the village. I have to give money for their studies. The cost of living here every day is so much. How do I give the money? I am having a lot of tension, a lot of tension"—he uses the English word.

In the South Asian context, *tension* refers not only to stress that a person feels due to specific circumstances but also to strained interpersonal and community relations. It is also used to describe spaces where communitarian or ethnic warfare might ensue; for example, one might say that the situation is tense, I am "taking tension," or that there was tension last night, which is why a curfew is in place. Used in this sense, tension can make or break community; it can also have a gendered aspect.[25] It stands separate from *pareshani* (worry, anxiety) in that *pareshani* is structural or internal and tension is interpersonal and political. Within the context of construction sites, tensions refer to the social and economic imbalances workers experience. Tensions allow employees and employers to negotiate issues within the larger structural circumstances of construction, and they are a site at which *mazdoori*'s exploitative tendencies and *majboori*'s frustrations often condense. Tension, not unlike the stresses born by TMT steel within concrete structures, is a live load, ever shifting and morphing due to the movements of those that dwell upon them. At times, when stress-bearing capacities reach breaking point, tensions can quickly escalate into violence.

INTO THE FURNACE

Darkness reigns in the electrical and service basement of Phase I. This is the heart of the project, where no light enters. Workers install electric panels. The wiring for the heavy-duty cables and the various boxes of meters is welded to the walls and ceiling. Workers haul in cartons shipped from as far away as Europe that will form the electrical infrastructure.

A group of men attach the caging for wires, and sparks stream from their blowtorches. Darkness envelops the room when they pause. The sparks reemerge from another corner, and the steel masks of two welders are momentarily lit orange-yellow. The torch sends intermittent red-hot showers across the room as they work.

"*Maruti Manesar plant mein workers ne GM ko zinda jala diya.* [The workers in the Maruti Manesar plant burned the general manager alive]." I turned to Mr. Kumar in astonishment at the scenario he was describing. It was the day after the incident and Mr. Kumar, the chief engineer, narrated the details on our way home. The severity of action and intent imbued in the statement shocked me. Maruti Udyog Limited, now known as Maruti Suzuki India Limited (MSIL), is India's premier car manufacturing company and was established in Gurgaon. The steady stream of cars the company produced drove straight into middle-class Indian hearts and budgets.

The unionized workers were protesting for changes including an increase in wages, laundry allowances, bonuses, and housing support.[26] They spoke of "harsh working conditions and extensive hiring of low-paid contract workers . . . paid half the minimum wage of permanent employees."[27] Tensions had recently escalated, as had police presence due to caste-based aggression on a supervisor's part (disputed by the company).[28] "The Maruti Manesar plant," the automobile manufacturing plant at which the protests were taking place, is located on the outskirts of Gurgaon. The phrase "burned the general manager alive," however, was entirely unexpected. News of ongoing labor strikes brought expectations of broken glass and limbs, destroyed property, and mass arrests. "Burned the general manager alive" indexed an unexpected side of class warfare and anger. This death was later ruled to be accidental, but there are strong and conflicting opinions regarding the incident, reflected in language such as "new 'militant workforce,'" by Maruti Suzuki's managing director, or "severest repression," by the workers' union.[29]

While the death and agitations at the car plant were a series of spectacular events, worker unrest in Gurgaon is not new. Tensions between unionized workers and management result in a preference for hiring of nonpermanent staff, allowing management to disempower and disperse difficult workers. This renders workers ephemeral and prevents them from forming unions. Many construction workers look upon labor unions favorably. They are seen as connected to steady pay and rights, as a tile worker describes: "In Star company, there was a labor union, whatever they decided that is what the company did, if payment was even a day late, they would agitate. The union was good. It paid well." Union activity in Haryana is growing. The state is now known as the hotbed of unions, largely because it is the car and motorcycle manufacturing hub of India.[30] Over two-thirds of passenger cars, 50 percent of tractors, and 60 percent of motorcycles in India are made in Haryana.[31] Although not India's largest producer, Haryana has emerged as the largest recipient of investment per capita in India since 2000.[32] In recent years the state legislature introduced several labor reforms in response to increased union activity and provided loopholes to suppress unions. An example is raising limits on the size of firms that can retrench their workers without permission from the government, making firing people easier.[33] The state legislative assembly also expanded the number of contract laborers who could be hired by one person without being subject to the Contract Labor Act and thus supported job precarity for workers. A labor law of the central government contains similar stances on retrenchment.[34] In addition, Haryana offers many incentives, such as the setting up of ten SEZs, exemptions from local area tax, and a promise of "bare minimum" strike outs and claims to house offices of 93 of the top Fortune 100 companies, among other multinational corporations.[35] The Maruti Manesar incident was the state's largest and most public scandal.

The day after the death, rumors of the union rebellion infiltrated our site, as laborers, supervisors, and engineers channeled gossip through their own personal networks. Curious to know more about what happened at the factory, on our drive home in the evening I ask Mr. Kumar about the details of the death of the general manager.

ME: How did they kill him?

MR. KUMAR: They burnt down the HR department. Everyone else ran off and forgot about him. He died of suffocation.

N: But what happened [to cause this violence]?

MR. K: In the morning shift, a supervisor stopped a worker from working [it was reported that the supervisor had hurled caste abuses, prompting the worker to protest]. He said you go home right now. This started a fight.

N: But why did they do this? What happened?

MR. K: These are all locals, they continue this thug-like [*gunde-garzi*] behavior. There is an FIR [First Information Report] out for ninety people and all of them are from [the local town]. . . . The problem that occurs is that locals are very powerful, and they are uneducated, so they indulge in thug-like behavior. It is better for an industry to bring people from another place.

The problem of "locals" articulated by Mr. Kumar is a frequent issue in industry operations. Considered too political, locals are those who get into fights. In response companies prefer to hire an ephemeral workforce who move so much that they cannot mobilize for their rights. In the days following the Maruti Manesar incident, workers on site and beyond shared with me their opinions about locals and violence. Jeevan explained that most of the laborers who were violent were local laborers linked to local political parties. Neelkanth Sir alleged that the protesting workers were connected to the then chief minister's home district and were politically powerful. Kishwar complained that no one wants to hire locals in their own areas, which is why they had to migrate to Gurgaon in search of jobs.

To solve the problems of "locals," industries conduct a well-known "corporate *jugaad*": subcontracting labor (*thekedari*), which involves hiring contractors to draw labor from rural areas in other states. A study of contract hires among manufacturing firms in India argues that this staffing model started booming in the early 2000s and expanded, as industries expressed a preference for out-of-state workers.[36] The proportion of informal labor continues to increase, because "most of India's labor regulations apply only to the formal sector and to formal workers."[37]

Drawing workers from distant rural areas produces a deliberate disembedding of workers from locale and enables the depoliticization of a construction site's labor force. It also makes workers more willing to be circulated between the various plants and sites a company owns once their contracts end. MD talks about the comings and goings of people on site. "Look at him, my Bengali mason, who is coming over. I do not even know what his *jhilla* [district] is. He was running for his money, so I fought for his money." (The Bengali mason had not received his dues from an employer; MD helped follow up and fight with the employer.) MD often presents a sentimental face, but he is clear about the temporary nature of friendships on site: "to make contacts [*pehchaan*] you have to be honest [*imaandaar*]. Tomorrow I go to Sonipat—the people from here are not going to come behind me." He emphasizes the mobility and ephemeral nature of workers in construction. "You make friends, work finishes, and where does the man go? This one goes. Will the next be as trustworthy? *Yeh falana aadmi hain joh kaam karta hain or karvata hain.*" The phrase literally means "so and so person who does work and gets work done" but in actuality refers to the ease with which coworkers and supervisors are moved and replaced.

As MD indicates, constant circulation is deliberate and built into the industry. Emerging solidarities are disbanded, and locals are avoided for their ability to connect with unions and local political factions. The discouraging of local hires as "too political" also forms the cover for working across the formal-informal boundaries of labor laws.[38] An increase in contract hires allows employers to avoid paying employee provident funds, medical insurance, and other legal requirements for permanent employees.[39] Of the more than three hundred employees at Wandering Woods, fewer than thirty were on permanent record and on the company's books (it is necessary to classify some employees as permanent).[40] The rest were part of a systematic series of contract hires that brought laborers to the region for periods as short as a week.

Malda labor subcontractor Abdul's own precarious presence in the city and his apparent informality expose the fallacy of labor laws in the industry. While his name appears as the labor contractor in the company books, and he is a licensed labor contractor, the vulnerable figure of this man is expected to absorb any governmental fallout from the mistreatment and conditions of Malda workers on site (including issues related to child labor, immigrants without legal status, lack of medical benefits, accidental deaths, and the lack of provident or welfare funds).[41] MD, who recently started small-scale contracting, describes the inequality of this system of risk and responsibility transference: "This site demands PPF [Public Provident Fund, an employer-supported retirement fund], ESI

[Employee State Insurance], et cetera, for all the workers—where am I supposed to get the money for that?"

A complex system of subcontracting that protects powerful employers prevails in the construction industry. A main site contractor will allocate work to several smaller subcontractors, who will allocate work to other subcontractors, who will in turn allocate work to small one- or two-member subcontracting teams. Sharanji, for example, subcontracts to MD and Munnalal (who bring family to the site to avoid the bureaucracy of hires). One or more of these subcontractors or the contractors might hire a labor contractor to bring in a bulk of labor that is then allocated to work with different contracting teams. The degree of subcontracting plays at the limits between formal industry responsibilities and the unorganized informality of small-scale contractors, whose lives are characterized by the daily hustle and are too small fish to fry. Labor inspectors are unlikely to pursue legal action against small-scale contractors and, it is rumored, take bribes to look the other way. Profit making and operational efficiency rely on the maintenance and exacerbation of worker circulations—a dependency that reveals itself at Haveli one day.

There is a commotion near the cement mixer, and I look over to see Mamun holding his son and yelling at Keshav. Shouts are emanating from that direction, and Shreelal gets up and runs over. The new supervisor screams at Mamun. The child is crying and holding his eye. Mamun shouts, claiming that Bittu's son beat his child. "That Bittu's son is a real bastard," says Shreelal under his breath. The perpetrator is standing at the back while the men are arguing. Mamun's wife is screaming at the top of her lungs at Keshav. "What if something bad had happened to her son?"

"That boy is a thug!" Ram quips to me. "It is good that [Mamun] is married, so his wife supports him—I wish I was married, then my wife would scream too." Jai agrees, and states (a little too valiantly, given his tiny frame): "The other day, if the women had not come in between, I would have given [the men] two or four slaps." Mamun comes over with his boy in tow: "Look Sir, Bittu's son, he threw a stone, so big [he indicates a fist-sized stone]—what if his eye went?" Shreelal acts nonchalant as he replies, "So [the child] must have also done something." "He is such a small child, and the stone is so big," Mamun cries, perplexed. Shreelal gives a vague reply: "You have also taken this [matter] in your hands, slap him—claps do not occur with one hand [*ek haath se taali nahi bajti*]." Mamun drags his crying son out of the site with one arm and heads to the Bengali doctor in the urban village nearby. People start going back to work. Shreelal turns to Jai and discretely says, "Get rid of these two."

Solidarities and friendships emerge on construction sites, but so too does anger and resentment. The sheer power of corporate *jugaad*'s subcontracting system allows for the circulation of people in and out of sites. It makes it possible to get rid of the angry and the insolent and serves to discipline those who stay into acceptable forms of behavior. The subcontracting system breaks attempts at solidarity and unionization. As Haveli and Wandering Woods are completed, the workers are moved to a new site, not en masse but distributed across various sites in NCR and even across the Indo-Gangetic plain. Even the supervisors move, taking those whom they most liked with them. Phone numbers change as new cell phone companies offer incentives. My own phone is inactive ten months of the year as I circulate between India and the United States.

INQUILAB ZINDABAD (LONG LIVE REVOLUTION)

I am standing at the gate one morning chatting with the Malda boys when a group of men run up and hand fliers to everyone. The site watchman sees them and darts out of his cabin, waving his stick. The young men run off but hand flyers to people standing on the street as they retreat. I look at the one stuffed into my own hand; it is a call for a general strike. A long paragraph in Hindi lists the causes of worker dissent and appeals to workers in industries both formal and informal. While speaking of the plight of workers in formalized industries, the pamphlet extends to those in formalizing industries such as construction, speaking of the difficulties workers face. It makes the following demands:

1. Pay a minimum wage of Rs.15,000 a month;
2. enforce labor laws, put names down on the attendance register, and establish ESI and PF accounts;
3. stop assaults on trade union leaders and register unions within five days;

4. end *thekedari* (contracting), fixed work–fixed people, same work–same pay; and

5. make provisions for housing laborers and legalize colonies.

The list extends to demanding the release of arrested workers from the Maruti Manesar plant, the establishment of land rights for displaced farmers, and the formalization of informal job contracts in government sectors. It calls for labor solidarity across local-migrant, formal-informal, and agrarian-construction lines. *Inquilab Zindabad* (long live revolution), it says.

Inquilab Zindabad—chanted on marches during India's freedom struggle—is a familiar call in protests across the country. *Inquilab Zindabad*, coined by Maulana Hasrat Mohani in 1921, was used by freedom fighter Bhagat Singh as a call for revolution in 1929.[42] The deployment and extension of the phrase, like the term *mazdoori*, is an extension of colonial-era critiques of exploitation into the present. In the flyers circulating across the construction sites, the phrase now indexes a renewed betrayal by the contemporary state.

Ahmed the tremixing mason is very vocal about this *amiron ki Sarkar* (the government of the rich) and has a wide distrust of all public provisions. He feels that government facilities serve the rich and has more faith in private development than public development. "*Sarkari aspataal garebon ke liyen nahi* [government hospitals are not for the poor]," he states. He tells a story of being bitten by a snake on one of the projects he worked on. A friend from his village took him to a public hospital, where the owner (*malik*) of the site turned up. "If he had not turned up, they would not have admitted me. . . . Then I had ten doctors and a first-class bed. . . . This is because there was a big man's hand on me." He shrugs his thin frame as he speaks. "There was a poor man there, he was almost about to die. None of the doctors even turned to look at him. . . . That is why I say they are for big men not poor men. . . . This too is *Angrezi-raj*."

The term *Angrezi* (literally, English) stands for both the language and the colonizer. In using this term, Ahmed once again ties colonial exploitation to contemporary forms of exploitation by the English-speaking elite castes and classes. At the same time, he accuses the state of partnering with and serving the rich. As buildings grow across the construction sites, material inequalities confront those who build them. The differential nature of lifestyles is recognized and received as well as appropriated. What MD told me—that workers are not allowed on site after the building is completed—is repeated by several people I speak with. This is accompanied by a loss of faith in state institutions, which are seen as serving the rich. These understandings of elitism, neglect, exploitation, and class difference inform work in construction. They fuel the recognition of inequity and the angers of *mazdoori*. As Pushpa, the wife of a carpentry worker, says, "*duniya ultnein wala hai, andar ka admi upar jayega, upar ka aadmi andar jayega* [the world is going to turn upside down, the downtrodden will rise up and the top will go under (world used in masculine form)]."

We do not only attune ourselves with our atmospheres; we also produce them as well as act in response to them. Construction atmospheres, through the processes of their own production, contribute to the making and breaking of political consciousness. They facilitate solidarities and help bridge ethnic, caste, and religious barriers. The affects produced within them stoke class anger. The practices of working and the environments of work facilitate a shared experience of rights and claims. On site, inequality is understood as historical, aesthetic, and material, and the experience of injustice is visceral. Continuous circulation helps disband collective organization. Workers themselves are rendered ephemeral. Yet at the same time, it is through this circulation that shared solidarities and understandings are born among differing communities. Languages of oppression and exploitation are learned and carried forward. The durability of historic inequality feeds the present. History and memory, too, circulate among the laboring atmospherics, reverberating and morphing slightly, but perhaps rising someday more strongly—heard in the rising calls of *Inquilab Zindabad*.

6 Concrete Love

The crowning glory of the Wandering Woods project is the slender, sinuous office tower under construction. The tower's undulating, half-built façade draws attention and moves the eye inward toward an unfinished concrete ramp. Stairwells spiral toward the topmost slab under construction, and columns divide the floor into neat working zones. The architect's organic vision extends into the large arcs of the bare, concrete floorplates. The curvilinear floor space forms an endless grey horizon of unfinished concrete. Above it, wall-less columns frame the stark fields, farms, and hills at the limits of NCR. The sunlit landscape saturates into a deep gold and azure against the gray architectural frame.

A building after it is built but before it is occupied is a haunting space. If hard labor, mechanical noises, heat and dust, and the movement of people and machines characterize spaces of activity on the Wandering Woods site, then the already-cast floors register the emptiness of the cessation of work. As a new phase of Wandering Woods grows, its constructed floorplates and towers await their future occupants. Sunlight streams silently through absent, external walls to cast shifting patterns on the bare surfaces and expansive slabs. Echoes of activity bounce off plastered walls, weaving between dangling wires and debris, to settle into the dank nooks and crannies of the structure. The dull sound of machines echoes through the structures and diffuses as white noise across the slab. As activity steps up in the midday heat, the empty slab awaits laborers who will seek respite in its cool darkness.

A long anticipation precedes the lunchtime whistle at Wandering Woods. Activity on-site slows down as workers' recognize proximity to the break. Tools are dropped and machines shut down as the break commences. The contractors and engineers return to their tin-walled, makeshift offices deep within the floorplate. The tin *tiffins* packed by their wives at 5:00 a.m. are now lukewarm. The men circulate the shiny, cylindrical containers, eagerly looking to swap their own drab lunches. Laborers' wives and young helpers arrive underneath the skeletal building, carrying afternoon meals. Hands, feet, and faces are washed near the pipe that pumps water up from the sandy soil. Shady nooks are sought. Brothers and kinsmen, husbands, wives, and travel companions pull out a plastic sheet and sit down to eat. Those who have neither kinsmen nor food wander the hot streets to look for an open food vendor at the nearby *chowk* (traffic junction).

The lunch hour extends into lethargy as stomachs weigh down with food and limbs grow heavy from the morning's labor. A husband-wife working team lean into each other at the edge of a floor slab, and workers spread newspapers to nap on the dusty slabs. They lie side by side, arms pulled over their eyes. Others smoke cigarettes or *beedis* on the edges of floorplates. Everyone drifts in and out of consciousness as the hour extends. Only a restless soul or two stay awake and listen to music on their cell phones. A cranky electronic voice wafts down the stairwell and bounces lithely off the glass façade: "*Tooooo, meri zindagi hai, tooooo, meri bandagi hai* [You are my life, you are my prayer]." When the overwhelming and all-encompassing sounds of construction equipment fall silent, it is then that the songs of love, joviality, desire, and betrayal dance through the architectures. They bounce off the slab, reverberating and resonating with the bodies and buildings on site. It is in these silences, moments of steadfastness and calm, inspired by the love songs that drift across the incomplete architecture, that I think through the political economy of *pyaar* (love).

Figure 16. Drawings on walls of a Gurgaon construction site, 2012. Photo by author.

Where and why do we find love on construction sites? It is hard to locate love in these speedily built spaces that hum with efficiency throughout the day; hard to articulate love in spaces meant to turn into urban spaces of middle-class domesticity. How do we imagine what home and family feel like when we walk onto an open, concrete slab mired in wires? Do we not leave love behind when we put our hard hats on? How is love evoked—and even revoked—on a construction site?

The subtleties of this omnipresent emotion are hard to capture and write of: by nature, love is fractured, invisible, affective, and ambiguous. It is incredibly difficult for an anthropologist to define and speak of. I never looked for love on construction sites. But it spoke to me from their walls: the walls of Wandering Woods's half-finished structure hold a cacophony of declarations of love. White chalk graffiti: drawings of women, children, homes, and flowers. Scribbled declarations of love: "I love you," "I love India," "I love Sumita." The walls bear drawings of hearts and detailed drawings of women. There are ducks, parrots, peacocks, roses, trees, and mangoes. Snakes, scorpions, and warnings of danger! They occupy the floor slabs, drawn surreptitiously during breaks and in times of darkness. A plethora of drawings rise from the skeletal structure, and they shout out the presence of love.

THE POLITICS OF *PYAAR*

The term for love in Hindi is deliciously vague. The move from *love* to *pyaar* creates an interpretive gap rich with emotive potential. *Pyaar* is a term with linguistic complexity.[1] The contexts, conditions, and formations within which it is deployed index different forms of power and different emotions. *Pyaar* can mean romantic love, a great passion for another (*hammein tumse pyaar kitna* [how much do I love you]); it can speak of a gentle tenderness extended to anyone (*pyaar se* [with love]); and it alludes to sexual desires and sex (*pyaar karna* [to make love])—but it also encodes paternal and maternal love (*bacchon ka pyaar* [for the love of your children]); it evokes our nearest and dearest friends or the communities we situate ourselves within through the term *mere pyaare* (my loved ones). It is paired or merged with terms such as *ishq* (romance), *luvs[h]ip* (love + friendship), *dosti* (friendship), and *pasandi/a* (liked one), and it blurs the boundaries between multiple forms of affection and affect, including for and between things, animals, and the nation.

"Who draws these drawings?" I ask the floor supervisor, curious about the artistry on these walls. It is hard to find someone engaged in the act of drawing; it is surreptitious, unapproved of, and denied. Unlike the map on the ground that workers drew for me, these drawings are secret, ornate, and passionate. Many are gone before the drawings are found, leaving signed names behind. "It is the painters," he replies; they draw with left-over bits of plaster that cakes walls into a glossy plane. Plaster turns into chalk as it dries and acts as a siren call for scribbles. "This is all their wickedness [*badmashi*]."

The very surreptitious and transgressive nature of the drawings makes them aesthetic significations of the emotional architectures of those who work in Gurgaon. Wall drawings dwell in the pauses of construction, in the unfinished-finished state of architecture; they are the mediators between work and home and form the connective threads between the architecture under construction and those who labor on it. The drawings are modes of claiming and proclaiming the labor of building the walls. The sheer volume of graffiti—the hearts, the animals, the slogans and poems—echoes with longing, desire, anger, and accusations, forming an ephemeral site of emotional expression on construction sites. The chalk scribbles are complex artistic and political acts; through their inscription and organization, they mediate sentiment. In an era when workers are being displaced from construction sites, these drawings remind us of the struggle of classed labor against erasure and of the emotion concretized into architecture. The multiplicities and overlapping sensibilities of love, an often-feminized emotion, I argue, form the site of class and caste struggle and aspiration in a male-dominated industry.

Each drawing I take to be a map of different forms of *pyaar*: domestic and familial, romantic, spiritual, or sexual. I juxtapose these drawings with conversations on site to link the affective capacities of *pyaar* to the political economy of construction. At the same time, I remain attuned to the fact that multiple significations of the drawings exist, depending on who views and draws them. *Pyaar* entangles the politics of social reproduction with architectural commodity production.[2] The ephemeral drawings and the *pyaars* they index, drawn in predominantly male spaces, I argue, in their ebbs and flows reinforce heteronormative understandings of family, property, and marriage that undergird the real estate and construction industries, while also challenging them with the multiplicity and contradictions that *pyaar* produces. It is this multiplicity that enables an ephemeral, affective excess that challenges concertizing norms.

THE ARCHITECTURE OF DESIRE

Chalk lines form the picture of a woman, hair wavy and face almond shaped. Her eyes gape wide open; she has spiky eyelashes and a large smile. Her long neck bears triangular jewelry. There are bangles on her elongated arms, and her sari flows sensual and strong down the gray concrete wall. A flower blooms next to her. It has concentric circles at its core and petals curling outward. Tendrils crawl from it and sprout delicate, teardrop leaves at regular intervals. This is a wall that celebrates femme form.

Figure 17. Femme drawings at a Gurgaon construction site, 2012. Photo by author.

Working in a space that is more than 90 percent male makes the few women on site hyper-visible. Among those who are most noticed are two young Banjara sisters, Beena and Parvati. The women arrive on site with their family during the summer months, hired at a labor *chowk* (square) on a temporary contract. Heavily adorned with jewelry and vibrant clothing, the two sisters and their mother, accompanied by the father and son-in-law, move mud to make embankments for landscape work by the site's main gate. The once nomadic Banjara community hails from Rajasthan and Gujarat. Work needs to be sped up on site, and this migrant family helps with excavation.

In the car on the way home, Mr. Kumar, the engineer, asks me whether I saw the Banjara women on site. I confessed I had already admired their clothes and adornments. Dressed in the vibrant colors of desert flowers, their long *ghagaras* (skirts) and *cholis* (blouses) formed a medley of blues, oranges, pinks, and purples, tailored in styles fit for the world's fashionistas. Upon Parvati's neck hung a beautiful silver heart-shaped necklace, thick and heavy. Mother and daughters wore sets of chunky bangles that gradually increased in size to accentuate their arms. They caught my gaze as well as those of many of the men. Determined to know more, I head down to the excavation site to talk to them the next day. It is noon and the sun is high in the sky. The workers walk back and forth, carrying tubs of soil on their heads to the edge of the site. Beena's mother and Beena's husband—Subas—tell me a little bit about their tribal community.

Banjaras migrate to the city for work in the summer when fields lie barren and there is no harvesting or sowing work. They generally serve as day-wage labor and till and harvest crops. The family arrived with some community members a few days ago and live in a plastic tarp tent, set up in an empty field nearby. They will stay there for three months until the summer ends. Subas and his mother-in-law tell me that Banjaras, traditionally a community that carried goods from one place to another, were replaced by trains. They have no land and tend to goats. As the forest decreases in size, so does their ability to make a living; piecemeal construction work makes up for that loss. The mother insisted on coming with her daughters to the site; she did not want to leave them alone and could not bear to part with them.

I remember construction sites from my childhood, full of Banjara women. Their numbers have decreased as machines gained strength; nevertheless, they remain visible. "These Banjara women, they are very bold. Did you see the way she spoke to her husband yesterday? She stopped working at exactly five. When he refused to stop, she told him, 'you see how you come home today!'" Mr. Kumar pauses to laugh as he talks about Subas. "He is not going to get anything to eat."

Beena publicly chides her new husband Subas and earns as much as he does. Her nonhierarchical attitude toward her spouse is shared by many in construction. Working on construction sites is often an agentive exercise for women who are able to live outside of the restrictions their extended families and communities enforce. Many become the primary decision-makers and entrepreneurs within their family. In Mahaab and Mohammed's relationship (see chapter 5), Mahaab is the chief bargainer for the couple, at least behind the scenes, and Bijli (see chapter 4) is the first contractor in her family. Both women are negotiators and are known as such on the construction site. In work, many women find additional empowerment and a change in their roles in the household. Through their labor on site they gain the power of an income. For many, work is an escape from the social orders of village life and a chance to learn and travel.[3]

Women are subject to the male gaze on construction sites. While most are tasked with unskilled work considered of lesser importance—carrying materials, sweeping, and helping masons—being a woman on a construction site means you tend to be noticed. Many women wear men's work shirts over their saris to avoid spoiling or entangling their saris, as well as to avoid being stared at. The two young Banjara women, with their jewelry and bright clothes, attract the eyes of many. That week, several engineers comment on the young Banjara women, their dresses, and their mannerisms. I become uncomfortable with the erotic undertones.

The property market, like capitalism, relies on multiple desires to propagate itself.[4] The desire for real estate increases consumptive practices, and late capitalism constructs new forms and fashions of desire.[5] Architecture as a prolific gallery of frames and vistas perpetuates and propagates the male gaze, eroticizing both people and architecture.[6] The lust for both bodies and buildings connects women with architectures and constructs the desire to own and accumulate both. Beena and Parvati are noticed and spoken about by the men on site, and I refuse multiple offers to go on solo drives. Love, lust, and longing collect on the construction site and propel the desire for property in violent ways. The etchings of women across the site stare open-mouthed at each other, their wild hair and breasts evoking laughter, anger, and dread, their eyes seeking another woman's body on the wall, carefully hidden from gaze.

There is a picture of a woman in a corner that sees no traffic. She is naked and wears only a *bindi* and a nose ring. She looks directly at us. Her breasts form two gentle arcs across her chest; her transparent underwear and genitalia are emphasized with neat lines in the now familiar white chalk on cement walls. A floating penis is etched next to her. The drawing is a road map for sex.

It is almost impossible for a young single woman to speak to men about sex on construction sites. I am expected to be the chaste, middle-class, Baniya Hindu girl: unmarried, unknowledgeable about sex, uncurious, and innocent. The women do not care about these protocols. "Do you know any of our Bhojpuri songs?" Pushpa, the Bihari wife of a carpenter,

Figure 18. A road map for sex on the wall of a Gurgaon construction site, 2012. Photo by author.

asks me one day as I visit the labor camp. I shake my head and she shares her cell phone. On the small screen a woman thrusts her breasts forward and wriggles restlessly on the floor as she sings in Bhojpuri. "What is she saying?" I ask. "*Meri choliya mein hota hain gud gudiya mai, mai ko bol raha hai* [There is tickling inside my blouse, she is saying to her lover]," she yells. There is wild laughter around me. Another day, as I sit in the camp, the group of women tease a woman walking by: "Come join us, come join us—today she does not want to sit with us!" The woman they are hollering at walks away. My curiosity is answered when they tell me her man stayed home from work today. "He is making a lot of demands," they joke. They continue to tease her and shout across the compound.

The staff at the Wandering Woods head office would continuously clean up my Mumbai *mishri* Hindi (a mix of Marathi, Gujarati, Hindi, and street slang)—most memorably, reminding me to use *beti* (daughter) instead of the cruder *ladki* (young female, which also stands for kept woman). Unlike the middle-class women and the men who cleaned up my language, the women on site openly joked and spoke about sex. They spoke of themselves and other women in masculine terms (*raha* not *rahi*) and used masculine forms more broadly. Greater sexual freedoms, queer practices, and lesser patriarchal controls may exist on site, but there are also many dark secrets related to sex. The empty buildings and damp corners hold memories of sexual violence perpetrated against all genders. There is a reason women tend to work in teams with their partners. Jitendraji tells me he does not want women on his construction site because he does not want to be responsible for their safety or behavior. The dual reference is not lost on me: women working in construction often opt for or are impelled into sex work as a means of controlling their own income and as a way to extract favors from employers.[7] Construction-heavy areas are known to boost sexual economies overall and often see parallel migrations or trafficking of women sex workers.[8] Same-sex abuses can occur, especially toward the younger apprentices, who are expected to cook, wash, and clean up, and some perform services for the craftsmen or masons they train under. A young man cryptically tells me he does not like the "*seva* [service]" his "*ustaad* [master craftsman]" makes him do to him at night.

Sexual desire is present not just at Wandering Woods but in the construction industry as a whole. Middle-class spaces in India thrive on strict divisions between erotic and nonerotic spaces, but construction has no such restrictions.[9] In constructing Chandigarh's Capitol complex, Le Corbusier compared interacting with architecture to interacting with a woman's body: "He would talk about the thighs of a woman and how you touch them. When you caress a column, a shiny round column, a voluptuous column, then you must touch the body . . . he saw beauty everywhere . . .

the big bosom and body of the Indian woman," narrates B. V. Doshi, his mentee.[10] The profession and its practices have historically encoded and enforced misogyny and patriarchy.[11] The material and formal properties of architecture serve as monuments and sensory indicators of gendered power structures: the tall skyscrapers, the long shafts, and the undulating curves stand in for masculine and femme forms, their power radiating into the built environment and reinforcing social norms. Architecture and sex have dangerous liaisons in the fact that property and patriarchy, and control and real estate, go hand in hand. The ownership of architecture demands the forced ownership of or claims on the sexualized other: sexual and real estate economies supplement each other, their power operations blurred and supported through the institutions of marriage, family, and kinship. Yet the blurred boundaries of desire—sexual, familial, material, economic—surpass these structures. Desire produces myriad values through its infusions and intersections and exceeds what it is meant to be.[12] Violent, celebratory, and unconstrained desire sprawls scrumptiously in unseen corners; runs redolent across the sexual diagrams, vaginas, and penises on the walls; intertwines in the urges of writhing snakes; and flowers through the tendrils and petals on the walls, merging into a lonely phrase.[13]

THE MARKET OF THE HEART

The expansive gray walls of Wandering Woods Phase I pulsate with scribbles. The phrases sprawl, uneven on the rough plastered face. I grow fond of a poetic one:

Dil ke bazaar mein sabsein gareeb hoon. Is duniya mein ek hi badnaseeb hoon. Main unkein sapnon mein bhi nahi tha, aur log kehtein hain ke main unke sabse kareeb hoon.

[In the market of hearts, I am the poorest. In this world I am the most unlucky. I wasn't even in their dreams, and people tell me that I am the closest to them.]

Shafi and Raveena found love on a bet in the *bazaar*, a love that drew them into the construction *bazaar*. The young couple dwell in the camp

Figure 19. "In the market of hearts," verses on the wall of a Gurgaon construction site, 2012. Photo by author.

behind the Wandering Woods construction site that houses the bulk of the project's construction workers. Construction sites with more than ten workers are required by law to provide housing for their laborers; at Wandering Woods this takes the form of a temporary housing colony built on a rented agricultural plot behind the construction site. The housing colony is referred to as the "labor camp" (without irony).

Raveena and Shafi hail from in and around a small town in Uttar Pradesh. Before he met and married Raveena, Shafi used to drive through small towns on his motorbike, repairing machines. In one of the town markets, a shopkeeper friend showed him a phone number. It was Raveena's. The shopkeeper said she was the same caste as them and that he had been calling her trying to chat her up (*patao*). The shopkeeper was having no luck: all Raveena did was shower abuse on him. Shafi teased his friend, "She abuses you, I will show you. I will chat her up (*pata ke loonga*). Give me a month."

He narrates their love story: "I went through so much trouble to meet her. I thought if I do not like her then I will not marry her, if I like her

I will." He must have liked her, I think to myself, as I head to the labor camp to meet Raveena and her mother, Bijli, the lightning fast *thekedarin*. Here they are, miles away from home, with a young child, married and happy together.

I cross the empty road behind the construction site and walk past the security guards into the labor camp. The undulating skyscraper under construction looms over my head in stark contrast to the informal rows of worker housing. About three meters long and two meters deep, the homes are arranged in a neat, militarized grid; they are made with cheap, exposed brick and mortar, and topped with corrugated tin sheets. A block of lavatories and bathing areas is situated behind the homes. There are two sections: one for the skilled staff of masonry workers and another for the Malda workers hired on three-month contracts.

The former section, where Shafi and Raveena live, looks more tended. The houses are allotted per family, whereas Malda workers sleep six to a room, dormitory style. The rows of houses are white and blue. The front of each house is personalized: some families have hung hand-stitched quilts from doorframes as curtains, and others have painted their space the color of their choice. I see bits and pieces of construction materials refashioned for domestic use: a bench made of plywood or steel bars supporting a plant. A few young children sit on doorsteps or run around with toys in their hands. It is summer, and every child's skin is covered in the gentle bumps of acute heat rash. A few have hair that is blond-brown from a nutrient-deficient diet. I wince at the sight of a blond child.

There is a hullabaloo in the camp as I arrive. I enter Raveena's home, and several women fill the small room in curiosity. The home is painted a deep blue inside, and her four-month-old daughter sleeps on a mattress on the floor. She is dressed in a princess-white dress and covered with black spots to ward off the evil eye. She sleeps with her two fists balled, like a brave baby warrior ready to do battle. The room is hot and muggy. Flies settle on the baby and swarm across the room; they settle on me as well. Raveena fans her baby's face. The clouds of swarming flies make it hard to concentrate, but nevertheless everyone is eager to chat. They came to this site through Raveena's mother Bijli, who procures small-scale contracting work; "I am a *thekedarin*," Bijli proudly proclaims, in her first meeting with me. It was she who got Shafi his job.

Workers on site point out Shafi to me as the young man who ran away from home because his father did not approve of his choice of wife. Raveena is from a much poorer background. Shafi tells me that his dad is a big political leader in their small town and has several businesses. He was shocked to see Shafi's choice of wife and threatened to banish him from the house if he married Raveena. Shafi had courted her in an act of male one-upmanship, liked her, and faced family disapproval when he wanted to marry her. "Leave her and we will give her family money to marry her to someone else," his father told him. "You want her family to have money, I will give you her dowry money," Shafi says, recalling their fight and his rebuttal. In the end there was no resolution. His mother-in-law got him a job in the city. He worked his way up the ranks, but his mother puts money from her household savings into his bank account to help out the young couple.

In a country driven so strongly by notions of arranged marriage and caste- and community-based marriages, falling in love seems to be a luxury that no one can afford, yet *pyaar*, *prem*, *mohabbat*, and love dwell in India among all classes, and their call rises. Flirtation and romance have long existed in Indian literary culture and gain even more traction through contemporary media.[14] The increasing presence and consolidation of romance between partners serves to foster rather than limit construction and real estate. It feeds the erotics of architecture and constructs a desire for an amalgamated triad of family, property, and home.

In Raveena and Shafi's case, their success in the market of hearts allowed them to challenge class hierarchies as well as to find love. The *pyaar bazaar* allowed them to challenge social norms but turned them into producers of real estate, thus harnessing their and their maternal *pyaars* to the construction industry. The ways of the heart support the real estate market through romance in construction. The case of Bansilal's *pyaar* is another example.

A rotund and jolly man, Bansilal is a financial director for Buildstrong, the developer behind Wandering Woods. Far from the camp, in his air-conditioned office, he offers me peanuts as snacks and narrates the story of how he met his wife. His wife works for the RBI. When they met, Bansilal was in charge of financial and legal compliance for his office. He visited the RBI for permissions. His wife's boss, from the same community as

Bansilal, began to like him very much. One day he told Bansilal that one of his employees was like a daughter to him. He asked Bansilal if he was interested in marrying her. Bansilal chuckles with male bravado as he tells me the story. "I handed him my file. You take care of this and I will take care of her. I went every day and handed her boss the files and took her out." I imagine the world of construction possibilities that that relationship facilitated.

Across professional and elite classes in North India, marriages further *bazaar* economies. "Gifts" of daughters across business households and the incorporation of entrepreneurial sons-in-law feed empires, through the generation of kin-based capital.[15] Within construction-related families, it is not uncommon to see business alliances coincide with marital ones: developers whose daughters are married to sons of other developers, politicians whose sons-in-law are developers, architect's children married to contractors, and daughters of cement suppliers married to contractors. Partnerships allow real estate and construction empires to consolidate and concretize. The *bazaar* works on kin-based *pyaar*.

Kinship draws extended families and domestic partnerships of masons and manual laborers (*kulis*) to construction sites and consolidates professional lineages of masons, steelworkers, and stone workers. Miriraj and his wife are one such couple. Miriraj and Mumtaz are a husband-wife mason-helper team from Chattisgarh. I first meet them, in my early days at the site, when I walk up the stairs of the tower block. Miriraj works alone on a column, and I stop to ask him about how he learned his craft. He yells at me, "*yehhi hamein sikhata hain*" (this one teaches me). He is chuckling, and I follow his pointed finger to find Mumtaz hiding behind a column clutching her sari across her face. "This [*yeh*] is my mason . . . look, look, how he/she [*yeh*] is holding the leveling tool [*fanti*]." His wife clutches the *fanti* and looks at me shyly as Miriraj laughs away, but she later tells me that she really does "know all the work." From then on, I keep an eye out for them on site.

The affective and emotive ties of *pyaar* build value in construction. They create business houses and familial lineages and yoke multiple forms of labor to each other. Domestic political-economic bonds—with their benefits of support, double incomes, and transforming gender roles, and drawbacks of reinscribing patriarchal power, doubling the vulnerability of a family, and erasing women's work—are enhanced in construction. The floors and slabs of Wandering Woods are steeped in *pyaar*'s affects, as the force of love embeds itself into work. In the scribbled phrase *Dil ke bazaar mein sabsein gareeb hoon* (In the market of hearts, I am the poorest), the term *bazaar*, denoting the vernacular Indian market, speaks to the political economy of the heart—an economy that is ignored in discussions of the speculative worlds of global finance, just as the *bazaar* economy was once ignored in discussions of colonial India's economy.[16] *Pyaar*— as the mediator of multiple forms of desire, kinship, partnership, family, and marriage—feeds the political economies of real estate. Its excess drips down the unfinished stairwells and pools into new creative practices and potentials. The hearts bouncing across Wandering Woods, the songs of love and pining, speak of the power of romance: the joy of finding each other or the melancholic heartbreak of unrequited love. The hearts on the walls yearn for each other through the framed architectural vistas, emphasizing the undulations and angularities, the smoothness of concrete and the harshness of steel, beating within the iron cages of gender norms, to lead us to new tensions of love in construction.

MANAGING TENSION

In one of the stairwells at the back of a building, an impertinent phrase proudly proclaims: "Tension *mat lo, kaam ho jayega* [do not stress out, the work will get done]."

Who gets tense about work to be done? And who does not stress? Most elders will point to the young men. In the grassy fields surrounding the site, laborers too young to be called men play cricket with a makeshift bat and ball. The boys break and huddle together, looking at pictures or movies on cell phones. Their hands rest on each other's shoulders, and their wiry frames lean on each other. The younger ones come and go. Many come to work in the city for a short time to earn some spending money. Others work in the summer when schools and colleges are on leave. It is easy to sort the married ones from the unmarried: married men tend not to disappear from the site as easily and take on greater responsibility, since they have wives and often children to feed at home (workers tell me).

Figure 20. "Do not stress, the work will get done," slogan on the walls of a Gurgaon construction site, 2012. Photo by author.

Marriage produces family, and family increases the need for income and homes and bring workers onto construction sites. Heteronormative conceptions of domesticity undergird both the production and the consumption of real estate. At the same time, the tensions created by familial and domestic *pyaar* threaten the stability of real estate economies and hence heteronormativity itself.

Conversations on marriage thrum through the air on construction sites, demanding you prove your allegiance to the institution. People discover my single status and offer volumes of unsolicited advice. Mr. Kumar, the site engineer, jokes with me on our car ride home: "Life is like a spider web . . . the more you enter it the more you get stuck." He feels he was carefree in his younger days: "First you get married [and] you feel 'now I am free,' but you start to worry about your wife. Then you worry about the kids."

Marriage, and conjugality, exist in many forms and transform ways of working on site; they draw new responsibilities into work.[17] Marriage increases monetary demands and demands more diligent labor. Gendered differences create labor, often shifting emotional and physical labor onto women. Most often, women bear the brunt of managing not only their commercial labor but also the household and children. Mahaab, for example, works as a *kuli* all day but washes clothes, cooks, and cleans during her hours off. Mrs. Singh, a planner, talks about middle-class marriage. "After marriage, life is very difficult for women. Husbands do not help at all. Look at this woman amongst my office staff," she says about her assistant. "She comes from Faridabad every day. On one hand she works here, then she takes the metro, and then the bus, and then another [bus] to reach home. She reaches [home] at about eight [p.m.]." Mrs. Singh talks about the unending labor women must do: "[She] does not even change her clothes, and has to look at her kids' homework. Cook food [and] feed them. She sleeps at two. And again in the morning she is back here." The labor is unequal in comparison to men, as Mrs. Singh describes: "Her husband owns a shop. He does not help at all. Now you tell me—nowadays they want that the women earn, but they do not help at all. And she, on top of that, has two bedridden elders in her house. The entire responsibility is on her." Mrs. Singh shares the story of her daughter's arranged marriage. A man who ran an arranged marriage bureau asked her for 5 percent of the dowry offered for her daughter as a commission. "You can afford it," he told her. "I told him are you arranging marriages or brokering property?" she says indignantly.

Mrs. Singh's sarcastic statement on marriage and property rings true. The industry grows through the reliability and popularity of Indian marriages: conjugality makes labor more efficient, combines domestic and commercial labor, and feeds the desire for property. The institution of marriage and the tensions arising from it do work on construction sites. The traction of marriage and the traction of the construction industry conspire in the fields of Gurgaon. Tensions related to marriage, work, land, and property intertwine with each other and spiral through the staircases in a heady rush. Tensions swirl down the empty apertures to fall into a chalky depiction of mother and child.

Sunlight streams across a wall, cutting an image in half. Hidden behind a stack of dust-covered glass and wire mesh is a drawing of a woman and her child. She wears a sari neatly tied and wrapped around her thin waist, its pleats etched with parallel lines. In her arms sits a child. Its hair radiates outward in all directions in singular lines. The child's features are

Figure 21. Mother and child on the wall of a Gurgaon construction site, 2012. Photo by author.

ambiguous, unlike the woman's defined doe-eyes and smiling mouth. The child's mouth is wide and open—maybe it is crying? The woman stares ahead into the space before them. A figure lurks off to the side, the father perhaps? Drawn by another painter in a rough abstraction much later? Or maybe it is the father who draws?

Amar, the marketing and sales director for Wandering Woods, speaks of his daughters. He lives in the affluent area of South Delhi with his wife and two kids. On a Diwali day, I head to a party at his house. The small-roomed but tastefully decorated home is pleasing to my architect's eye. Marbles floors and white walls offset blue-gray aluminum doorframes. The living room is large, with white sofas. Chic decorative plates, design books, and a good music system add flourishes. Amar leads me upstairs to show me a warm study with cane curtains and wooden chairs. Brass antiques decorate shelves, and a white desk occupies the end of the room. I see his two daughters in an adjacent bedroom, and they look up at me with the distracted eyes of children at play.

Amar is a jovial person with a lot of ambition and an equally fierce temper. The son of a middle-class Punjabi family, he developed expensive tastes in business school. Wandering Woods was his path to success. As Buildstrong grew, so did Amar's affluence: he bought and renovated this new home, got himself a brand-new car, and took his children to Europe on summer vacations. One day he describes his family's visit to Bombay (Mumbai), where they stayed at the Oberoi hotel, a prominent five-star hotel by the city's famous sea promenade, Marine Drive.[18] "Do you know that movie where Amitabh, where he sits on Marine Drive and stares at the Oberoi . . . ?[19] When I had first come to Bombay . . . I used to come sit on Marine Drive and stare up at the Oberoi." Amar talks about his dreams of upward mobility and his joy at achieving them, "so Nilima and I decided we wanted to take our daughters to live in it—to show them what life is like. So we stayed there for three days—next time I bring them I want them to stay at the Taj."

At his home during Diwali we play cards.[20] It is a custom, I am told, among Delhiites to play cards at Diwali. Each of us places a 10 rupee note in a bowl at the center of the table and receives a set of cards. We work toward creating the perfect hand; the winner picks up the entire stash. I win big and then lose it over the course of the night. I make a sum total of 30 rupees (50 cents) that night and pay for my auto-rickshaw home. The emotional rollercoaster of the game courses through my veins during the cool, breezy ride.

"Will you go take a picture of my Gudiya?" asks Miriraj when he sees me with my camera on site. "Yes," I promise, and head over to the camp where his daughter plays in the crèche. Gudiya is an infant and is crawling on the floor; I recognize her as a mix of her two parents. The old woman caretaker holds her up as I take her photograph. Gudiya stares at me with serious eyes. I return with a hard-copy photograph a month later. "Do you recognize this person?" I ask, as I show Miriraj the photograph. A smile breaks across his face. "*Yeh toh meri gudiya hai*! [This is my doll!]" he laughs. I smile back at the proud love that glints in his eyes. I know that, as Gudiya grows up, she will not be brought to the city; the only reason she travels now, Mumtaz informs me, is because she is breastfed. The labor camp and the city, the women tell me, are not safe spaces to bring prepubescent girls.

Shreelal, the site supervisor at Haveli, left his wife and young daughter back home, declaring this area unsuitable for both of them. He pulls his wallet out when I ask about them and shows me a picture of his daughter. "If I do not go home for a month then she stops eating. Right now she must have come home, thrown her bag, and must be playing train in her room . . . or maybe cops and robbers." I look at a girl with thick curls, heavily adorned with lipstick and *kajal* (kohl) for a special photography day; all the family gold seems to hang from her neck. "Her uncle lives with them; he also has two kids. They are her age. They play the whole day," Shreelal describes his child. To work in construction, for Amar, Miriraj, and Shreelal, is to draw a connection between family and work; despite being of three different classes and castes, Amar, Miriaj, and Shreelal share a love for their families and children. Through their work and *pyaars*, they tie together their families and the real estate they construct.

As a woman anthropologist in a predominantly male space, it is hard to use heteronormative masculine tropes to create bonds with men. In order to gain acceptance into the community, I adhere to the religious and social protocols of a conservative, middle-class, dominant-caste woman, which makes drinking alcohol, talking about sex, or smoking taboo.[21] So men talk to me about fatherhood and of the wives they leave behind, of people they love and the responsibilities they feel toward them: the mother who needs medicine for her cancer treatment; the alcoholic father who died too soon; the sisters they need to marry off; the heavy financial weight that marriage, death, birth, and other rituals of life carry with them. Despite being performative at times, these narrations attest at some level to the connection between their work and their loves. Their roles as fathers, sons, brothers, and uncles are fulfilled by work. The tensions of work form part of the net that binds workers and enables them to care for the ones they love. *Pyaar* celebrates the loves, holds these tensions, and even produces the desire to break free. All these emotions thrum in the heart of the home.

On one wall at Wandering Woods, buried in the depths of the twelfth floor, there exists a wistful drawing of a home. An elongated rectangle is topped with a conical roof, its tiles depicted with a neat, tilted grid. A door marks the front of the house. It has a latch. Beside the door is a square window. A path leads into the foreground. The words "*shubh*

Figure 22. Drawing of home on the wall of a Gurgaon construction site, 2012. Photo by author.

laabh [auspicious gain]" flank the house on each side. On the right, a large flowerpot sprouts four stems, with leaves that evoke four-leaf clovers. Two hearts with arrows through them flank the humble home; they are inscribed "S. P." The drawing is signed "Painter S. K." Perhaps this is the home that rests in his heart?

Where does one find home in Gurgaon? The city teems with architectures of different classes: the towering middle-class apartments, the old-style village *havelis* (ancestral bungalows) in which local farmers live, the candy-colored migrant dormitories, and the makeshift brick and corrugated-aluminum-roofed structures that provide labor housing and informal housing for those who cannot afford the dormitory structures.

Mahaab and Mohamed built their urban home on the Haveli construction site. When I first meet them, the thirty-something mason (*mistri*) and helper (*kuli*, coolie) couple from West Bengal are constructing a temporary house along the back wall of the site upon which they will work for over a year. Picking a strategic corner, bounded by two compound walls and under a small tree, they gather debris from across the site for construction materials. They align notched bamboo poles and dig them into the ground to act as verticals, which rest against the corner of the compound walls. Old pipes and thin steel bars form the horizontals. Corrugated tin sheets are tied to the horizontals and verticals to create walls and a roof. The roof juts out two feet and hangs over a small area. The couple cordons off this area with discarded flowerpots from the bungalow they have demolished. Mahaab sets up her kerosene cooking stove by the pots. The couple climb the sides of the house and place a blue tarp over the roof to protect it from the rain. They weigh it down with stones and broken bricks. This is their home on site.

Mahaab and I talk inside this small home on days when work is slow. The dark room is barely the size of two full beds. On hot afternoons, light streams in from the gap between the roof and the gray, patchy compound wall. I sit on a bed made from pilfered wood battens and plywood from the site. It is the main piece of furniture in the small home and is draped with a bright orange bedsheet printed with bold black circles. A salvaged bookshelf sits next to it, holding a motley collection of items: large aluminum cooking pots, glasses, a plastic cane basket of vegetables, and a number of bottles filled with oils and spices. A clothesline swings along the back wall. Saris and shirts hang upon it.

Mahaab often talks about her home in the village as we sit amid the flotsam and jetsam of her construction-site home. We communicate in Hindi and my broken Bengali. We swap pieces of our lives over the course of our daily conversations. She talks of her home in the village often and tells me how they built it. She, her husband, and her father-in-law built the home themselves; hiring masons in the village is expensive. "Plus they are masons themselves," she says, reminding me of her husband's skill set. Cement in the village is expensive too, so the village home was built from bamboo and tin. It is much bigger than this house, she tells me, disdainful of the space she lives in. The family used their savings to build the house and government subsidies to build a latrine. They bought two solid beds. Not like the makeshift one in this room, she explains.

I imagine her village home as she has described it. A house that rests at the corner of the fields where her in-laws cultivate tobacco and rice and her children pretend to help. Her two boys, aged four and six, attend a private school, English-medium, in town. In the afternoons they run home through the fields and hover around their grandmother as Mahaab and Mohamed grasp the cell phone and speak loudly into it. On speaker I can hear a crackling child's voice as he brags about his day. I hear Mahaab respond in a mellifluous voice. One day I see her worried and red-eyed. Her boy in the village is ill. Home is too far away.

"We do all this for their education, so that they can have a better life?" I nod to agree. They have two homes, these two. One idealized and the other required; one that they work to build and the other that they build for work. The cell phone connects their homes and streams love from one into the other. The village home is the one she recalls, the one that she would draw upon those walls; the home that carries the heartbreak of *pyaar* left behind.

The productive economies of real estate and construction link together love for family and the desire for a home.[22] Contemporary real estate dynamics are constituted through a contrivance of property and domesticity. The fantasy of buying some land, building a home, or owning an apartment or other property is enhanced on construction sites. Working in the real estate and construction industry causes you to fall conspicuously on the fault line between production and consumption, of desiring that which you build. Gautam's search for an appropriate apartment also ties to marriage: he wants to have a permanent home for his spouse. "I need to build a house before I marry," jokes Veer, the young mason who wants to roam. Workers save to build homes on the lands they own. "We divided our ancestral property. Our wives started fighting too much," recounts Prakashji the mason. As Mahaab and Mohamed build a luxurious bungalow with a swimming pool and multiple bedrooms, they reshape the economies, the form, and the social structure of their own home. The two homes are linked through the systems of production and consumption. The stark differences between them, however, are a source of exploitation.

Contemporary real estate harnesses *pyaar*, embedding it into concretized property that the slabs at Wandering Woods multiply. The political economic intimacies of *pyaar* enable the heteronormative, upper-class, and dominant-caste construction and consolidation of notions of marriage, family, and home. They propel the demand for land and real estate. Architectures multiply across the Indo-Gangetic plains; a multiplicity of homes—S. K. Painter's, Mahaab and Mohamed's, Amar's, and Mohan's—grow through the accumulative and exploitative politics of *pyaar*.

Feminist literature on property relations has long pointed out the dangerous liaisons between property accumulation and patriarchy.[23] Property, accompanied by domesticity, is responsible for not only gendered but also intersectional—including, I would argue, caste-based—social subjugation.[24] Speculative economies of advanced neoliberalism marshal the sentiments of kinship.[25] Real estate thrives on heteronormative ideals of courtship and family.[26] Intimacy and capital both demand "an ever-expanding market" and "connect the micro-practices of certain forms of love to the macro-practices of certain forms of state governance and certain forms of capital production, circulation, and consumption."[27] Love, however, is not without conflicts and tensions, and it is these discontents within the politics of love, romance, marriage, and real estate that challenge the violent dynamics they are embedded in and produce. *Tension mat lo* (do not bear the tension)—for it is what furthers exploitation and accumulation. The ephemeral intensities of *pyaar* cure the industrial strength of speculative architecture but also instill the fine lines of tension across it. *Pyaar* strengthens the durability of the institutions and architectures it constructs, while rendering invisible cracks of rebellion and tension within it.

LABORS OF LOVE

> *Gareeb ka paseena, khoon choosta hain ussein kameena kehtein.*
>
> [The one who sucks the sweat, blood of the poor, they call him a bastard.]

Can love be exploitative and hungry? Like the love for money and capital? Ram, a site supervisor, explains how *pyaar* can be instrumental within the political economy of construction work. He explains to me how he gets workers to work: "Labor is hungry for love and to get them to work we must speak to them with love/affection [*pyaar se baat karna*]. This is

Figure 23. "The one who sucks the sweat and blood of the poor . . . ," saying on the wall of a Gurgaon construction site, 2012. Photo by author.

the method [*tareeka*] . . . with a little love we have to get them to work." He explains how he speaks with love, "It is like this, if an educated architect or engineer speaks to them at their level, they feel good. I talk to them like they are my brothers—[if I say] brother, please do this—then he will do the work properly." According to him it is the most effective way of getting laborers to do work. "Yesterday, what happened, he [the contractor] talked to him [the worker] and abused him verbally. Then he [the worker] began working loosely [*kaam dhila karne laga*]," he describes an incident on site and how it was mediated. "Then the senior contractor said to him, son please do this—this work is going on, so please get yours done before that . . . [then] he finished it in one or two hours. Basically this is what talking with a little love is."

My brother (*bhai*), my son (*beta*), my daughter (*beti*), and my child (*baba*): these are common terms used to get work done on site. Like love, they are ambiguous shapeshifters. At times they symbolize the emotive relationship between contractors and laborers, who often share bonds of affection and companionship. At other times they are used to encourage someone who is reluctant to work. Patronizing or not, they mobilize affective energies, constructing groups of workers as cross-class families and kin.

To talk with love is to be both instrumental and emotive: The "marked boundaries between labor and love, affection and exploitation, and desire and decency . . . [are] constantly blurred in practice."[28] On construction sites *pyaar* gathers a slipperiness, an intimacy, a coercive weight, a longing, and a political-economic leaning. Talk to workers with love or affection and they will walk up twelve stories carrying the heavy bars of scaffolding on their heads. Evincing love wins hearts and acts as a tool of exploitation and economic gain. The site contractor Jitendraji is loved for his calm mannerisms and his genteel way of talking to people. Workers work hard for him because he treats them with respect and affection; they follow him from site to site. "We love Amar," rave his staff to me. No one would tell me otherwise: public love for your employer is compulsory. The politics of love can strangle protests on construction sites, where the walls scream of the political-economic weight of *pyaar*.

As I walk across the floor slab, I pause momentarily to breathe in the cement dust. The talcum powder–like quality of cement tickles my nostrils and unites with a single word on the wall, *Ma* (Mother). The fine, dusty smell of cement reminds me of my mother's hair. Every night as I grew up, the construction site came to my childhood bed, in the smell of sawdust, cigarettes, and cement embedded in my mother's hair. Her workday as a landscape architect echoed in our evening rituals, as she sang my sister and me lullabies in a voice so discordant that it roused us from our hazy dreams. I slept comforted by the smell of cement. We were children who occupied construction sites, dragged from project to project after school when we insisted that we wanted to accompany her. Contractors and masons became our uncles, buying us treats and watching over us as our mother gave instructions on site. There were other children there too—the children of masons, like Mahaab and Mohamed.[29] Construction worlds were both their playgrounds and their homes. They played on heaps of gravel, sleeping within the structures under construction when activity halted at night.

There are children all across construction sites. On smaller sites, they play on the unfinished floorplates and in the gravel and sand. Their toys are bricks, bars, stones, and wood—the careless leftovers of construction. On larger sites, children are kept in mandated day-care centers. The protests of human rights activists and the increasing enforcement of child labor laws have caused large-scale construction sites to bar children from their sites. They are required by law to build a crèche and to provide childcare.[30]

Miriraj and Mumtaz's daughter Gudiya spends her days at the crèche at the Wandering Woods labor camp along with the smaller children at the site. An elongated tin-walled and -roofed structure, the crèche has an unfinished mud floor covered by cheap plastic mats. The walls of the crèche are plastered with educational posters—Hindi alphabet tables, typical Indian animals and birds—and the regulations from the labor department. A tube light illuminates the space, and a few children play around an older woman attendant. There are no children of school age, just the young ones, still being breastfed, or who still need hands-on care. The breastfeeding mothers leave the construction site and walk over to the crèche every few hours to feed their children. They too carry construction in their clothes and hair.

Construction is an act of caregiving and nurturing. Like children, growing buildings require constant care and attention. The surveying of materials, the watering of curing cement, the meticulous mapping of foundations, and the monitoring of architecture's gradual growth all require constant techniques of care. As parents nurture, mold, and grow both architecture and children, they blur the boundaries between construction and kin. The skin and bones of architecture grow with those of their children. They carry both child and building on their clothes and hair, producing a bridge between the two worlds.

As the five o'clock siren sounds through the site, my female companions rush to nurse their children or buy vegetables at the market nearby. Their laboring day, they remind me, isn't over yet: they must cook dinner, feed the family, and wash vessels and clothes for the coming day. "The water supply will go," they say as they rush. I am left alone as I wait for my ride home—alone with the images and evocations of women on the walls. Mothers, wives, daughters, lone women, naked women call silently to each other across staircases and landings. I read the writing on the walls.

Wandering Woods grows at a breakneck pace. Every fifteen days, a new floor is added to the building. The scaffolding moves higher, and a new floorplate is poured into place. As it dries, it needs water to cure: water triggers the exothermic reaction that generates heat to harden the concrete. Constant watering increases strength and decreases porosity. This makes the slab durable for forty-odd years. For twenty-eight days we must cure the concrete until it achieves its durability, watering and watching it every few hours, covering it with wet gunny sacks and chipping away at its deformities once hardened.

The wall drawings serve as aesthetic formulations of the affects and affective labors that infuse the workings of construction. Affect, understood through affective labor, is a vital aspect of nurturing, nourishing, and growing someone or something.[31] This intensity is constructed not only between living beings but also between beings and materials.[32] Affective labor and affective atmospheres on site concretize heteronormative conceptions of family, home, and marriage that further social reproduction and the accumulation of property. *Pyaar*, while often located in the figures of parents, children, family, kin, and home, also dwells within the materialities of architecture and in the atmospheres of labor. *Pyaar* is a word embedded with tensions and rife with multiplicity. Love, intimacy, desire, and kinship are malleable categories under *pyaar*; this malleability helps them nourish and exploit, trap and liberate, lend agency, and add value to the architecture they create.[33]

The ephemeral rests both in the rising and falling affect of *pyaar* and the temporariness of the drawings themselves. Like the many forms of the ephemeral presented in this book, *pyaar* represents how kinship and atmospheres in construction undergird the political economy of construction but simultaneously produce the possibility of dissent and change. Affects of *pyaar* cure concrete materialities and the economic realities around them, seeping into molecular, architectural, and social structures. They form the thin, invisible cracks of social tension and change.

Happiness and sadness, desire and despair, the lightness of carefree laughter and the weight of responsibility—all are drawn into the architecture of Wandering Woods as workers tie steel bars, shovel, and plane concrete. The labor, the construction work, the architecture, the real estate industry, all created through forms of *pyaar*.

Conclusion

Inquilab Zindabad. Cries of "long live revolution" resound through the streets of India. Heard in the farmers' protests of 2021, in the National Register of Citizens' protests of 2020, in the union strikes of 2016, in mill-workers' protests in the 1990s, in anti-dam protests in the 1980s, and dating back to freedom fighter Bhagat Singh in the 1920s, *Inquilab Zindabad* has been the rallying cry against injustice. Emerging in British India as an anti-colonial slogan, today *Inquilab Zindabad* encompasses critiques of state injustices and neoliberal privatization policies alike, its durability maintained through the affective connections it draws as a historical call for freedom and justice.[1] *Inquilab Zindabad* is an ephemeral sound— simultaneously fleeting yet durable. Even when used temporarily—in protests that are clamped down on or that fade out—the term rises again in a new space with new voices, still indexing the intentions and emotions, the history and shared solidarities of those who have said it in the past. The continuity of present and historical struggles is registered through a sound that rises and then fades.

I evoke this slogan, printed on a unionization pamphlet handed to me on a construction site, as an instance of the ephemeral that speaks to many of the ways in which the concept works in this book. A sound that is a call to action and social change but is nevertheless temporary, a sound that circulates from space to space and eventually dissipates, and a sound that has affective connections and shapes the sensibilities of those who hear it for decades to come. A sound that creates community. The rising call of *Inquilab* is only one of many instances of the ephemeral outlined in this book—including the erasure and displacement of laborers from construction sites, the aesthetics and atmospheres of construction sites, material transformations, the constant circulation and erasure of documents and money in construction, and the changing affective states that accompany these processes. *Inquilab Zindabad*, however, captures both the injustice that the ephemeral perpetuates as well as the possibilities of justice and solidarity it creates. It demands basic change with speed or urgency, and acknowledges that there are systematic issues that require action; it is an ephemeral that is temporary but leaves long-term effects.[2]

Inquilab, understood as a revolution, an uprising, or a sweeping change, was used by freedom fighter Bhagat Singh after he and an associate bombed the Legislative Assembly in British-governed India; it encodes a call to political action.[3] Bhaghat Singh was viewed as a terrorist by the British, and the phrase remains the object of the same punitive gaze: many who publicly utter it are looked at suspiciously by state and corporate actors. While the phrase is now also part of the register of middle-class social justice activism that does not necessarily support revolution, there are many—like Pushpa, the carpenter's wife—who want to turn the world upside down, as she fights against her own erasure and hopes for an unjust world rectified.

Inquilab Zindabad. This book remembers a place and process that no longer exist. Like the poet Maulana Hasrat Mohani, who coined the phrase *Inquilab Zindabad*, the familiar landscapes of the jeweled pit, the sounds of the diesel generator, the clouds of dust and cement, and most importantly the people I returned to during my fieldwork, are all gone. The pit lies buried under piles of mud, and the once-bare architecture is now coated with paint and plaster, occupied by people I do not recognize, while those I do know have dispersed across sites throughout the Indo-Gangetic plain. All have packed up and gone, the urban region has been renamed from Gurgaon to Gurugram, and the NH8 is now the NH48; even the city of Gurgaon and its arterial road no longer exist.

The drawings on the walls at Wandering Woods undergo a slow erasure at the end of my time on site. I see the painters move downward, one floor at a time. They start from the top floor and every few weeks move to a lower floor. They cover the drawings with smooth, white plaster to create an ivory wall. The white plaster spreads over the drawings in thicker and thicker layers, to provide an even surface for paint. The gray palate of concrete smoothens into a shiny papyrus-white, as plaster and paint extend across the bare faces of walls and ceilings. Whiteness and glass, smoothness and shine, replace the grime and grit of construction. The very operations of construction encode the erasure of its own work. From the first act of digging up the earth to the last polishing of furniture, workers bury foundations, cement over steel reinforcement, plaster walls, tile floors, hide wires and ducts, and cover over ceilings. Each stage erases the evidence of the work done in the last; each stage, once complete, displaces those who labored upon it onto different floors and eventually to different construction sites. Mahaab and Ahmed, MD and Munnalal all expected this erasure. They knew from experience that they too would soon be removed from the architecture they helped build; they often reminded me that their time at the site was only temporary, like the drawings on the walls.

My presence is temporary, too. The final days of my fieldwork end, and I pack my bags for home in Mumbai. Weeks later, the army of machines beat a slow retreat, moving on to another construction site. Nazeem joins the banks of Malda workers in an unreserved train compartment home. MD starts a new project, and Mahaab and Mohamed go home for the holidays. The air-conditioning system turns on at Wandering Woods and slowly pushes the heat and dust out to the peripheries of the building. Security guards anchor themselves at the gates with guest ledgers and guard this ethereal kingdom. Even with my class status and educational credentials, I have no excuse to wander within.

I have explored what it means to be disciplined, exploited, and controlled by an ephemeral atmosphere in construction. The constant shifting of people and materials, the transformation of money and plans, the sounds and emotions that filter through construction worlds control workers in invisible and surreptitious ways. Can it be proven in court that the sound of a machine forces workers to work faster and harder, to the point that they cannot cope? Or that emotions are harnessed into real estate logics? It is precisely the intangibility of the ephemeral that allows industries to deploy it: ephemeral affects, aesthetics, and material transformations are fundamental to the workings of contemporary capital. We have seen how the material shifts in capital make its movement harder to track, and how the circulation of drawings allows for a variety of individuals to make money. Naming and identifying these hard-to-capture ephemeral devices of power provides an important counterweight to the political effects of their deployment.

While this book presents the contributions of those rendered ephemeral in the construction of urban India, it has also sought to think through the transformative state that constitutes the ephemeral. Construction atmospheres—and, by extension, construction aesthetics—bear a heightened temporality. The changing states of concrete; the shifting material forms of money; the drawing-redrawing of plans; and the sounds, smells, and actions of work construct an atmosphere that is powerful and all-encompassing, albeit ephemeral. This state of heightened affects and aesthetics, imbued with the ability to shape our sensibilities and actions, lends the ephemeral its power.

The ephemeral within industrial workings is even more important in contemporary times, as multisited and distributed industrial operations rise. Contemporary industries rely on their ephemeral atmospheres as much as they do on their durable infrastructures. In construction, the aesthetic qualities that characterize the production and consumption of the built environment—the urban and natural landscapes produced, the mobilities through them, the textures, sounds, smells, and imagery—manage and manipulate labor and capital and hence structure industrial political economy. Industries harness the heightened, processual nature of ephemeral atmospheres disciplining workers, creating obfuscations that mask accumulations, and perpetuating accumulative knowledge only to a chosen few.

And yet. As I have argued throughout these chapters, the same atmospheres also contain the potential for protest and for political action. Like *Inquilab Zindabad*, the ephemeral is a register of injustice and inequality. In its momentariness and heightened intimacies, it forms affects, agencies, and solidarities. In the intensity of work and atmospheres of work, the ephemeral generates alliances, consolidates class affinities, and empowers people who speak against exploitation. In this respect, *The Industrial Ephemeral* is very much a story about class, and by extension caste, gender, and religious relations. In a country whose urban spaces grow divided, gated, and enclaved, this study of the production chain of the construction industry demonstrates the interreliances, the shared solidarities, and the unequal exchanges that drive the nation's urban expansion. It shows how an industry controls Indian urbanism.

Though it appears solid, strong, and permanent, the built environment—architecture, landscape, and infrastructure—is undergirded by and produced through ephemeral atmospheres and individuals. As the tenants of Haveli sit by their swimming pool and the offices of Wandering Woods are filled with workers typing with the confidence that the floor will not give way underneath them, and as we move smoothly across the architectures and infrastructures of our everyday lives that MD, Mahaab, and Mohamed built, we do not remember them. Attending to the ephemeral helps us trace the movements of the many workers who built this environment. We move through the memory and history of atmospheres far different from those we occupy, and through the memory and history of those who undergird the social structures we live in. *Inquilab Zindabad*: those who cried it once may be long dead, but the legacies of their struggle remain. *Inquilab Zindabad*: the ephemeral may dissipate, but it always rises once again.

Appendix

Table 1 Master Plans Affecting Gurgaon

Year	Output	Validity (Date)	Area (Hectares)	Area Added (Hectares)	Source
1964	Controlled area declared around municipal Gurgaon town				Haryana government, Town and Country Planning Department notification, 29 April 1982
1971	First Development Plan for Gurgaon	1991			Haryana government, Town and Country Planning Department notification, 29 April 1982
1977	Revised Development Plan for Gurgaon (two controlled areas)	2001			Haryana government, Town and Country Planning Department notification, 29 April 1982
1982	Revised Draft Development Plan for Gurgaon (all controlled areas, I–IV)	2001	9,372		Haryana government, Town and Country Planning Department notification, 29 April 1982
1996	Final Development Plan for Gurgaon	2001			Haryana government, Town and Country Planning Department notification 9, 1996.
1999	Draft Development Plan for GGN (areas I–IV)	2021			CCP(NCR)/FDP-2001/GGN/82/6528, dt.08/01/1996
1999	Draft Development Plan for GGN (areas I–IV) placed before SLC and rejected because contemplated population far in excess of actual population	2021			
2001	National Capital Region Regional Plan				National Capital Region Planning Board
2005	National Capital Region Regional Plan 2021	2021	55,083 sq. km.		National Capital Region Planning Board

Year	Plan	Target year			Source
2007	Gurgaon–Manesar Urban Complex Final Development Plan 2021	2021	21,733		Haryana government, Town and Country Planning Department notification, 5 February 2007
2011	Gurgaon–Manesar Urban Complex 2025	2025	22,223		Haryana government, Town and Country Planning Department notification, 24 May 2011 https://tcpharyana.gov.in/DevelopmentPlan.htm
2012	Gurgaon–Manesar Urban Complex 2031	2031	22,957		Haryana government, Town and Country Planning Department notification, 15 November 2012
2017	Gurgaon–Manesar Urban Complex 2031 (amended)	2031		66,913	Haryana government, Town and Country Planning Department notification, 24 January 2017 (amendment) https://tcpharyana.gov.in/DevelopmentPlan.htm

SOURCE: Created by Namita Vijay Dharia, Tarun Sharma, and Arjun Rajagopal.

Notes

1. Reader One points this out in their review of the manuscript.

2. Early writing on Indian urbanism focused on history (e.g., Chattopadhyay, *Representing Calcutta*; Evenson, *Indian Metropolis*; Hosograhar, *Indigenous Modernities*; Nair, *Promise of the Metropolis*; Rao, *House but No Garden*); this emphasis moved to informal settlements and streets in the 1990s (e.g., Roy, *Urban Informality*; Rao "Proximate Distances"; Tarlo, *Unsettling Memories*). In recent years expanded topics have included land politics (e.g., Levien, *Dispossession without Development*; Searle, *Landscapes of Accumulation*), the ecologies and beautification of public space (e.g., Baviskar, "City Limits"; Ghertner, *Rule by Aesthetics*; Rademacher and Sivaramakrishnan, *Ecologies of Urbanism*), the fallout of deindustrialization (e.g., Adarkar, *Chawls of Mumbai*), and infrastructural development (Anand, *Hydraulic City*; Björkman, *Pipe Politics*). Very few scholars consider industries and labor as central to contemporary urbanism (exceptions include Anjaria *Slow Boil*; Finklestein, *Archive of Loss*), when in fact they are central to it. In addition, as Anjaria argues, studies of urbanism in India frequently focus either on the affective or political economic dimensions of urban life (*Slow Boil*, 67–71) often representing it in binaries such as the static and kinetic (Mehrotra, "Negotiating the Static"); building on this insight, *The Industrial Ephemeral* presents the mutual constitutive-ness of the affective and political economic and the transient and permanent.

3. Gururani, "Flexible Planning."

4. The construction industry has two arms—infrastructure and real estate—but the two cannot be wholly separated. I focus on real estate (except for chapter 1).

5. For more on techno-aesthetic conditions see Benjamin and Tiedmann, *Arcades Project*, 7, 895, 938–39; and Masco, *Nuclear Borderlands*.

6. Stewart "Atmospheric Attunements," 14.

7. Ephemeral atmospheres are a "form of capital," similar to Ahmed's discussions of emotion ("Affective Economies," 120).

8. Atmosphere's ability to shape the world is central to the work of the industrial ephemeral. Atmospheres, composed of aesthetics and materialities, combine affect and political-economic power. As an architect attuned to aesthetic registers who learned how to manipulate aesthetics to generate emotion, I believe that material and sensory environments—smells, sounds, images and textures, objects, and even human performances—are tangible and manipulable material and aesthetic registers. My interest lies in how humans draw on the agency of these nonhuman entities and elements to do their work (De León, *Land of Open Graves*, 43). Affective atmospheres are an active site of the control and disciplining of Indigenous and non-dominant-caste communities in construction, while also creating space for collective mobilization. Atmospheres are affective and are generated by bodies (Anderson, "Affective Atmospheres," 80). They are "a psychosomatic climate, ... the overall perceptual, sensory, and emotive impression of a space or a situation" (Bressani and Sprecher, "Atmospheres," 2). Atmospheres add sociopolitical dimensions to architecture's atmospherics (Bieber, "Atmospheric Pressures," 32). Atmospheres lend attention to "the peculiar materialities of things" and are "at once abstract and concrete, ephemeral and consequential" (Stewart, "Atmospheric Attunements," 4). Studying atmospheres emphasizes "our long contemporary as a material and existential embroilment in atmospheres" (Choy and Zee, "Condition-Suspension," 212). Atmospheres encompass a study of aesthetics and are understood as the new aesthetics (Böhme, *Aesthetics of Atmospheres*).

9. It is useful to begin with Chen's nonrestrictive definition of affect: "Affect is something not necessarily corporeal. . . . [I]t potentially engages many bodies at once, rather than (only) being contained as an emotion within a single body" (*Animacies*, 11). As Parreñas emphasizes, affect is about interfaces between humans and nonhumans (*Decolonizing Extinction*, 62–79). Affect's relations to political economy—the creation of affective economies (Ahmed, "Affective Economies"); the production of "imaginaries, feelings, futures, and phantasma" as part of the "work of quantification" (Murphy, *Economization of Life*, 7); and their relation to colonial economies and labor (Parreñas, *Decolonizing Extinction*, 62–79)—are relevant in construction. Affect, and by extension atmospheres and new materialisms, are now white imaginaries that elide discussions of race (Chin, *My Life with*

Things, 23), as affect studies erased the contribution of women of color (Garcia-Rojas, "(Un)Disciplined Destinies"). Affect theory is linked to new materialisms due to the shared precognitive space of assemblages of humans-nonhumans (Latour, *Pandora's Hope*). I take seriously the ability of material environments to exhibit their power, issue calls, produce effects, and intervene in social processes (Bennet, *Vibrant Matter*, 4, 5, 9) and am interested in how the combined intensities and agencies of assemblages of humans-nonhumans do political work (Navaro-Yashin, *Make-Believe Space*). I broaden the understanding of nonhumans to include toxins and DNA (Chen, *Animacies*; Tamarkin, *Genetic Afterlives*), untraceable chemicals (Shapiro, "Attuning to the Chemosphere"), and "our own constitution as vital materiality" (Bennet, *Vibrant Matter*, 10).

10. The term *aesthetics* commonly refers to "bundles of indeterminate stimuli" (Adorno, *Aesthetic Theory*, 335) that constitute artworks or a "distribution of the sensible" (Rancière, *Politics of Aesthetics*), where *the sensible* refers to political regimes set up through the circulation of works of art in society. Aesthetics, in a series of combinatory actions, produce subjective human conditions (Guattari, *Chaosmosis*) and are powerful in their ability to evoke human emotion and integrate the senses. Aesthetics are a fundamental part of capitalist political economies (Adorno and Horkheimer, "Culture Industry"; Deleuze and Guattari, *Thousand Plateaus*) and are inherently political (Rancière, *Politics of Aesthetics*) but are often only associated with art. The political economy and politics of aesthetics are integral to construction work, as the aesthetics are atmospheric (Böhme, *Aesthetics of Atmospheres*) and occur in the every day (Dewey, *Art as Experience*). Within the Indian context, Dutta demonstrates how aesthetics emerge through a "cluster of pedagogical theories emanating from Europe's self-described 'Enlightenment' of the eighteenth century" (*Bureaucracy of Beauty*, 4). These enlightenment ideals continue into the present, as Ghertner argues, through the establishment of a "'rule by aesthetics,' a mode of governing space on the basis of codes of appearance" (*Rule by Aesthetics*, 6). Aesthetics in modern India served as forms of domination and governance, but top-down aesthetic ideals can also be adopted by the working classes (Harms, "Beauty as Control," 742); aesthetics as atmospherics and sensations evoke *rasa*. Aesthetics assert power but can also invert and challenge it (Mbembe, "Aesthetics of Vulgarity"), I demonstrate that they do so through the affective and material agencies they encode.

11. Infrastructure conjures powerful images of stability and permanence (Graham, *Disrupted Cities*, 8).

12. *Oxford English Dictionary*, 1989, s.v. "Ephemeral."

13. Mehrotra and Vera consider the ephemeral as a property of informal urbanism in India ("Ephemeral Urbanism"), while Ginsburg describes it as a "rich sensorium of everyday life in Delhi" that builds "fleeting, everyday familial intimacies" ("Chronicles of the Ephemeral," 455, 457). While powerful in their depiction and analysis of social and material practices, these texts serve to cleave

the permanent and durable from that which is dynamic, practiced, and ephemeral, thus inadvertently celebrating the exoticness of and makeshiftness in the Global South. This can be otherizing.

14. The ephemeral constitutes the "affective and phenomenological orientations that are the often unreflected upon form and content of daily life" (McGlotten, "Ordinary Intersections," 50). It can be attributed to ghosts, possessions, and other transcendental experiences. Despite being marginalized, the ephemeral is a powerful, transitory and transformative state (e.g., Turner, *Ritual Process*; Bellamy, *Powerful Ephemeral*) and a vital site for the production of knowledge (Salzburg, *Ephemeral City*) and the construction of publics (Steedly and Spyer, *Images That Move*, 18, 33). The ephemeral aligns with discussions of increased speed (Harvey, *Conditions of Postmodernity*) and mediation (Appadurai, *Modernity at Large*) in contemporary societies.

15. Muñoz, "Ephemera as Evidence," 10 (minoritarian culture and criticism makers); and Siddiqui, "Ephemerality," 24.

16. Steedly, *Hanging without a Rope*, 20.

17. See Raheja, *Poison in the Gift*; Raheja, and Gold, *Listen to the Heron's Words*; Trawick, *Notes on Love*; and Pinto, *Where There Is No Midwife* and *Daughters of Parvati*.

18. See Birla, *Stages of Capital*; and Chari, *Fraternal Capital*.

19. Ilaiah Shepherd, *Why I Am Not a Hindu*, 66.

20. Govindrajan uses the term *relatedness* to index kinship that emerges "through situated regimes of routinized and ardorous labor in capitalist contexts" (*Animal Intimacies*, 63).

21. Yengde, "Being a Dalit."

22. Rawat's identification of occupational stereotyping of Dalits, for example, assuming all Chamars are leather workers (*Reconsidering Untouchability*, 11), reminds readers that while community lineages exist in construction, they are small in number and undergoing change. As Ramberg writes, "Forms of power and possibility can be entangled with stigma in the embodiment of caste-specific labor" (*Given to the Goddess*, 17).

23. Workers describe their condition in relation to terms such as poverty (*gareebi*), necessity (*majboori*), or labor (*mazdoori*). These terms intersect with self-identifications such as Adivasi (Indigenous), *aurat* or *ladeej* (woman), scheduled caste, *musalmaan* (Muslim), and specific caste communities. As Walley argues, class "is a form of inequality that takes on its meaning in relation to other forms of inequality" (Introduction to *Exit Zero*, 8), and seeing "social reproduction . . . solely in terms of class obscures the intersections of class and caste" (Subramanian, *Caste of Merit*, 11). Breman argues that factory organization in India derives from the social institution of caste (*At Work in the Informal Economy*, 218); he quotes Morris's claim that "those who have studied caste have ignored industry, and those who studied industry have ignored caste" (*At*

Work in the Informal Economy, 230). Women have always formed a critical site of Dalit politics (e.g., Ramberg, *Given to the Goddess*, 24; Rao, *Caste Question*, 65); this holds particular poignancy in construction industries where the participation and skilling of women is denied, devalued, and erased, but where gendered regimes of emotions, aesthetics, and affect are critical to power struggles. *The Industrial Ephemeral* depicts the deliberate erasure and eventual absence of nondominant caste workers from the urban areas they construct, a spatial parallel to the erasure of Dalits from history (Rawat, *Reconsidering Untouchability*, 12).

24. Balaskrishnan, *Contesting Shareholder Cities*.

25. Kumar, "Construction of the Ahir Identity," 19.

26. Kasmir and Carbonella discuss an academic division that moved studies of labor, trade unions, and theories of class formation into sociology and other disciplines ("Dispossession and the Anthropology of Labor," 8).

27. Deamer, "Architectural Work," 143.

28. Ilaiah Shepherd argues that Hindu castes (dominant castes) "do not understand the meaning or value of knowledge that emerges from work"; he speaks of two systems of knowledge in India, drawing a distinction between Brahmanical knowledge systems that emphasize reading and writing and the productive knowledges of Dalitbahujan castes (Iliah Shepherd, *Why I Am Not a Hindu*, 63).

29. Thank you to Kevin O'Neill for suggesting this method.

30. Rao, "Proximate Distances."

31. Weinstein, *Durable Slum*.

32. Census of India, "Economic Activity (2001)."

33. Roy, Manish, and Naik. *Migrants in Construction*, 1.

34. World Bank Group, "GDP (Current US$)—India."

35. "Financialization is neither a single process nor an event but an ongoing set of speculative, adaptive and malleable power relations (Goldman and Narayan, "Through the Optics of Finance," 210). Land in India's urban centers and peripheries increased in value after the country's neoliberal economic restructurings. Dispossession occurred in many forms, such as slum redevelopment projects (e.g., Bhan, *In the Public's Interest*; Björkman, *Pipe Politics*; Weinstein, *Durable Slum*), redevelopment of deindustrialized lands (e.g., Finklestein, *Archive of Loss*), and the acquisition of agrarian lands for real estate projects or special economic zones (Levien, *Dispossession without Development*). This was largely uneven and connected to the democratic intent and political power of local governing bodies (Balakrishnan, *Contesting Shareholder Cities*). Searle argues that this was not a natural rise in value; instead, several individuals in real estate worked to turn Indian land into an international commodity (*Landscapes of Accumulation*, 8–9). Real estate was supported by a variety of financial instruments that switched from equity to debt in the second decade of the 2000s (Goldman and Narayan, "Through the Optics of Finance," 221). Mass-based financialization

such as housing mortgages and a "shadow banking sector" aided land financialization (Goldman and Narayan, "Through the Optics of Finance," 212). In the 2000s, real estate developers owned thousands of acres of land reserves in what they called "land banks" (Searle, *Landscapes of Accumulation*, 7). Bhattacharya ("Hoarding Land") describes the longer history of this financialization. See also Goldman "Speculative Urbanism."

36. NASA Earth Observatory, "Urban Growth of New Delhi."

37. The table in the appendix provides this data.

38. Ministry of Commerce & Industry, "Fact Sheet." Roy refers to these as "geobribes" ("Why India Cannot Plan," 79).

39. Oxfam International, "India: Extreme Inequality."

40. Roy, Manish, and Naik, *Migrants in Construction*, 1.

41. Ong ("Gender and Labor Politics) critiques this division, arguing that postmodern industries are characterized by feminization of labor and that patriarchy, domestication, and kinship are central to industrial operations. Nash and Fernández-Kelly (*Women, Men*) share these critiques questioning the gendered division between production and reproduction.

42. I borrow from Wilson, who uses the term *intimate economies* to describe "the interactions between economic systems and social life, particularly gender, sexuality, and ethnicity"; *intimate* here refers to "features of people's daily lives that have come to seem noneconomic, particularly social identities" (Wilson, *Intimate Economies of Bangkok*, 9–11). Further, using Povinelli's (*Empire of Love*) work on the "intimate encounter," I describe intimate workings or intimacy as social features, practices, and aesthetics that shape and form behavior, emotion, and subjectivity in invisible yet very proximate ways. Dave, inspired by Geetha, also believes that feminists must take "the realm of the intimate seriously: as a realm of violence and hurt, and also of radical creative political possibility" (*Queer Activism in India*, 118). I also borrow from Herzfeld, who defines *cultural intimacy* as an understood, unspoken insider sociality (*Cultural Intimacy*, 3).

43. Gendered critiques of political economy and industry focus on women's work or femme labor. Walley, for example, critiques histories of industry and class for devoting disproportionate attention to men ("World of Iron and Steel," 18). She stresses the importance of "nonwork" and "kin work" in the functioning of industries and class ("World of Iron and Steel," 18; "It All Came Tumbling Down," 5). Besky (*Darjeeling Distinction*) emphasizes the role of affect and care in industries, collapsing the division between reproductive and nonreproductive work. The construction industry deploys gendered forms of work—intimacy, kin work, and affect—to enable industrial political economy. Industries and industrialization—long understood as part of the formal, economic workings of a patriarchal state—work through ephemeral, intimate, and affective devices. This problematizes the gender of capitalism not only through the presence and lifestories of women, but by examining femme forms of power.

CHAPTER 1. EPHEMERAL INFRASTRUCTURES

1. DMIC, "Introduction."
2. DMIC, "Introduction."
3. Bear, *Lines of the Nation*, 288. Postindependence infrastructural development focused on dams and big industries: The setting up of steel and cement towns and hydroelectric power projects was a way to build a self-sufficient nation. A critical shift occurred in 1999 with the proposal of the Golden Quadrilateral Project, which expanded highways connecting India's four metropoles. In the late 1990s and early 2000s India increased its emphasis on building roads through funding made available by international organizations such as the International Finance Co-operation and International Bank for Reconstruction and Development. Indian national budgets shifted away from rail development to emphasize road construction. This is not to deny that the railways serve as integral transportation channels, but to point out that roads gained a greater emphasis. India rose to become the fourth-largest consumer of cars in the world (Mukherjee, "India Pips Germany;" Hayakawa, "India Zooms Past Germany") and the world's biggest two-wheeler consumer (Doval, "India Is Now"). Annual economic surveys in the Union Budget of India steadily increased the budget for infrastructural development and construction in the years between 2002 and 2011. The union budget allocations of public funds to infrastructure went from ₹37,919 crore in 2002–3 to ₹2,14,000 in 2011–12 (Ministry of Finance, "Key Features of Budget, 2002–2003" and "Budget Speech, 2011–12"). National highway and expressway projects were funded. In rural India, the Mahatma Gandhi National Rural Employment Guarantee Act (NREGA) launched rural road construction projects. The eleventh five-year plan from 2007 to 2012 placed roadways as a "high priority" (Planning Commission, *Eleventh Five Year Plan*, 290). In accordance, road construction ranked only second to electricity in infrastructural investment (IBEF, "Indian Infrastructural Sector," 4). The culmination of this emphasis was in the voting of the Bharatiya Janta Party into national government in 2014, with Prime Minister Narendra Modi's claim to fame being the roadways he built in Gujarat. His election promise led to the doubling of the road budget in 2015, while the railway budget only increased by one-third. "India's highest ever kilometers of new highways were awarded in 2015" (Union Budget, "Union Budget Highlights,"13), and the 2016–17 budget saw 10,000 kilometers of highways approved, much higher than in any of the previous years (Union Budget, "Union Budget Highlights,"14). It is only in the 2018 budget that the neglect of railways for two decades came to be recognized and emphasized as a developmental agenda. Nevertheless, financial year 2017–18 saw the launch of the BharatMala project that promises to develop 24,800 kilometers of India's road network (National Information Centre, "Bharatmala Pariyojana," 1).
4. Studies of materiality in anthropology emphasize a focus on the material as well as social and symbolic aspects of architecture and infrastructure (Vellinga,

"Review Essay"). "Materials and technologies . . . are not politically neutral" but relate to "different (but related) forms of political subjectivity" (Anand, *Hydraulic City*, 11); see also Arora and Ziipao, "The Roads (Not) Taken" and Harvey and Knox, "Enchantments of Infrastructure." "Urban matter becomes political and urban politics become material" (Pilo' and Jaffe, "Political Materiality of Cities"), I challenge the stability of materiality by exploring its ephemeral dimensions. Anand, *Hydraulic City*, 6 ("a social-material assemblage").

5. See, for example, Coleman, *Moral Technology*; Graham and Marvin, *Splintering Urbanism*; and Harvey and Knox, *Roads*, for studies of infrastructure and state-society relations.

6. Rabinow (*French Modern*), Holston (*Modernist City*), and Scott (*Seeing Like a State*) critique the totalitarianism of modernist architecture and urban planning, while Ingold (*Life of Lines*) and Mitchell (*Colonizing Egypt*) believe that straight roads and grids have disciplinary capacities. In British India roads allowed access to remote areas to subdue territories, while contemporary roads enact new forms of domination such as the militarized control of the Indian Northeast (Ziipao, *Infrastructures of Injustice*).

7. Agrarian areas suffer state neglect and receive attention only during acute distress or through protests (e.g., Vasavi, *Shadow Space*; Aga, "Demonetization and Normalization"; Sethi, "Mahadev's Gift").

8. Most of the skilled laborers on site have studied till the eighth or tenth grade and can read. It is hard to be upwardly mobile in construction if you cannot read drawings.

9. As opposed to Yusef, who was supported by governmental schooling and scholarships, rural India saw the rise of "private" schools, in the years after India's neoliberal economic reforms. Workers in the construction industry indicated that they would rather send their children to private school than have them waste away in public school. This seems to mirror opinions about other state institutions such as health care, indicating broader state mistrust that often unites with a reading of the state as corrupt (Gupta, "Blurred Boundaries").

10. City and country (or urban and rural) are "interrelated social formations" (O'Neill, "Hands of Love," 171), most spaces are "neither rural nor urban, neither wholly inside nor outside, but uncomfortably both" (Harms, *Saigon's Edge*, 3).

11. Chattaraj, "Roadscapes," 46.

12. Chattaraj, "Roadscapes," 46.

13. Some Ahir and Jat communities qualify for affirmative action. This indexes that they are not Dalits but have faced structural inequality. The fact that many of them are landowners in a lucrative land market has given some Ahir and Jats mobility (Kumar, "Construction of the Ahir Identity").

14. Channing, *Land Revenue Settlement*, 31, 84.

15. The gender distribution in construction is different in North India than in South and West India. I was struck by the lack of middle-class women on

construction sites and the overall dissuasion of women of all classes from construction sites in North India.

16. Elyachar, "Phatic Labor"; Simone "People as Infrastructure"; and Sopranzetti, *Owners of the Map*, argue that social relations are infrastructures.

17. Ministry of Law and Justice, "Gazette of India . . . Special Economic Zones Act, 2005";" and Make in India, home page.

18. National Information Centre, "List of Notified SEZ."

19. Donthi, "How Brokers of Land and Power Built."

20. Kumar, "Paupers & Princes of Realty"; and Rao, "Manesar Land Release."

21. The green revolution increased the affluence of Jat farmers as well as their land holdings (Cowan, "Urban Village;" Jodhka, "Agrarian Changes and Attached Labour"), allowing them entry into politics (Bhalla, "Development, Poverty, and Policy," 2620).

22. Balakrishnan (*Contesting Shareholder Cities*) describes the caste complexities around land acquisition and development.

23. See Wahi (*Right to Property*) and Vaidya ("India's Forest Rights Act") for discussions of property legislation and its transitions in India.

24. Agricultural costs increase with the use of fertilizers, high-yield grain varieties, and technological requirements such as bore wells and water pumps. The vagaries of climate change add new difficulties. Expenses and desires in rural India increase; private school and English-language school costs, cancer treatments, weddings of siblings (dowries), and funerary costs cannot be met by agricultural work. Unemployment levels in nearby, small towns hit a new high (Jeffery, *Timepass*). A booming 2000s NCR construction industry welcomed the unemployed, landless, and those who wished to supplement their agricultural income.

25. In 2020–21 large-scale farmers' protests took place against changes in agricultural laws. The new laws deregularized trade in produce; a key concern was the end of the minimum support price (MSP) and the undermining of existing procurement systems that would leave farmers vulnerable to private buyers (Dhaliwal, "Critical Analysis on the Farmer Bills"). Many believe this is another step in the undermining of agriculture and enhacing of farmers' distress, calling it a "death warrant" for small farmers (BBC News, "Bharat Bandh").

26. A growing number of rural households are multilocal or translocal, relying on various circuits of long- and short-term migration (Gidwani and Ramamurthy, "Agrarian Questions," 996).

27. Thakur, "Scientists Wage War on Colonial Kikar."

28. These *jhils* or lakes were formed through the construction of small dams by farmers cultivating the fertile flood plains of the Jamuna (Dewey, *Anglo-Indian Attitudes*, 64–65). This points to a historical relationship of construction and ecology in the area.

29. Business Standard, "Jaypee Infratech Ltd."

30. Sharma and Rai, "Yamuna Expressway."

31. Vidal, "As Flood Waters Rise."

32. Saini, "Haryana Khap Blames Consumption" (lead to rape).

33. "Kinship exogamy" exists in Haryana, which is extended by territorial exogamy (Chowdhry, "Caste Panchayats," 4). "[V]illage exogamy means that all men and women of the same clan, the same localised clan and the same village are bound by the morality of brother-sister and, therefore, that both sex and marriage are prohibited between members of any of these units" (Hershman quoted in Chowdhry, "Caste Panchayats," 5). This village exogamy is practiced in tandem with caste endogamy for marriages; cross caste marriages are also punished. Here women's honor comes to be tied with community honor and is often protected with extreme violence by Khap panchayats (nonelected, caste-based organizations). If anyone judicially challenges caste-based panchayats, they are considered Westernized and urbanized (Chowdhry, "Caste Panchayats," 35).

34. I am unsure of the veracity of the statement, but the beliefs expressed in the statement are under analysis, not the actual event.

35. Changes in gendered behavior as well as social and economic change occur in every generation and can create conflict between them (Raheja and Gold, *Listen to the Heron's Words*).

36. Gurgaon has the highest number of rapes in Haryana but falls below other states in reported numbers (National Crime Records Bureau, "Table 3A.3"). Yet the city is considered a "rape capital." While Gurgaon does have a high percentage of rapes, the focus on Gurgaon and not other cities in other states is part of elite Indians' belief that Gurgaon is a space of uncivilized, patriarchal populations (e.g., Dhingra, "Patriarchy, Popular Culture"). Note that this discussion relies on reported rapes, and rapes of Dalit women are underreported if at all.

37. Haryana is known for its high rate of female feticide (see George and Dahiya, "Female Foeticide"). The state is defensive about supporting the girl child. Affirmative action for women in political positions, teaching, and health care, as well as growing ruro-urban cooperative economies, affect the roles women play within the household.

38. Singh, "Uttarakhand Bans Trishul."

CHAPTER 2. THE FINANCIAL SUBLIME

1. The blackness of black money no doubt has racialized roots, as India's approach to race is influenced by Euro-American history. The term *kala* or black can refer to moral dirt as well as being a derogatory term for Black people: *Kala pani* or black waters references a proscription of ocean crossing, and crossing *kala pani* means losing one's respectability. Black money tends to be mapped on not the bodies of poor but those of the rich and serves as moral judgment of the

rich, among other nuances, as this chapter shows. Several scholars write of the solidarities of African American and Dalit experience, thus adding a caste bias and complexity to the pairing of *kala* and corruption (see, e.g., Pandey, *History of Prejudice*; West and Yengde, "Shared History of Struggle").

2. The state is often discursively constituted through corruption talk (Gupta, "Blurred Boundaries").

3. Hazare was protesting the inadequate framing of a government of India anti-corruption bill—the Lokpal and Lokayutkta Bill—which sought to create a tribunal that would try cases of political corruption. The drafting of the bill generated a Jan Lokpal Bill movement, or a people's Lokpal bill movement (also known as Team Anna), led by Gandhian and social activist Anna Hazare. Team Anna sought critical changes in the bill, including allowing members of Parliament to be tried within these tribunals, providing greater protection for whistleblowers, and giving the Lokpal Committee control over the Central Bureau of Investigation for the cases they oversaw (PRS Legislative Research, "All about the Lokpal Bill"). The protests took place in central New Delhi but filtered into everyday conversation.

4. Times News Network, "Kejriwal Escalates Attack."

5. Ministry of Finance, "White Paper on Black Money."

6. Indian Express, "India 5th Largest Exporter."

7. The Hindu, "Black Economy."

8. Patnaik, "Demonetization."

9. Speculation, as a component of formal finance and banking, is tied to a knowledge economy where increased speculation is often a reaction to the illegibility of economic working (Stout, "Petitioning a Giant") and can create deception (Walsh, "In the Wake of Things"). Speculative markets are not abstract entities but operate through localized individuals, legalities, networks, and spaces while simultaneously negotiating international ones (e.g., Elyachar, "Phatic Labor"; Ho, *Liquidated*; Peterson, *Speculative Markets*; Stout, "Petitioning a Giant").

10. Kant, *Observations on the Feeling*.

11. Nye (*American Technological Sublime*) describes American technological endeavors and the awe they produce as sublime, such as the imagery of nuclear bomb explosions that overtook the US imagination (Masco, *Nuclear Borderlands*, 3).

12. Dunbar-Ortiz, *Indigenous Peoples' History*.

13. De-aesthetization, or in this case revealing the aestheticization of the sublime, critiques the sublime (Manning, "Spiritualist Signal," 70), as does revealing the material and "dirty" processes of the sublime (Anderson, "Excremental Colonialism"). A focus on the material processes of the sublime amplify tensions within the sublime (Shapiro, "Attuning to the Chemosphere," 381).

14. Larkin, *Signal and Noise*, 36, 38.

15. Larkin, *Signal and Noise*, 43.

16. A policeman in a Delhi market collected his *hafta*—a protection fee from shop owners—and stuffed the cash into his back pocket. I met with a liaison officer who paid government officials on behalf of developers, charging the latter a hefty "liaison-ing fee" for the same; he spoke of carrying cash in suitcases. An architect met a new client in a peri-urban area who asked her how much she would charge for a particular task and then proceeded to pull the large sum out in cash from his garland-adorned safe as a down payment. A young engineer boasted about handing ₹500 out of his car window to policemen who stopped him for a breathalyzer test.

17. "Accumulating capital through the built environment has entailed not just constructing buildings, but engaging with finance capital" (Searle, *Landscapes of Accumulation*, 25).

18. Sai Baba is a popular saint in India.

19. Bear describes this restructuring as occurring in three stages. First, through Indira Gandhi's acceptance of an IMF loan in 1981; second, through the creation of a payment crisis due to tax reductions, and third, through a spike in oil prices during the first Gulf War, combined with the collapse of the Soviet Union, India's main trading partner. This led to the IMF loan of "US$1.2 billion in return for the adoption of economic reforms." A whole host of reforms that emphasized private investment followed the 1991 restructurings (Bear, "For Labour," 76).

20. Chandrasekhar and Ghosh, *Market That Failed*, 20 (foreign direct investment); and World Bank Group, "Structural Adjustment in India."

21. Gurgaon Workers News, "List of Companies Situated in Gurgaon."

22. The cost of apartments in a luxury tower escalated from ₹2,800 (US$40) per square foot in 2005 to ₹15,000 (US$210) per square foot in January 2012; a more affordable set of apartments increased from ₹1,800 (US$25) per square foot to ₹8,750 (US$122) per square foot (Donthi, "How Brokers of Land and Power Built").

23. Sahni, "Real Estate Sector, 2."

24. World Income Distribution, "Evolution of Average Income," para. 4.

25. The top 10 percent of India's population had a 56 percent share of its income in 2012. World Income Distribution, "Evolution of Average Income," para. 4.

26. Two banking institutions lead the home mortgage and project finance sector since the liberalization of banking. The Housing and Development Finance Corporation (HFDC), set up in 1977 (Money Control, "Company History"), and ICICI Bank was promoted in June 1994 by ICICI Limited (ICICI Bank, "History"). "The Industrial Credit and Investment Corporation of India Limited (ICICI) [was] incorporated with the objective of creating a "development financial institution for providing medium-term and long-term project financing to Indian businesses" (ICICI Bank, "History"). The bank expanded into home loans as well as construction finance. HDFC provides "long-term housing loans mainly

to low- and middle-income individuals and corporate bodies. It has also provided a modest amount of construction finance to housing developers" (Money Control, "Company History").

27. The middle class in India is different than the middle class in the United States: the upper middle classes constitute an elite majority with disposable income, while the lower middle class is more aligned with populations in the United States with disposable income for consumer goods. Overall the middle class in India expanded from thirty million in the 1990s to between three and six hundred million in 2015 (Roy, "Middle Class in India," 33).

28. Sreenivasan, "Gold's Own Country."

29. See, for example, Seth, "Indian Farmers Shun Volatile Gold."

30. My landlord owned eight apartments across the National Capital Region. The professor I consulted at the local university invested in a small shop in Gurgaon that generated rental income. Gurgaon farmers described selling their land to developers and buying land in Rajasthan a few miles away. An advertisement at a new housing project read: "Investors include . . . [an] endowment fund of a top US University."

31. Singh and Menon, *Whatever the Odds*, 99–101.

32. "The formal and the legal are perhaps better understood as fictions, as moments of fixture in other- wise volatile, ambiguous, and uncertain systems of planning" (Roy, "Why India Cannot Plan," 84). In India "different segments of the workforce are cross-cut by broader social relationships . . . [and] cannot be reduced to a simple dichotomy" (Breman, *At Work in the Informal Economy*, 18). "Drawing a line around the formal and informal, the legal and the illegal," as though they constitute "distinct and bounded sectors[,] is . . . deeply problematic" (Goldstein, *Owners of the Sidewalk*, 21). We must recognize the perpetual slippage and fluidity between the formal and informal (Goldstein, *Owners of the Sidewalk*, 23; Gandalfo, *City at Its Limits*). It is often the formal that regulates and produces the informal (Bhan, *In the Public's Interest*, 21; Roy, "Urban Informality," 149). Formal and informal categorizations are an act of power (Shah, *Street Corner Secrets*, 81).

33. This is an example of the locale of global real estate. As Sassen writes, "global economic activities are not hypermobile and are, indeed deeply embedded in place" (*Global City*, 31).

34. RBI, "Master Circular on Finance."

35. "Dubai money" references mafia-based funding, evoking mafia heads who lived in Dubai, such as Dawood Ibrahim. Ibrahim's rise to power is linked to Mumbai's property boom and the drug trade between India and the Middle East.

36. India's financial lending and credit history involved local firms combining "moneylending, brokerage, wholesale and retail trade, and, later, speculation and industry" (Birla, *Stages of Capital*, 18). They did so through systems such as *hundis* and *chittis* (Birla, *Stages of Capital*, 61). Moneylenders were dominant caste

and Hindu (Birla, *Stages of Capital*; Metcalf, "British and the Moneylender"), much of their power was enabled by the fall of village communities made possible by the British (Metcalf, "British and the Moneylender," 391). Moneylenders played a key role in the development of a real estate economy, as they bought and secured mortgages of tenant rights as well as became leaseholders of periodic marketplaces in the nineteenth and early twentieth centuries in India (Yang, *Bazaar India*, 247). The 1950 Rural Credit Survey found that moneylending accounted for 70 percent of rural credit (Thorner, "All-India Rural Credit Survey," 961). Land financialization and rents from migrant markets promoted the growth of moneylenders to fund real estate purchases on ruro-urban peripheries (Shah, "Crowning of the Moneylender"). In contemporary times moneylenders are well embroiled in credit schemes due to their ability to interlock markets (Shah, "Crowning of the Moneylender") and are especially active due to a rise in farming distress. Qazi ("Inside the World") argues that "farming distress has attracted a new breed of moneylenders. Anyone with some disposable cash—from shopkeepers, government officials, and policemen to village teachers—now lends in the hope of making a killing" (Qazi, "Inside the World").

37. Singh and Menon, *Whatever the Odds*, 118–19.

38. Singh and Menon, *Whatever the Odds*, 119.

39. Singh and Menon, *Whatever the Odds*, 120.

40. Goldman and Narayan, "Through the Optics of Finance," 213.

41. Maruti Suzuki India Limited (formerly Maruti Udyog Ltd.) traces to a 1982 Indo-Japanese collaboration, initiated after the state-owned Maruti Motors Limited company was incorporated in 1971 and then liquidated in 1978 (Bhargava with Seetha, *Maruti Story*).

42. The statement is a popular rumor; it points less to truth and more to public perceptions.

43. Oldenberg (*Gurgaon*, 32–39) describes the Gandhi family's and the Congress Party's role in Gurgaon's development.

44. Oldenberg argues that the urban development boom should be attributed to urban development minister Sanjay Gandhi's initiative to build the Maruti-Suzuki car manufacturing company there and not to DLF (*Gurgaon*, 25).

45. Singh and Menon, *Whatever the Odds*, 182.

46. Singh and Menon give details of Gandhi's support. Searle (*Landscapes of Accumulation*, 217) also writes of facilitations after this meeting. It is rumored that the urban land ceiling policy of Gurgaon changed due to this event, but I could not find a record of the change or amendment until 2011 (Siwach, "Ashok Khemka"). Instead, I share Gururani's ("Flexible Planning") opinion, that creative interpretations of the 1972 act allowed several developers to procure property far beyond the ceiling. Oldenberg also states that a reliable source says this was "wishful exaggeration" and that plans for expansion were well under way (*Gurgaon*, 67, 55).

47. Srivastava, *Entangled Urbanism*, xxviii.

48. This is the same family as Sanjay Gandhi, reemphasizing the role of dynastic politics.

49. See, for example, Kaul "Explained"; Times News Network, "Kejriwal Escalates Attack"; and Searle, *Landscapes of Accumulation*, 217.

50. Brosius writes, "according to architect Fredrick R. Gurgaon will be have to be rebuilt completely in a few years ahead from now, or will become a ghost city. It is already 'drowning' in chaos, mostly due to the fact that Gurgaon consists mainly of privatised land, acquired by private developers such as DLF, one of the largest real estate developers in India. Unlike Noida, says Fredrick, Gurgaon has not been planned for a sustainable future. Instead it was put together haphazardly in a patchwork way, without an overall vision in profit-oriented manner. Investors and developers consciously banked on profits over a very short time span, and promoted the vision of an exhaustive lifestyle for the elite" (*India's Middle Class*, 55).

51. RBI ("Press Note 2") details the exact terms of this investment.

52. RBI, Press Note, September 9, 2016 (cited in RBI, "Foreign Exchange Management").

53. Espinoza, "Chris Hohn and Investor Group."

54. Das and Malhotra, "The Trail."

55. Das and Malhotra, "The Trail."

56. Jost and Sandhu ("The Hawala Alternative," 14, 19) outline these connections in a report to the US Treasury Department. Property is not the only site to launder money in India, but it does have a wider reach as it is more accessible than other industries.

57. The Hans India, "IL&FS Imbroglio."

58. The Hans India, "IL&FS Imbroglio."

59. HT Correspondent, "Panama Papers."

60. Hazare is an anti-corruption activist.

61. Financial and cultural systems or morality and economics are not separate but intertwined (e.g., Fischer, *Cash on the Table*; Maurer, *Mutual Life, Limited*; Zaloom, "Evangelical Finance Ethic").

62. Moore's definition of terrain is useful here: "Terrain conjures the historical sedimentation of discursive and material practices, at once locally grounded and translocally embedded" (*Suffering for Territory*, 23).

63. Circle rates are routinely revised according to district. The difference between circle and market rates varies depending on the revisions and the market; on rare occasions (e.g., in 2015 in Gurgaon) circle rates equal market rates and can also go higher than market rates.

64. Land and natural resource sectors comprised a "toxic mixture of oppressive regulation, regulatory incapacity, and ill-defined rules for allocation" that create space for corruption (Vaishnav, *When Crime Pays*, 58). Levien describes

special economic zones in India as "directly coercive, state orchestrated dispossession" (*Dispossession without Development*, 6). Even seemingly protectionist laws such as the 2013 Land Acquisition Act establish "foundations for a 'compromise'" and enable "the long-term advance of neoliberal restructuring" (Nielsen and Nilson, "Law Struggles," 131).

65. Here we witness what Ferguson (*Anti-politics Machine*) calls "etatization," whereby state representatives act in their own interest rather than that of their office.

66. The kind of inspector is deliberately obscured. The quote and who it is attributed to are also slightly altered to obscure the department and people involved.

67. Some of these opportunities no longer exist due to changes in governance structure and digital governance.

68. DLF established DLF power in 2016 (Bloomberg, "DLF Power & Services Ltd.").

69. First Post Staff, "Ponty Chadha Raids."

70. Gupta (*Red Tape*) and Parry ("'The Crisis of Corruption'") argue that the Indian state is experienced through corruption. Anjaria argues that corruption, along with the discussions, protests, and negotiations that accompany it, might lead to new forms of democratic politics (*Slow Boil*, 133).

71. Appadurai, "Introduction."

72. Nakassis and Searle, "Introduction," 170 ("economic . . . entangled"); and Herzfeld, *Body Impolitic* (multiscalar).

73. Maurer, *Mutual Life*.

74. Ferry, *Not Ours Alone*, 18 ("forms of value appear simultaneously"); and Jauregui, "Provisional Agency in Northern India," 88.

75. Land can bear the *hau* or *mana* of a person and can be both alienable and inalienable (Mauss, *The Gift*; Munn, *Fame of Gawa*; Myers, *Empire of Things*; Weiner, *Inalienable Possessions*). Ancestral property, due to its connections with commemoration and even material remains of ancestors, embeds inalienability (Shipton, *Mortgaging the Ancestors*; Smith, *Urban Furnace*).

76. This refers to Evans-Pritchard and Gillies's (*Witchcraft, Oracles, and Magic*) linking of causality and witchcraft; Steedly's (*Hanging without a Rope*) discussion of possessions as fragmented forms of reckoning with violent pasts; and Ong's (*Spirits of Resistance*) discussion of spirit possession as a critique of industrial capitalism.

77. Ajantha Subramanian voiced this critique of occult economies in a talk at Harvard University on March 9, 2020.

78. The sublime was introduced as a concept by Burke (*philosophical enquiry*) and emerges from Emmanuel Kant's theorizations. Kant attaches the sublime to natural phenomena or mathematical work, where the experiencer grapples with their own morality and reason. Key sites of the sublime are the American

landscape (via the work of the Hudson Valley painters) (Eagleton, *Ideology*), the economy (Amariglio, Childers, and Cullenberg, *Sublime Economy*), and technology such as engineering feats and the nuclear bomb (Nye, *American Technological Sublime*). Zizek (*Sublime Object of Ideology*, 229) emphasizes the dialectical relations of wonder and discomfort present in the sublime. In many ways landscape and architecture in Gurgaon serve as expressions of both the mathematical and natural sublime that encodes both the horror and wonder of fast-paced urban growth. Srinivas makes a similar connection to the sublime through the concept of wonder in the urban development politics of Bangalore and reminds us that sublimity is born out of the experience of difference (*Cow in the Elevator*, 7).

79. Amariglio, Childers, and Cullenberg, *Sublime Economy*, 7.

80. Shapiro's description of how the chemical sublime differs from the Kantian, applies to the financial sublime: in its lack of separation between the sensible-insensible, its ability to corrode the optimism of the Kantian sublime, and in its lack of complete rational control (Shapiro, "Attuning to the Chemosphere," 381).

81. Srinivas writes of the "economy of wonder" that is linked with the demonstration and discourse of plentitude and excess (*Cow in the Elevator*, 103, 107–11).

82. Marx, "Capital"; and Berman, *All That Is Solid Melts*.

CHAPTER 3. DRAWING FANTASIES

1. The plan, its lines, and the spaces they inscribe come lined with rationalized vision and imbued with totalitarian power (as argued in Holston, *Modernist City*; and Rabinow, *French Modern*) but can also descend into a murky political and contested terrain (Hull, *Government of Paper*; Perez, "Urbanism as Warfare"). Plans and drawings produce a representation of space (Lefebvre, *Production of Space*, 38)—the utopic space of planners and dreamers alike—and are aesthetic devices of seduction and control. Plans encode ideology and agency; they form the material means of producing significance (Hull, *Government of Paper*, 27). Plans colonize space and are a "totalizing stage" (de Certeau, *Practice of Everyday Life*, 121). The transmutability of plans reveals a "phantasmagoria," a techno-aesthetics, that serves to deceive and control society (Benjamin and Tiedmann, *Arcades Project*, 7, 895, 938–39; Masco, *Nuclear Borderlands*). A line, and by extension plans and drawings, inscribes movement, affect, observation, and translation into the unity of its slender form (Ingold, *Life of Lines*, 1–10).

2. Drawings in construction enable and produce fantasies. Fantasies can be understood as scripts "that can be dramatized," "take a visual form," and "involve the subjects themselves as key actors" (Gammeltoft, "Silence as a Response," 436). Weiss writes, quoting Appadurai, "Fantasy is now a social practice" ("Thug

Realism," 198); lived worlds "are increasingly constructed through fantasies and fabrications" ("Thug Realism," 96). Fantasies form collectives as they secure the commonalities of groups (Scott, "Fantasy Echo," 288). It is the vital fantasy work done by planning and real estate drawings that I explore in this chapter, arguing that real estate and construction perpetuate fantasies through their drawing processes and that these fantasies enable social reproduction, real estate accumulation, and industrial operations, keeping in mind that fantasies can produce violence (Hansen, *Saffron Wave*). Wilson argues that "phantasy and peristalisis (swallowing) are coeval. That the gut is always minded" (*Gut Feminism*, 22). This is salient in the context of Indian labor politics, as the stomach is considered the reason for labor; feeding the stomach or filling the stomach are used as reasons for work in construction. Fantasy by extension of Wilson's argument is connected to need, necessity, and labor and is therefore the site of labor politics. Irani discusses how design maintains a fantasy of improving the world (*Chasing Innovation*, 19–20); building on Irani I argue that the act of drawing constructs the fantasy of participating in real estate. Akin to Chen's comments on the fantasy of licking lead toys, drawing as fantasy produces both participation in real estate economies as well as a denial of their violence (Chen, *Animacies*, 207).

3. Scholars adopt the emic Hindi word *basti*, a term chosen by *basti* inhabitants versus the label of slum or *jhuggi-jhopdis* applied to them by others (Srivastava, *Entangled Urbanism*, 4–5). The Delhi Urban Environment and Infrastructure Improvement Project lists seven types of unplanned settlements or informal settlements in the city (Center for Policy Research, "Categorisation of Settlement"). Many informal settlements are razed and thus erased from maps (The Missing Basti Project).

4. This is not a comprehensive description, just a gloss for readers unfamiliar with the region. For an in-depth commentary on NCR's spatial history see Vanaik, *Possessing the City*). Datta ("'Mongrel City'"), Menon-Sen and Bhan (*Swept Off the Map*), and Grover (*Marriage, Love, Caste*) write on *bastis*; Brosius (*India's Middle Class*), Srivastava (*Entangled Urbanism*), and Weston (*Animate Planet*) offer contemporary urban narratives.

5. NCRPB, "NCR Constituent Areas."

6. NCRPB, *National Capital Region Growth and Development*, 25–27.

7. Master plans demarcate the boundary of an urban area and allocate functions or land use for all the spaces within this boundary. Master plans can propose new transportation systems, allot space for public utilities and recreation, and delineate housing, commercial, industrial, and governmental land use. In this case the master plan was for transportation infrastructure for the region.

8. This can be understood as cultural intimacy or "the recognition of those aspects of a cultural identity that are considered a source of external embarrassment but that nevertheless provide insiders with their assurance of a common sociality" (Herzfeld, *Cultural Intimacy*, 3).

9. Planning itself is a fantastical act, as it comes with the "territorial impossibility of governance, justice, and development" (Roy, "Why India Cannot Plan," 81). Caldeira (*City of Walls*), Escobar (*Encountering Development*), Low (*Behind the Gates*), Low and Smith (*Politics of Public Space*), and Rabinow (*French Modern*) critique the totalitarian and technocratic vision of planners and development; recent work builds on the work of these authors but addresses greater subtleties of planning processes, including agencies of populations and sensoriums of governmentality (Gandalfo, *City at Its Limits*; Navaro-Yashin, *Make-Believe Space*), ideological dispersion (Hull, *Government of Paper*), securitization (Low and Maguire, *Spaces of Security*), conflict and sectarianism (Bou Akar, *for the War Yet to Come*; Perez, "Urbanism as Warfare"), and corporatization of the planning process itself (Doherty, *Paradoxes of Green*; Kanna, *Dubai*; Menoret, *Joyriding in Riyadh*). Harms argues that citizens can also have some degree of agreement with planning proposals ("Beauty as Control," 738). Here I explore the political economic power that acts of drawing produce through the lens of fantasies.

10. Bhan's insights that we must rethink plans and planning as a site of subaltern politics (*In the Public's Interest*, 85), and Anand's belief "that paper is a critical force of claims making" (*Hydraulic City*, 88) extend to drawing and plans.

11. The appendix depicts the number of and changes in plans related to Gurgaon since 1981. I count seven proper plans for NCR and Gurgaon, but several changes were made in the interim.

12. The 1970s saw electrification drives in Haryana; the electric infrastructure, combined with subsidies for tube wells, led to an increase in the number of tube wells in the region in the 1980s. Year-round farms are a legacy of this drive. Ironically, it is illegal tube wells dug by construction sites and tube wells by residents in Gurgaon that now suck the water table dry.

13. *Patwaris* are local government officials who keep land records in rural areas. They are very powerful in the real estate industry, as official documentation of land holdings in India is messy; *patwaris* often broker land deals.

14. Traditionally, women in North India are incorporated into their husband's family at marriage and are part of the economic unit of the husband's extended family. They join the women of the household in the gendered division of labor. Matriarchs gain authority in the household as they age. The love between husband and wife is considered subordinate to that of the husband for his male kin and mother (Raheja and Gold, *Listen to the Heron's Words*), but women have historically expressed resistance to these norms (Raheja and Gold, *Listen to the Heron's Words*). In contemporary times, resistance can take the form of the separation of nuclear families from extended households.

15. "In order to restrict the expansion of the villages [into agricultural lands]. . . , the prevalent norms since imperial times, defined a *lal dora* [literally a red line] as the boundary of the village. This usually coincided with a *phirni* [a

circulatory road]. Within the *lal dora*, the land was earmarked as either *abadi deh*, i.e. privately owned parcels of land where residential/commercial establishments can be constructed, or as *shamlat deh*, which was collectively owned land for community activities" (Ojha, "Nested Cohabitation").

16. Bhojpuri cinema and song use a juxtaposition of city and village to construct the ideal home space (Hardy, "Constituting a Diffuse Region," 154–55). Images of real estate "shape, and even fire, the imagination of innumerable individuals who have access to those forms of media" (Brosius, *India's Middle Class*, 3; see also Zhang, *In Search of Paradise*). Affective, consuming desires are very much part of the construct of the postliberalization middle class (Irani discussing Mazzarella, *Chasing Innovation*, 71)

17. Court-ordered injunction. This was lifted in 2015, and Gautam flipped the house to buy one closer to town.

18. Sharma, "YearEnder."

19. Developers decorate the boundary walls of properties with computer-generated images of to-be-built properties.

20. Dharia, "Artifacts and Artifices of the Global."

21. In India it is called "Chinese Whispers," which indicates racism toward the Chinese.

22. The planners may have been reluctant to share them, not knowing who I was. The destruction of plans and documents related to urban planning in state offices was fresh in my mind in the field, as an accidental fire burned down the office of the Housing, Urban Development, and Town Planning departments of the Maharashtra state government in Mumbai (Rajput, Malik, and Bhatt, "Mantralya Fire"). Many believed the fire to be a deliberate destruction of records.

23. In his study of Pakistani plans and documents of urban production, Hull speaks of plans as bureaucratic artifacts (*Government of Paper*, 21). Documents and related artifacts such as files, he argues, do shape relations, but also have their own functions and deployments; their circulation allows for a "multiparty interaction" that distributes authorship and agency across several functionaries (*Government of Paper*, 138). Deleuze and Guattari celebrate drawing as "an act of creation" that blazes a trail or "opens a road" (*Thousand Plateaus*, xvi): to draw is to embrace the tactile, the relational, and the incomplete (Sennett, *Craftsman*, 43–44); it is to celebrate the *Life of Lines* (Ingold). Drawing these readings together, I argue that drawings and the fantasies they enable not only are a site of deception and control but also form the construction of new political imaginaries.

24. Within art silences are read as profound moments where the artist refuses interpretations of their art and opens it up to unconscious experience (Sontag, *Styles of Radical Will*, 6). "The 'silence,' of things, images, and words is a prerequisite for their proliferation" (Sontag, *Styles of Radical Will*, 28). Within sociohistorical frameworks, however, silences are seen as a gauge of "how history

works" (Trouillot, *Silencing the Past*) and reveal the gendered translations and commemoration of violence in the everyday (Das, *Life and Words*). "The presences and absences embodied in sources or the archive," Trouillot writes, "are neither neutral or [*sic*] natural. They are created" (*Silencing the Past*, 48). Akin to language and art, drawings in Gurgaon produce gaps that can act as sites of the proliferation of power as well as gaps that mark collective erasures and silences. The micro-ellipses that embed themselves in acts of drawing consolidate alliances, enable accumulation, construct social mobility for some, and distance others from the products of their labor.

CHAPTER 4. THE INDUSTRY OF SOUND

1. Bijsterveld ("Listening to Machines") discusses the health and efficiency effects of early industrial noise in Europe and North America, especially the role of rhythms, music, and noise in these debates.

2. Feld, *Sound and Sentiment*, xxvii. Authors work on sound in spirituality (e.g., Feld, *Sound and Sentiment*; Stoller, "Sound in Songhay"); sound in scientific research (Helmreich, "Gravity's Reverb"); sound as pollution (Peterson, "Atmospheric Sensibilities"); and sound, noise, and rhythm in music or poetry (e.g. Caton, *"Peaks of Yemen"*; Larkin, *Signal and Noise*; Hirschkind, *Ethical Soundscape*).

3. Helmreich "Anthropologist Underwater," 626.

4. Peterson and Shipley's ("Audio Work") discussion of sound becoming meaningful through practices is useful here.

5. Peterson and Shipley "Audio Work," 399 (production of sounds); Stoller, "Sound in Songhay" (forces of sound); and Feld, *Sound and Sentiment* (aesthetic and compositional qualities).

6. I use the term *rationalization* from Weber, Parsons, and Henderson's (*Theory of Social*) comments on bureaucracy, the "subjection of the natural world to the machine transpires in conjunction with the rationalization of the human sensorium and of human social relations" (Fisch, "Introduction," 8). Machines on construction sites create rationalized technological atmospheres of work that are complicated by variant life rhythms. Like Millar (*Reclaiming the Discarded Life*, 92), I am interested in the rhythms of labor and the ways in which the body relates to machines (Finkelstein, *Archive of Loss*, 66).

7. While Komatsu is a brand name of a construction equipment manufacturer, not the actual machine. On site the excavator was referred to as "the Komatsu," as is often done in India; for example, toothpaste is referred to as Colgate.

8. Haryanavi is the name for locals from the state of Haryana. Gurgaon is a city in the state of Haryana.

9. A lakh is 100,000 rupees, a little over US$2,000.

10. This refers to the monthly payments on loans to buy the machine.

11. Tata Steel, "Evolution Story."

12. Rao, "Brief History of the Indian Iron," 4–5.

13. Ministry of Steel, "Development of Indian Steel Sector," 1.

14. Pandey, "Importance of Cement Industry, 30, 36" (decontrolled, delicensed). India has 188 large-scale and more than 365 small-scale cement plants. Cement production in India was expected to increase at a compound annual growth rate (CAGR) of 9.7 percent over the financial years 2007–17 to reach 272 metric tons. Production capacity of cement in India became 444 metric tons (Mekha and Reddy, "Experiences of Cement Industry," 72–73).

15. Pandey, "Importance of Cement Industry, " 36.

16. ACC Limited, "Ready Mix Concrete."

17. IBEF, "Cement Industry in India."

18. Oldenberg, *Gurgaon*, 38.

19. Planning Commission, *Twelfth Five Year Plan (2012–2017)*, 18. The union budget allocations of public funds to infrastructure went from ₹37,919 crore in 2002–3 to ₹2,14,000 in 2011–12 (Ministry of Finance, "Key Features of Budget, 2002–2003" and "Budget Speech, 2011–12").

20. Several people in the construction sector reiterate that road construction technology is responsible for the changing technologies of real estate construction: the cost, volume, and modularity of road construction is optimal for machine-led production. India's emphasis on road building spurred fast-paced real estate construction.

21. Haryana was part of the Indian state of Punjab and came to be a separate state in 1966. The green revolution saw affluent farmers grow less dependent on sharecroppers, allowing farmers to consolidate land parcels and self-cultivate through the use of cropping systems and machines (Jodhka, "Agrarian Changes," 103). These landholdings allowed easy acquisitions for construction. As landowning Jat politicians acquired social and political mobility, they pushed for rural development, including investments out of agriculture into small-scale manufacturing. This led to 100 percent rural electrification and tube-well drives (Bhalla, "Development, Poverty and Policy," 2620). In contemporary times tube wells, and the network of tube-well installers and suppliers, emerged as important facilitators of the construction industry, creating quick and cheap access to nonbrackish water that would cure concrete.

22. ICEMA, "About ICEMA."

23. IBEF, "Construction Equipment."

24. J. C. Bamford Excavators, "Company Overview."

25. Business Standard, "India Will Emerge as Hub."

26. "Revenues increased at a CAGR of 6.6% during FY07–12" and were expected to rise (Fawad and Nath, "Infrastructure & Construction Equipment.")

27. Fawad and Nath, "Infrastructure & Construction Equipment."

28. Harvey, *Conditions of Postmodernity*, 285. Harvey argues that the techniques and economies of contemporary forms of production produce an aesthetics of speed. Speed or a sense of acceleration, he believes, is essential to the postmodern condition. It creates an accelerated rush, a "volatility and ephemerality," that reshapes our "thinking, feeling, and doing" (*Conditions of Postmodernity*, 285). Techniques such as outsourcing create a space-time compression and reduce the time it takes to communicate and move things across distances. This acceleration, Harvey believes, is the key marker and aesthetic of our times. Through speed, the "values and virtues of instantaneity" come to govern our worlds (Harvey, *Conditions of Postmodernity*, 286).

29. Virilio, *Speed and Politics*, 84. Virilio speaks of speed as a core component of militarized, technological warfare. "Speed is no longer just a by-product of capitalist value production but has become a commodity in and of itself" (Stein, "Selling Speed," 105); speed is a condition of politics and a threshold of attention (Zee, "Holding Patterns," 224). The "different pacings of labor accumulation are more significant to global capitalism than time economy or speed" (Bear, "Time as Technique," 488).

30. "Entrepreneurs had to sense, envision, and build intensely, seizing opportunity before its time passed" (Irani, *Chasing Innovation*, 131). The narrative of entrepreneurial elite Indians is linked to a teleology of national development (Amrute, *Encoding Race*, 115–16).

31. He uses the Hindi word *karigar* (craftsman) for worker. Though there is a slippage here, it indicates that the worker possesses a skill but does not necessarily index a craft practice.

32. I align with authors such as Desjarlais (*Shelter Blues*), Merleau-Ponty (*Phenomenology of Perception*), and Sennet (*Craftsman*), who argue that there is no Cartesian dualism between mind and body.

33. This is one of two preferred contracting systems. In item work, a person is given a specific amount of money to finish a piece of work within an agreed upon time (for example, build a 3-foot-by-4-foot wall that is six inches deep with certain material specifications in a week). Workers prefer item work contracts, as they are paid better for the same amount of work, but most are hired under the contracting system known as "day rate." Day rate contracts are affordable for contractors and developers, and most contractors submit costs based on day rates. Supervisors often complain about day rates; they claim workers stretch work out longer in order to extend the number of days they are paid for.

34. Sahil was lucky to escape the widespread mistreatment of migrant workers that took place after the 2008 real estate crash in Dubai.

35. Harvey, *Conditions of Postmodernity*.

36. De Certeau, *Practice of Everyday Life*, 99.

37. Deleuze and Guattari, *Thousand Plateaus*, 312–15. As Fisch argues in his work on trains and commuters, "Managing the gap is the technique of

commuting, eliciting a constant, embodied, and active attention to the network's fluid order"("Introduction," 3). The gap represents an ontological incommensurability between humans and machines: "It is a space in which perspective transpires as a material force that elicits novel organizations of becoming with the machine" (Fisch, "Introduction," 10).

38. See Liep (*Locating Cultural Creativity*) and Moten (*In the Break*) on improvisation and music; Ingold (*Life of Lines*) on improvisation as creativity; Herzfeld (*Cultural Intimacy*) for creative modeling of semiotic structures or "social poetics"; and Lavie, Narayan, and Rosaldo (Introduction to *Creativity/ Anthropology*) for discussions on process, creativity, and anthropology. See *jugaad* in chapter 5.

39. Construction companies often refer to the "labor problem"; that is, labor is considered the Achilles' heel of the construction industry. Employers rely on the availability of a cheap labor bank but also fear labor protests and dread managing populations. Technology is celebrated because it reduces the dependency on labor.

40. Activists and NGOs monitoring human rights abuses warned of the dangers of having children on construction sites. The government of India in 1996 passed regulations for crèches (day-care centers) on worksites, further amended in 2017 under the Maternity Benefit Act (Ministry of Law and Justice, "Gazette of India . . . Maternity Benefit (Amendment) Act, 2017," 2), but not everyone provides them.

41. In speaking of road infrastructure, Menoret (*Joyriding in Riyadh*) and Chattaraj ("Roadscapes") critique theories of speed and argue that different geographies have differential speeds or conditions of development.

42. Sharma, "Slowdown in Real Estate."

43. Different time and tempos among societies enact and produce inequality. Examples include bodily time zones (Solomon, *Metabolic Living*, 232), water time (Anand, *Hydraulic City*, 99), ritual time, memory (Das, *Life and Words*), tempos of work (Herzfeld, "Rhythm, Tempo"), and even a crisis of temporality (Finkelstein, *Archive of Loss*, 13). Here I argue that the interaction of several temporal rhythms with the rationalization of mechanical sound is a disjunctive and violent experience for many in the industry, as mechanical rhythms do not recognize and incorporate life rhythms. "The circulation of capital will repeatedly emerge as an ethical, affective problem of attempting to reconcile diverse, recalcitrant rhythms and representations" (Bear, "For Labour," 86). "At the centre of this discussion of capitalist time will be a theoretical emphasis on the act of labour as a mediation of conflicting rhythms, representations, and technologies of time" (Bear, "For Labour," 72).

44. The JanLokpal bill, proposed to change the Lokpal Bill; see chapter 2 for an explanation.

45. Within spirit-calling traditions noise is understood as chaos or substance from which patterns must be read (Santo, "Fluid Divination," 51), noise can

be "illegitimate" like the impure sound of "parasitic" non-humans (Manning, "Spiritualist Signal," 88), noise can appear as mutations or distortions (Masco, "Mutant Ecologies," 522), or form the sticky static of busy hums of the universe (Helmreich, "Gravity's Reverb," 482). Noise in urban India is also tied to class markers (Kaviraj, "Filth and the Public Sphere," 110).

46. Hainge, *Noise Matters* (oppositional cultural form); and Kunreuther, "Sounds of Democracy," 21 (civil democratic processes). Noise indexes the failure of the state (Larkin, *Signal and Noise*, 239); it has political connotations (Khan, "Acoustics of Muslim Striving," 581).

47. Kunreuther, quoting Novak ("Sounds of Democracy," 19).

48. Barbara Browning's *Infectious Rhythms* makes associations between social discontents and rhythms in her study of the AIDS pandemic and African diasporic cultural practices (7).

CHAPTER 5. INSIDE THE PIT

1. "Atmospheres are generated by bodies" (Anderson, "Affective Atmospheres," 80) and are understood as "the overall perceptual, sensory, and emotive impression of a space or a situation" (Bressani and Sprecher, "Atmospheres," 2). They "are at once abstract and concrete, ephemeral and consequential, fully sensory and lodged in prolific imaginaries" (Stewart, "Atmospheric Attunements," 4). Specific atmospheres on construction sites encode inequity and bear the potential to create collective subjectivities.

2. Garcia-Rojas argues that women of color feminists produce a "language of self" that enables a deidentification from and subversion of the dominance of a universal whiteness in affect studies ("(Un)disciplined Destinies," 2). Garcia-Rojas critiques affect studies for creating epistemic practices that erase historically marginalized women of color ("(Un)disciplined Destinies," 5). Affect and by extension atmospheres are often white imaginaries and encode an implicit whiteness (Chin, *My Life with Things*, 23). Here I demonstrate how affect and by extension atmospheres are systems of domination, and how workers create their own reorientations (Garica-Rojas quoting Ahmed, "(Un)disciplined Destinies," 8–9).

3. I agree with Böhme (*Aesthetics of Atmospheres*), who argues that atmospheres are the new aesthetics.

4. See Gill (*Of Poverty and Plastic*) for task-based discussions of the concept.

5. Elyachar ("Phatic Labor") and Simone ("People as Infrastructure") read these as infrastructures.

6. *Pehchaan* among workers also relies on what Asef Bayat calls the "passive network," a "tacit recognition of ... common identity" when occupying a public space ("From 'Dangerous Classes,'" 552). Physical proximity in Indian settlements can bring together a mix of castes, religions, and ethnicities (Datta,

"'Mongrel City,'" 746). It can foster politics as everyday practice (Chance, *Living Politics*).

7. Gupta, *Postcolonial Developments*, 141.

8. Pandey (*Bonded Histories*) and Singh (*Poverty and the Quest for Life*) discuss *mazdoori* as colonial and agrarian labor respectively.

9. Raheja, *Poison in the Gift*, 210.

10. Singh, *Poverty and the Quest for Life*, 121.

11. Within the Indian context this does not necessarily indicate same-sex relationships. It is common for heterosexual, cisgender men to hold hands or lean on each other in affection.

12. Marx, "Working Day."

13. Weber, *Protestant Ethic*, 123–24.

14. According to the Child Labor (Prohibition and Regulation) Act of 1986, employing children between ages fourteen and eighteen in nonhazardous work is legal, as is employing children of any age in a family related business; this is why sons are brought to sites. Children between fourteen and eighteen are required to have more frequent work breaks, shorter hours, and no overtime. They are also required to be kept away from hazardous materials such as timber handling and cement. (Ministry of Labour and Employment, "Child Labour").

15. While several speak of *majboori*, there are also those such as Nazeem who say they came to see the city.

16. Farmer, "An Anthropology of Structural Violence," 307, building on Farmer, *Pathologies of Power*; Gilligan, *Violence*; and Galtung, "Violence, Peace, and Peace Research."

17. Murthy and Sheshu, "Feminist and the Sex Worker," 39 (economic pressure; quoting Shabana Kazi of VAMP); and Shah, *Street Corner Secrets*, 125 (exercising force).

18. Majumdar, *Transnational Commercial Surrogacy*, 22–23. See Pande (*Wombs in Labor*) for a discussion on sex work and *majboori* as agency. Commercial surrogacy is paying a woman to carry your child, made possible by in vitro fertilization. This has emerged as an industry in India, as it costs less than in the United States and is permitted by law. It is accompanied by debates about exploitation of poor women.

19. Agrawal, *Jugaad Urbanism*.

20. Radjou, Prabu, and Ahuja, *Jugaad Innovation*; Ashoka, "Jugaad"; and Schomer, "Getting to Mars through 'Jugaad.'"

21. Jauregui, "Provisional Agency in India," 82 ("provisional agency"); and Jeffery and Young, "Jugad" ("shrewd improvisations").

22. Rai, *Jugaad Time*, 30 ("premodern; law of precarity"); and Irani, *Chasing Innovation*, 183 ("evidence . . . free will").

23. *Jugaad* has some elements of "hustling." Labor is hustling." Hustling has a "dual morality, defining both life's possibilities and its constraints" (Shipley,

Living the Hiplife, 221). Largely emerging from African American communities across the United States and the Caribbean, the term *hustle* is often seen as a social-structural attribute of poverty or "project living." In this context, hustling is not only a form of survival and identity construction; it also frames the way in which practices and people are read (Venkatesh, "'Doin' the Hustle,'" 93 and 106–7); for example, life is seen as an endless hustle.

24. "The social production of *wealth* is systematically accompanied by the social production of *risks*" (Beck, *Risk Society*, 19). In construction "risk becomes 'distributed' and 'individualized' across the population" as workers "are forced to incorporate practices of risk management into their own daily decision-making processes" (Fisch, "Ninety Seconds," 6). Risk is increasingly mediated by turning the life of poor people into financial collateral (Kar, *Financializing Poverty*, 167–98). I argue elsewhere that physical and economic risk is the dangerous excess of real estate speculation, managed by the life and labor of the working classes (Dharia, "Embodied Urbanisms"),

25. For Solomon tension or *tenshun* creates interfaces between body and environment (*Metabolic Living*, 49). Managing tension has a gendered dimension according to Ring (*Zenana*, 60–102), who describes women mitigating tensions between ethnic communities sharing domestic space in Pakistan.

26. Prasad, "Case Study," 135–36.

27. Prasad, "Case Study," 136.

28. Prasad, "Case Study," 136.

29. Prasad quoting Nakanishi, "Case Study," 138 ("new militant workforce"); and Maruti Suzuki Workers Union, "An Appeal to Workers" ("severest repression").

30. "The Gurgaon-Manesar belt of Haryana is often referred to as [a] notorious belt because of the number of recurring . . . labor disputes during the last five years. Though there are no concrete figures on the estimated losses due to the unrest, it is believed that they are to the tune of Rs 800–1000 crore, the biggest brunt being borne by Maruti Suzuki India Ltd. and Honda Motorcycle and Scooter India (HMSI)" (All India Organisation of Employers, *Industrial Unrest*, 4).

31. IBEF, "About Haryana."

32. While Haryana falls far behind the manufacturing levels of big states such as Maharashtra, Andhra Pradesh, and Tamil Nadu, it maintains a strong position with respect to states of its own size. RBI, "Table 26"; Prasad, "Case Study," 139.

33. Firms with up to three hundred workers can now retrench workers without permission from the government, as opposed to the earlier limit of one hundred workers (Haryana Government, "Industrial Disputes Act," 69–70; Upadhyaya and Kumar, *Amendments in Labour Laws*, 8). See also Haryana Government, *Haryana Government Gazette*).

34. Ray, "Modi Government Is Working."

35. Ministry of External Affairs, "India in Business."

36. "While a legal framework for the deployment of contract labor has been in existence since the early 1970s, the staffing model only started booming in the early 2000s . . . , a decision by the Indian Supreme Court in 2001 (Steel Authority of India Ltd. v. National Union Water Front Workers), which clarified that employers were not required to automatically absorb their contract workers into regular employment if forced to abolish their reliance on such contract work, played an important role in explaining the explosion of contract labor in India, particularly . . . the intensive margin" (Bertrand, Hsieh, and Tsivanidis, "Contract Labor and Firm Growth," 1). By 2013 contract workers comprised 50 percent of the workforce for 30 percent of large firms (with more than one hundred employees) as compared to 10 percent in the 1990s. While the preceding data focuses on manufacturing, this was likely exacerbated among construction firms, as construction has a longer legacy of temporary labor (Bertrand, Hsieh, and Tsivanidis, "Contract Labor and Firm Growth," 1–2).

37. Mitra, "Indian Labor Regulations." In addition, restrictions on layoffs for firms with over one hundred employees by the Industrial Development Act of 1947 and its subsequent amendments of 1976 and 1982 kept salaries competitive among permanent employees (Bertrand, Hsieh, and Tsivanidis, "Contract Labor and Firm Growth," 2–3). According to a report in 2012 by the international labor organization, "the informal percentage of employment in non-agricultural employment is 83.6%" (Mitra, "Indian Labor Regulations").

38. The hiring of interstate contract workers is a long-established practice in construction. The bulk of construction workers are migrant workers from rural areas; their number expands seasonally in relation to agricultural patterns. National- and state-level regulation for interstate migrant workers emerged in 1979, amid concerns over the high percentages of contract hires and abuses in the construction industry. The Interstate Labour Act of 1979 outlines these unethical hiring patterns, many of which continue in contemporary times: "In Orissa and in some other States the system of employment of Inter-State migrant labour known as Dadan Labour is in vogue. In Orissa Dadan Labour is recruited from various parts of the State through contractors or agents called *Sardars* or *Khatadars* for work outside the State in large construction projects. At the time of recruitment Sardars or Khatadars promise that wages calculated in piece-rate basis would be settled every month but usually this promise is never kept. Once the worker comes under the clutches of the contractor, he takes him to a far-off place on payment of railway fare only. No working hours are fixed for these workers and they have to work on all the days in a week under extremely bad working conditions. The provisions of the various labour laws are not being observed in their case and they are subjected to various mal practices" (Government of India, "The Inter-State Migrant Workmen,"3).

39. Benefits for interstate employees in Haryana remained frozen according to 1970 stipulations. Out-of-state workers are required to have housing,

emergency medical facilities, and travel fare (Government of India, "Contract Labour"). More often than not laborers do not know their rights, and employees play with the boundaries of what constitutes good housing, medical aid, and travel fare: housing workers in badly made homes turned ovens in high temperatures, providing doctors who do not even look up at the patients they treat, and moving people like cattle in general train compartments (all of which occurred on the site I spent time on). The 2021 amendment is criticized as being altered for the worse (Reddy, "New Labour Codes").

40. The Haryana Government passed a new law in 2022 requiring local companies to hire local workers for all jobs below INR 50000 a year, in all likelihood responding to the pressure of joblessness among their constituents. Business leaders criticized this as the downfall of Haryana.

41. Haryana labor contract laws state that the principal employer is liable to provide welfare and other amenities for contract labor, if the contractor fails to provide the same, and can recover the expenses involved from the contractor (Government of India, "Contract Labour," 8).

42. Zee Media Bureau, "India Remembers"; and Singh and Dutt, "Full Text of Statement."

CHAPTER 6. CONCRETE LOVE

1. See Orsini (*Love in South Asia*) for a discussion of love terminologies and etymologies in South Asia. In particular, Gold's discussion of *prem* shares *pyaar's* linguistic origin, and they are substituted for each other in the introduction (*Love in South Asia*, 36). While *pyaar* is a Hindi word, it is recognized in the many languages spoken on site, and most workers also have a working knowledge of Hindi. Much of love language is adopted from both Hindi and regional cinemas, such as Bhojpuri (linguistic community of a bulk of workers). As Hardy describes, regional cinema such as Bhojpuri produces its own "cinematic language" that is widely comprehensible across North India but different from standard Hindi ("Constititing a Diffuse Region," 151). *Pyaar* is commonly used in Bhojpuri films.

2. Love and family tie to social reproduction. Social reproduction is "a set of structured practices that unfold in dialectical relation with production, with which it is mutually constitutive and in tension" (Gidwani and Ramamurthy quoting Katz, "Agrarian Questions," 1000). By analyzing love in the production of architecture I foreground the role of love in production and production's entanglement with social reproduction. Thank you to Sarah Besky for asking me to make this stance clearer.

3. This is not to imply that rural or small-town life is oppressive for women, but that women expressed feeling freer of domestic work and social conformities

on site. Discussion of gendered life in rural India can be found in Raheja and Gold (*Listen to the Heron's Words*), Trawick (*Notes on Love*), and Wadley (*Struggling with Destiny*).

4. McGowan, *Capitalism and Desire*.

5. Deleuze and Guattari, *Anti-Oedipus*.

6. Colomina ("Split Wall") demonstrates how architecture frames sexuality: Modern architecture with its multiple frames and prescribed sightlines propagates the male gaze and sexualizes women.

7. "Soliciting clients for sexual commerce and soliciting contractors for construction work are . . . neither fundamentally distinct nor . . . essentially the same" (Shah, *Street Corner Secrets*, 76); see Vijayakumar ("Sexual Laborers") and Parry ("Sex, Bricks," 1271).

8. Goodman, "Construction Industry Cited."

9. Gender and sexual relations are not universal in India; a diversity of sexual practices and relations exist (Singh, *Poverty and the Quest for Life*, 141–45). See also Manyanath, "Shameless Marriage."

10. Weber, *Le Corbusier*, 617.

11. See Mary Woods (*Women Architects in India*) for discussion of women architects in India.

12. Ramberg (*Given to the Goddess*) calls for a focus on value over agency in her study of kinship, sex, and property among Dalit devdasis in Tamil Nadu.

13. Kareem Khubchandani, "Snakes on the Dance Floor."

14. Orsini, *Love in South Asia*. "Homo-love and the people who make it have always existed in India" (Dave, *Queer Activism in India*, 18).

15. Marriage and political-economic alliances are common in Indian upper-class worlds, a legacy not only relevant to kings and queens but also to community-centric traders. You hire your own kin to do work to create stable and reliable working groups. Marriage between trading families builds corporations through kinship (e.g., Birla, *Stages of Capital*; Chari, *Fraternal Capital*).

16. Jain describes the *bazaar* as "forming a crucial interface with the colonial administration," managing both foreign trade and peasants and artisans (*Gods in the Bazaar*, 79). Birla argues that "the legal histories opened by inside/outside status of indigenous capitalists . . . evince a defining feature of Indian modernity . . . the staging of difference between public and private as a distinction between economy and culture" (*Stages of Capital*, 3). The political economy of *pyaar* dissolves the fallacy of this modernity and accompanying distinction of economy and culture.

17. Indian states through their judicial procedures have recognized many different forms of conjugality in different communities and geographies. State laws recognize broader notions of conjugality (Solanki, "Registering Marriage," 244).

18. The city of Mumbai is often referred to as Bombay. The choice in nomenclature has political connotations that differ across generations.

19. Amitabh Bachchan is a popular Bollywood actor.

20. Diwali is the Hindu festival of light.

21. I was also afraid to cross these taboos as an Indian woman, lest I be identified as promiscuous and invite inappropriate conduct (several men did make inappropriate comments or offers). It was a form of cultural norm-keeping as well as safeguarding myself; inevitably this was violent to my own identity.

22. Brosius argues that "the range of economic liberalization, circulated and shaped by the media, by transnational groups and globalized concepts, make sure that notions such as 'world city' or 'world-class' reach more than 15 percent of the Indian population who may fall into the category of 'middle class' in India" (*India's Middle Class*, 3).

23. For example, Engels ("Origin of the Family"), Rubin ("Traffic in Women"), and Massey (*Space, Place, and Gender*) examine links between patriarchy, property, and labor.

24. Anna Tsing argues that the control of women, racial discrimination, the domestication of animals and crops, and the enclosure of the commons are linked to a shared history of capitalist relations ("Unruly Edges").

25. Stout, *Dispossessed*, 79–80.

26. Wilson, *Intimate Economies of Bangkok*, 124.

27. Povinelli, *Empire of Love*, 190–91.

28. Stout, *After Love*, 3; see also Carrier-Moisan ("'I Have to Feel Something'"), who argues that money and intimacy intersect.

29. The sites my mother supervised were small projects and did not have many children at them. Construction work in Mumbai was far more visible than it is now, and there were children on the sites.

30. The Building and Other Construction Workers Act of 1996 requires crèches to be constructed by employers who employ more than fifty employees. The number of women was reduced as the industry formalized and women were replaced by machines (Ministry of Law and Justice, "The Gazette of India, . . . Maternity Benefit").

31. Affective labor is often understood as material or immaterial labor involving "'labor in the bodily mode'" (Hardt quoting Smith, "Affective Labor," 96). Parreñas (*Decolonizing Extinction*, 208) criticizes Hardt for a limited understanding of affective labor and defines it as a "surge of sensation" (208n25). According to Hardt, "affective labor produces . . . biopower" (Hardt, "Affective Labor," 98); along with Negri he sees affect as a form of value or value-affect: "Labor finds it value in affect" (Negri and Hardt, "Value and Affect," 79). Affect can be a potential tool of liberation: "On the basis of affect the enemy must be destroyed" (Negri and Hardt, "Value and Affect," 88). Affect drives a global economy (Hardt, "Affective Labor," 98). Laborers and their labor are not divisible from the environment; affinity and affect are cultivated (building on Besky, *Darjeeling Distinction*, 86).

32. Dave, Govindrajan, and Sethi discuss human-animal intimacies in the South Asian context. Dave examines the "sensorium of political engagement between human and animals" ("Witness," 434), while Govindrajan explores how "knots of connection produce a sense of relatedness between humans and non human animals" (*Animal Intimacies*, 5). The connection between human-animals can serve as "heightened arenas of social praxis and representation" (Sethi, "Mahadev's Gift," 1191).

33. Pinto describes "intimacy and kinship as malleable" (*Daughters of Parvati*, 28).

CONCLUSION: INQUILAB ZINDABAD (LONG LIVE REVOLUTION)

1. Habib, *Inquilab*.
2. Ashraf, "Revisiting Bhagat Singh's Slogan."
3. Habib, *Inquilab*.

Bibliography

ACC Limited. "Ready Mix Concrete." Accessed September 5, 2016. www.acc limited.com/products/ready_mixed_concrete.

Adarkar, Neera, ed. *The Chawls of Mumbai: Galleries of Life*. Gurgaon, HR: ImprintOne, 2012.

Adorno, T., and M. Horkheimer. "The Culture Industry: Enlightenment as Mass Deception." In *Dialectics of Enlightenment*, edited by T. Adorno and M. Horkheimer, translated by John Cumming. New York: Herder and Herder, 1989. First published 1944.

Adorno, Theodor. *Aesthetic Theory*. New York: Continuum, 1997.

Aga, Aniket Pankaj. "Demonetization and the Normalization of Agrarian Distress." Hot Spots, Fieldsights. September 27, 2017. https://culanth.org /fieldsights/demonetization-and-the-normalization-of-agrarian-distress.

Agrawal, Kanu. *Jugaad Urbanism: Resourceful Strategies for Indian Cities*. New York: Center for Architecture, 2011.

Ahmed, Sara. "Affective Economies." *Social Text* 22, no. 2(2004): 117–39. https:// doi.org/10.1215/01642472-22-2_79-117.

All India Organisation of Employers. *Industrial Unrest: Past Trend & Lessons for Future*. New Delhi: All India Organisation of Employers (AIOE), n.d. http://aioe.in/html/Industrialunrest.pdf.

Amariglio, J., J. Childers, and S. Cullenberg. *Sublime Economy: On the Intersection of Art and Economics*. London: Routledge, 2009.

Amrute, Sareeta Bipin. *Encoding Race, Encoding Class: Indian IT Workers in Berlin*. Durham, NC: Duke University Press, 2016.

Anand, Nikhil. *Hydraulic City: Water and the Infrastructures of Citizenship in Mumbai*. Durham, NC: Duke University Press, 2017.

Anderson, Ben. "Affective Atmospheres." *Emotion, Space and Society* 2. no. 2009): 77–81.

Anderson, Warwick. "Excremental Colonialism: Public Health and the Poetics of Pollution." *Critical Inquiry* 21, no. 3 (April 1995): 640–69. https://doi.org/10.1086/448767.

Anjaria, Jonathan Shapiro. *The Slow Boil: Street Food, Rights and Public Space in Mumbai*. Palo Alto, CA: Stanford University Press, 2016.

Appadurai, Arjun. "Introduction: Commodities and the Politics of Value." In *The Social Life of Things: Commodities in a Cultural Perspective*, edited by Arjun Appadurai. Cambridge: Cambridge University Press, 1986.

———. *Modernity at Large: Cultural Dimensions of Globalization*. Minneapolis: University of Minnesota Press, 1996.

Arora, Vibha, and Raile Rocky Ziipao. "The Roads (Not) Taken: The Materiality, Poetics and Politics of Infrastructure in Manipur, India." *Journal of South Asian Development* 15, no. 1 (2020): 34–61. doi:10.1177/0973174119896470.

Ashoka. "Jugaad: The art of converting adversity into Opportunity." *Forbes Magazine*. March 23, 2014. www.forbes.com/sites/ashoka/2014/03/23/jugaad-the-art-of-converting-adversity-into-opportunity/?sh=708cb6843844.

Ashraf, Asif Arslan. "Revisiting Bhagat Singh's Slogan 'Inquilab Zindabad.'" Video interview with Fabeha Syed. The Quint, Facebook. Accessed June 15, 2021. https://nb-no.facebook.com/quintillion/videos/podcast-revisiting-bhagat-singhs-slogan-inquilab-zindabad/226388044908431/.

Balakrishnan, Sai. *Contesting Shareholder Cities: Agrarian to Urban Land Transformations in Globalizing India*. Philadelphia: University of Pennsylvania Press, 2019.

Baviskar, Amita. "City Limits: Looking for Environment and Justice in the Urban Context." In *Rethinking Environmentalism: Linking Justice, Sustainability, and Diversity*, edited by Sharachchandra Lele et al. Cambridge, MA: MIT Press, 2018.

Bayat, A. "From 'Dangerous Classes' to 'Quiet Rebels': The Politics of the Urban Subaltern in the Global South." *International Sociology* 15, no. 3 (2000): 533–57.

BBC News. "Bharat Bandh: India Farmers Strike to Press for Repeal of Laws." September 27, 2021. www.bbc.com/news/world-asia-india-54233080.

Bear, Laura. "For Labour: Ajeet's Accident and the Ethics of Technological Fixes in Time." *Journal of the Royal Anthropological Institute* 20 (2014): 71–88. https://doi.org/10.1111/1467-9655.12094.

———. *Lines of the Nation: Indian Railway Workers, Bureaucracy, and the Intimate Historical Self*. New York: Columbia University Press, 2007.

———. "Time as Technique." *Annual Review of Anthropology* 45, no. 1 (2016): 487–502. https://doi.org/10.1146/annurev-anthro-102313-030159.

Beck, Ulrich. *Risk Society: Towards a New Modernity*. Translated by Mark Ritter. London: Sage Publications, 1992.

Bellamy, Carla. *The Powerful Ephemeral: Everyday Healing in an Ambiguously Islamic Place*. Berkeley: University of California Press, 2011.

Benjamin, Solomon. "Occupancy Urbanism: Radicalizing Politics and Economy beyond Policy and Programs." *International Journal of Urban and Regional Research* 32, no. 3 (2009): 719–29.

Benjamin, Walter, and Rolf Tiedmann. *The Arcades Project*. Translated by H. Eiland and K. McLaughin. Cambridge, MA: Harvard University Press, 1999. First published 1972.

Bennet, Jane. *Vibrant Matter: A Political Ecology of Things*. Durham, NC: Duke University Press, 2010.

Berman, Marshall. *All That Is Solid Melts into Air: The Experience of Modernity*. New York: Penguin Books, 1982.

Bertrand, Marianne, Chang-Tai Hsieh, and Nick Tsivanidis. "Contract Labor and Firm Growth in India." Semantic Scholar. August 16, 2021. www .semanticscholar.org/paper/Contract-Labor-and-Firm-Growth-in-India -Bertrand-Hsieh/7c29d9137c28f14439fd4845247b0e359d384f5b.

Besky, Sarah. *The Darjeeling Distinction: Labor and Justice on Fair-Trade Tea Plantations in India*. Berkeley: University of California Press, 2014.

Bhalla, Sheila. "Development, Poverty and Policy: The Haryana Experience." *Economic and Political Weekly* 30, nos. 41/42 (1995): 2619–34.

Bhan, Gautam. *In the Public's Interest: Evictions, Citizenship and Inequality in Contemporary Delhi*. New Delhi: Orient Blackswan, 2016.

Bhargava, R., C., with Seetha. *The Maruti Story*. Delhi: OBI Publishers, 2011.

Bhattacharya, Debjani. "Hoarding Land: Interwar Housing Speculation and Rent Profiteering in Colonial Calcutta." *Comparative Studies of South Asia, Africa and the Middle East* 36, no. 3 (2016): 465–82.

Bieber, Susanneh. "Atmospheric Pressures." *Journal of Architectural Education* 73, no. 1 (2019): 32–45. https://doi.org/10.1080/10464883.2019.1560796.

Bijsterveld, Karin. "Listening to Machines: Industrial Noise, Hearing Loss and the Cultural Meaning of Sound." *Interdisciplinary Science Reviews* 31, no. 4 (2006): 323–37. https://doi.org/10.1179/030801806X103370.

Birla, Ritu. *Stages of Capital: Law, Culture and Market Governance in Late Colonial India*. Durham, NC: Duke University Press, 2009.

Björkman, Lisa. *Pipe Politics, Contested Waters: Embedded Infrastructures of Millennial Mumbai*. Durham, NC: Duke University Press, 2015.

Bloomberg. "DLF Power & Services Ltd." Accessed March 10, 2020. www .bloomberg.com/profile/company/1639316D:IN.

Böhme, Gernot. *The Aesthetics of Atmospheres: Ambience, Atmospheres and Sensory Experiences of Space*. Edited by Jean-Paul Thibaud. London: Routledge, 2017.

Bou Akar, Hiba. *For the War Yet to Come: Planning Beirut's Frontiers*. Stanford, CA: Stanford University Press, 2018.

Breman, Jan. *At Work in the Informal Economy of India: A Perspective from the Bottom Up*. New Delhi: Oxford University Press, 2013.

Bressani, Martin, and Aaron Sprecher. "Atmospheres." *Journal of Architectural Education* 73, no. 1 (2019): 2–4. https://doi.org/10.1080/10464883.2019.1560792.

Brosius, Christiane. *India's Middle Class: New Forms of Urban Leisure, Consumption and Prosperity*. New Delhi: Routledge, 2010.

Browning, Barbara. *Infectious Rhythms: Metaphors of Contagion and the Spread of African Culture*. New York: Routledge, 1998.

Burke, Edmund. *A Philosophical Enquiry into the Origin of Our Ideas of the Sublime and Beautiful*. London: Penguin Books, 1998. First published 1767.

Business Standard. "India Will Emerge as Hub for Construction Equipment: CII." Last updated November 19, 2013. www.business-standard.com/article /companies/india- will-emerge-as-hub-for-construction-equipment-cii -113111901171_1.html.

———. "Jaypee Infratech Ltd." Accessed September 20, 2021. www.business -standard.com/company/jaypee-infratech-34663/information/company -history.

Caldeira, Theresa. *City of Walls: Crime, Segregation, and Citizenship in São Paulo*. Berkeley: University of California Press, 2000.

Carrier-Moisan, Marie-Eve. "'I Have to Feel Something': Gringo Love in the Sexual Economy of Tourism in Natal, Brazil." *Journal of Latin American and Caribbean Anthropology* 23, no. 1 (2018): 131–51. https://doi.org/10.1111 /jlca.12243.

Caton, Steven. *"Peaks of Yemen I Summon": Poetry as Cultural Practice in a North Yemeni Tribe*. Berkeley: University of California Press, 1990.

Census of India. "Economic Activity (2001)." The Registrar General and Census Commissioner India. Accessed June 15, 2021. https://censusindia.gov.in /census_and_you/economic_activity.aspx.

Center for Policy Research. "Categorisation of Settlement in Delhi." Center for Policy Research India. Accessed January 15, 2021. www.cprindia.org/sites /default/files/policy-briefs/Categorisation-of-Settlement-in-Delhi.pdf.

Chance, Kerry Ryan. *Living Politics in South Africa's Urban Shacklands*. Chicago: Chicago University Press, 2017.

Chandrasekhar, C. P., and Jayati Ghosh. *The Market That Failed: A Decade of Neoliberal Reforms in India*. New Delhi: Leftword Books, 2006.

Channing, F. C. *Land Revenue Settlement of the Gurgaon District*. Lahore: Central Jail Press, 1882.

Chari, Sharad. *Fraternal Capital: Peasant Workers, Self-Made Men, and Global- ization in Provincial India*. Palo Alto, CA: Stanford University Press, 2004.

Chattaraj, Durba. "Roadscapes: Everyday Life along the Rural-Urban Continuum in 21st Century India." PhD diss., Yale University, 2010.

Chattopadhyay, Swati. *Representing Calcutta: Modernism, Nationalism, and the Colonial Uncanny.* London: Routledge, 2005.

Chen, Mel. *Animacies: Biopolitics, Racial Mattering, and Queer Affect.* Durham, NC: Duke University Press, 2012.

Chin, Elizabeth. *My Life with Things: The Consumer Diaries.* Durham, NC: Duke University Press, 2016.

Chowdhry, Prem. "Caste Panchayats and the Policing of Marriage in Haryana: Enforcing Kinship and Territorial Exogamy." *Contributions to Indian Sociology* n.s., 38, nos. 1 & 2 (2004).

Choy, Timothy, and Jerry Zee. "Condition-Suspension." *Cultural Anthropology* 30 (2015): 210–23.

Chu, Julie. *Cosmologies of Credit: Transnational Mobility and the Politics of Destination in China.* Durham, NC: Duke University Press, 2010.

Coleman, Leo. *A Moral Technology: Electrification as Political Ritual in New Delhi.* Ithaca, NY: Cornell University Press, 2017.

Colomina, Beatriz. "The Split Wall: Domestic Voyeurism." In *Sexuality and Space*, edited by Beatriz Colomina. New York: Princeton University Press, 1992.

Cowan, Thomas. "The Urban Village, Agrarian Transformation, and Rentier Capitalism in Gurgaon, India." *Antipode* 50 (2018): 1244–66. https://doi.org/10.1111/anti.12404.

Das, Goutam, and Sarika Malhotra. "The Trail: How Is Black Money Made White." *Business Today.* October 11, 2015. www.businesstoday.in/magazine/cover-story/black-money-trail-around-trusts-hawala-tax-havens-shell-companies/story/223900.html.

Das, Veena. *Life and Words: Violence and the Descent into the Ordinary.* Berkeley: University of California Press, 2006.

Datta, Ayona. "'Mongrel City': Cosmopolitan Neighbourliness in a Delhi Squatter Settlement." *Antipode* 44, no. 3 (2012): 745–63.

Dave, Naisargi. *Queer Activism in India: A Story in the Anthropology of Ethics.* Durham, NC: Duke University Press, 2012.

———. "Witness: Humans, Animals, and the Politics of Becoming." *Cultural Anthropology* 29, no. 3 (2014): 433–56. https://doi.org/10.14506/ca29.3.01.

de Certeau, Michel. *The Practice of Everyday Life.* Berkeley: University of California Press, 1988.

De León, Jason. *The Land of Open Graves: Living and Dying on the Sonoran Desert Migrant Trail.* Oakland: University of California Press, 2015.

Deamer, Peggy. "Architectural Work: Immaterial Labour." In *Industries of Architecture*, edited by Katie Lloyd Thomas, Tilo Amhoff, and Nick Beech. Critiques: Critical Studies in Architectural Humanities, 11. London: Routledge, 2016.

Deleuze, Gilles, and Felix Guattari. *Anti-Oedipus*. Minneapolis: University of Minnesota Press, 1983. First published 1977.

———. *A Thousand Plateaus: Capitalism and Schizophrenia*. Translated by Brian Massumi. Minneapolis: University of Minnesota Press, 1980.

Delhi Mumbai Industrial Corridor (DMIC). "Introduction." DMIC India. Accessed March 6, 2022. http://delhimumbaiindustrialcorridor.com /introduction.html.

Desjarlais, Robert. *Shelter Blues: Sanity and Selfhood among the Homeless*. Philadelphia: University of Pennsylvania Press, 1997.

Dewey, Clive. *Anglo-Indian Attitudes: The Mind of the Indian Civil Service*. London: Hambledon Press, 1993.

Dewey, John. *Art as Experience*. New York: Putnam, 1934.

Dhaliwal, Kirpen. "Critical Analysis on the Farmer Bills 2020." Lexforti Legal News Network. September 27, 2020. https://lexforti.com/legal-news/farmer -bills/.

Dharia, Namita Vijay. "Artifacts and Artifices of the Global: Practices of US Architects in India's National Capital Region." *Global South* 8, no. 2 (2014): 49–64. https://doi.org/10.2979/globalsouth.8.2.49.

———. "Embodied Urbanisms: Eating and Excreting in India's Real Estate Economies." *Cultural Anthropology* 36, no. 4 (2021): 708–32. https://doi.org /10.14506/ca36.4.11.

Dhingra, Sanya. "Patriarchy, Popular Culture, Unemployment: Why Haryana Is India's Rape Capital." *Hindustan Times*. June 25, 2018. www.hindustantimes .com/india-news/patriarchy-popular-culture-unemployment-why-haryana -is-india-s-rape-capital/story-MGXBCioEeVZ9yNYEXmKsFJ.html.

Doherty, Gareth. *Paradoxes of Green: Landscapes of a City-State*. Oakland: University of California Press, 2017.

Donthi, Praveen. "How Brokers of Land and Power Built the Millennial City." *Caravan Magazine*. December 31, 2013. https://caravanmagazine.in /reportage/road-gurgaon.

Douglas, Mary. *Purity and Danger*. New York: Routledge, 2002. First published 1966.

Doval, Pankaj. "India Is Now the World's Biggest Two-Wheeler Market." *Times of India*. May 7, 2017. https://timesofindia.indiatimes.com/auto/bikes/india -is-now-worlds-biggest-2-wheeler-market/articleshow/58555735.cms.

Dunbar-Ortiz, Roxanne. *An Indigenous Peoples' History of the United States*. Boston: Beacon Press, 2014.

Dutta, Arindam. *The Bureaucracy of Beauty: Design in the Age of Its Global Reproducibility*. New York: Routledge, 2006.

Eagleton, Terry. *Ideology: An Introduction*. London: Verso, 1991.

Elyachar, Julia. "Phatic Labor, Infrastructure, and the Question of Empower-ment in Cairo." *American Ethnologist* 37, no. 3 (2010): 452–64.

Engels, Frederick. "The Origin of the Family, Private Property and the State."
Marx/Engels Internet Archive. Accessed March 10, 2020. www.marxists.org
/archive/marx/works/1884/origin-family/index.htm.

Escobar, Arturo. *Encountering Development: The Making and Unmaking of
the Third World*. Princeton, NJ: Princeton University Press, 1995.

Espinoza, Javier. "Chris Hohn and Investor Group Step Up $1.6bn Indian
Battle." *Financial Times*. December 12, 2018. www.ft.com/content/96667b8a
-fdfb-11e8-ac00-57a2a826423e.

Evans-Pritchard, E. E., and Eva Gillies. *Witchcraft, Oracles, and Magic among
the Azande*. Oxford: Clarendon Press, 1976.

Evenson, Norma. *The Indian Metropolis: The View toward the West*. New Haven,
CT: Yale University Press, 1989.

Farmer, Paul. "An Anthropology of Structural Violence." *Current Anthropology*
45, no. 3 (2004): 305–25. https://doi.org/10.1086/382250.

———. *Pathologies of Power: Health, Human Rights, and the New War on the
Poor*. Berkeley: University of California Press, 2003.

Fawad, Ajmal, and Rajesh Nath. "Infrastructure & Construction Equipment
Industry in India." NBM&CW. Accessed March 10, 2020. www.nbmcw.com
/report/construction-infra-industry/32396-infrastructure-construction
-equipment-industry-in-india.html.

Feld, Steven. *Sound and Sentiment: Birds, Weeping, Poetics, and Song in Kaluli
Expression*. Philadelphia: University of Pennsylvania Press, 2012.

Ferguson, James. *The Anti-politics Machine: "Development," Depoliticization, and
Bureaucratic Power in Lesotho*. Cambridge: Cambridge University Press, 1990.

Ferry, Elizabeth Emma. *Not Ours Alone: Patrimony, Value and Collectivity in
Contemporary Mexico*. New York: Columbia University Press, 2005.

Finkelstein, Maura. *The Archive of Loss: Lively Ruination in Mill Land
Mumbai*. Durham, NC: Duke University Press, 2019.

First Post Staff. "Ponty Chadha Raids: Official Who Led the Raid, Transferred."
First Post. February 17, 2012. www.firstpost.com/india/ponty-chadha-raids
-official-who-led-the-raid-transferred-217275.html.

Fisch, Michael. "Introduction: Toward a Theory of the Machine." In *An Anthropology of the Machine: Tokyo's Commuter Train Network*. Chicago: University of Chicago Press, 2018.

———. "Ninety Seconds." In *An Anthropology of the Machine: Tokyo's Commuter
Train Network*. Chicago: University of Chicago Press, 2018.

Fischer, Edward F. *Cash on the Table: Markets, Values, and Moral Economies*.
Santa Fe, NM: School for Advanced Research Press, 2013.

Galtung, Johan. "Violence, Peace, and Peace Research." *Journal of Peace
Research* 6 (1969): 167–91.

Gammeltoft, T. M. "Silence as a Response to Everyday Violence: Understanding
Domination and Distress through the Lens of Fantasy." *Ethos* 44 (2016): 427–47.

Gandalfo, Daniella. *The City at Its Limits: Taboo, Transgression, and Urban Renewal in Lima*. Chicago: University of Chicago Press, 2009.

Garcia-Rojas, Claudia. "(Un)Disciplined Destinies: Women of Color Feminism as a Disruptive to White Affect Studies." *Journal of Lesbian Studies* 21, no. 3 (2016): 254–71. https://doi.org/10.1080/10894160.2016.1159072.

George, Sabu M., and Ranbir S. Dahiya. "Female Foeticide in Rural Haryana." *Economic and Political Weekly* 33, no. 32 (1998): 2191–98. http://www.jstor.org/stable/4407077.

Ghertner, Asher. *Rule by Aesthetics: World-Class City Making in New Delhi*. New Delhi: Oxford University Press, 2015.

Gidwani, Vinay, and Priti Ramamurthy. "Agrarian Questions of Labor in Urban India: Middle Migrants, Translocal Householding and the Intersectional Politics of Social Reproduction." *Journal of Peasant Studies* 45, nos. 5–6 (2018): 994–1017. https://doi.org/10.1080/03066150.2018.1503172.

Gill, Kaveri. *Of Poverty and Plastic: Scavenging and Scrap Trading Entrepreneurs in India's Urban Informal Economy*. New Delhi: Oxford University Press, 2009.

Gilligan, James. *Violence*. New York: Vintage Books, 1997.

Ginsburg, Faye. "Chronicles of the Ephemeral: Some Thoughts on Delhi at Eleven." *Asia Pacific Journal of Anthropology* 15, no. 5 (2014): 455–57. https://doi.org/10.1080/14442213.2014.952058.

Goldman, M. "Speculative Urbanism and the Making of the Next World City." *International Journal of Urban and Regional Research* 35, no. 3 (2011): 555–81.

Goldman, M., and D. Narayan. "Through the Optics of Finance: Speculative Urbanism and the Transformation of Markets." *International Journal of Urban and Regional Research* 45 (2021): 209–31. https://doi.org/10.1111/1468-2427.13012.

Goldstein, Daniel M. *Owners of the Sidewalk: Security and Survival in the Informal City*. Durham, NC: Duke University Press, 2016.

Government of India. "Contract Labour (Regulation and Abolition) Act, 1970." Government of India. Accessed February 20, 2022. https://legislative.gov.in/sites/default/files/A1970-37_0.pdf.

———. "The Inter-State Migrant Workmen (Regulation of Employment and Conditions of Service) Rules, 1979." Labor Department, Haryana. Accessed March 10, 2020. https://hrylabour.gov.in/staticdocs/labourActpdfdocs/Inter_State_Migrant_Act.pdf.

Govindrajan, Radhika. *Animal Intimacies: Beastly Love in the Himalayas*. Gurgaon, Haryana: Penguin Random House, 2019. First published 2018.

Graham, Stephen, ed. *Disrupted Cities: When Infrastructure Fails*. New York: Routledge, 2010.

Graham, Stephen, and Simon Marvin. *Splintering Urbanism: Networked Infrastructures, Technological Mobilities and the Urban Condition*. London: Routledge, 2001.

Grover, Shalini. *Marriage, Love, Caste and Kinship Support: Lived Experiences of the Urban Poor in India*. New Delhi: Social Science Press, 2011.

Guattari, Félix. *Chaosmosis: An Ethico-Aesthetic Paradigm*. Translated by Paul Bains and Julian Pefanis. Bloomington: Indiana University Press, 1995.

Gupta, Akhil. "Blurred Boundaries: The Discourse of Corruption, the Culture of Politics, and the Imagined State." *American Ethnologist* 22, no. 2 (1995): 375–402.

———. *Postcolonial Developments: Agriculture in the Making of Modern India*. Durham, NC: Duke University Press, 1998.

———. *Red Tape: Bureaucracy, Structural Violence, and Poverty in India*. Durham, NC: Duke University Press, 2012.

Gurgaon Workers News. "List of Companies Situated in Gurgaon." Accessed August 7, 2014. http://gurgaonworkersnews.wordpress.com/list-of-companies -situated-in-gurgaon/.

Gururani, Shubhra. "Flexible Planning: The Making of India's 'Millennial City,' Gurgaon." In *Ecologies of Urbanism in India: Metropolitan Civility and Sustainability*, edited by Anne M. Rademacher and K. Sivaramakrishnan. Hong Kong: Hong Kong University Press, 2013.

Goodman, Jennifer. "Construction Industry Cited in Human Trafficking Study." Builder Online. March 30, 2017. www.builderonline.com/money/economics /construction-industry-cited-in-human-trafficking-study_o.

Habib, Irfan, ed. *Inquilab: Bhagat Singh on Religion and Revolution*. Delhi: Yoda Press, 2018.

Hainge, Greg. *Noise Matters: Towards an Ontology of Noise*. London: Blooms- bury, 2013.

Hans India, The. "The IL&FS Imbroglio: Lessons to Be Learnt." December 28, 2018. www.thehansindia.com/posts/index/Opinion/2018-12-28/The-ILFS -imbroglio-Lessons-to-be-learnt/465524.

Hansen, Thomas Blom. *The Saffron Wave: Democracy and Hindu Nationalism in Modern India*. Princeton, NJ: Princeton University Press, 1999.

Hardt, Michael. "Affective Labor." *Boundary2* 26, no. 2 (1999): 89–100. www .jstor.org/stable/303793.

Hardy, Kathryn C. "Constituting a Diffuse Region: Cartographies of Mass-Mediated Bhojpuri Belonging." *BioScope: South Asian Screen Studies* 6, no. 2 (2015): 145–64. https://doi.org/10.1177/0974927615600623.

Harms, Erik. "Beauty as Control in the New Saigon: Eviction, New Urban Zones, and Atomized Dissent in a Southeast Asian City." *American Ethnologist*, 39 (2012): 735–50. https://doi.org/10.1111/j.1548-1425.2012 .01392.x.

———. *Saigon's Edge: On the Margins of Ho Chi Minh City*. Minneapolis: University of Minnesota Press, 2011.

Harvey, David. *Conditions of Postmodernity*. Boston: Blackwell, 1990.

Harvey, Penny. "The Materiality of State Effects: An Ethnography of a Road in the Peruvian Andes in State Formation." In *Anthropological Explorations*, edited by C. Krohn-Hansen and K. Nustad. Cambridge, UK: Pluto, 2005.

Harvey, Penny, and Hannah Knox. "The Enchantments of Infrastructure." *Mobilities* 7, no. 4 (2012): 521–36. https://doi.org/10.1080/17450101.2012 .718935.

———. *Roads: An Anthropology of Infrastructure and Expertise*. Ithaca, NY: Cornell University Press, 2015.

Haryana Government. "Contract Labour (Regulation and Abolition Act)." Labour Department Haryana. Accessed March 10, 2020. https://hrylabour .gov.in/content/contract_labour.

———. *Haryana Government Gazette, Extraordinary*. No. 118-2020/Ext. August 22, 2020. LexComply. Accessed October 4, 2021. https://lexcomply .com/rsjadmin/news/202008253846Notification%20No.%20Leg.%2025-2020 -%20Factories%20(Haryana%20Amendment)%20Ordinance%202020.pdf.

———. "Industrial Disputes Act 1947." Labour Department Haryana. Accessed October 4, 2021. https://hrylabour.gov.in/staticdocs/labourActpdfdocs/ID _Act.pdf.

Hayakawa, Akira. "India Zooms Past Germany as Fourth-Largest Auto Market." *Nikkei Asian Review*. January 12, 2018. https://asia.nikkei.com/Business /Automobiles/India-zooms-past-Germany-as-fourth-largest-auto-market2.

Helmreich, Stefan. "An Anthropologist Underwater: Immersive Soundscapes, Submarine Cyborgs, and Transductive Ethnography." *American Ethnologist* 34, no. 4 (2007): 621–41.

———. "Gravity's Reverb: Listening to Space-Time, or Articulating the Sounds of Gravitational-Wave Detection." *Cultural Anthropology* 31, no. 4 (2016): 464–92.

Herzfeld, Michael. *The Body Impolitic: Artisans and Artifice in the Global Hierarchy of Value*. Chicago: University of Chicago Press, 2004.

———. *Cultural Intimacy: Social Poetics in the Nation-State*. New York: Routledge, 1997.

———. "Rhythm, Tempo, and Historical Time: Experiencing Temporality in the Neoliberal Age." *Public Archaeology: Archaeological Ethnographies* 8, nos. 2–3 (2009): 108–23.

The Hindu. "Black Economy Now Amounts to 75% of GDP." September 3, 2016. www.thehindu.com/news/national/Black-economy-now-amounts-to-75-of -GDP/article60515670.ece.

Hirschkind, Charles. *The Ethical Soundscape: Cassette Sermons and Islamic Counterpublics*. New York: Columbia University Press, 2006.

Ho, Karen. *Liquidated: An Ethnography of Wall Street*. Durham, NC: Duke University Press, 2010.

Holston, James. *The Modernist City: An Anthropological Critique of Brasília*. Chicago: University of Chicago Press, 1989.

Hosograhar, Jyoti. *Indigenous Modernities: Negotiating Architecture &* *Urbanism*. New York: Routledge, 2005.

HT Correspondent. "Panama Papers: 500 Indians in Global List of Secret Firms in Tax Havens." *Hindustan Times*. Updated on April 5, 2016. www.hindustan times.com/india/actors-tycoons-politicians-among-indians-named-in-global -list-of-secret-firms-in-tax-havens/story-uGXipxzdJL3kuMf8iGg8DK.html.

Hull, Matthew. *Government of Paper: The Materiality of Bureaucracy*. Oakland: University of California Press, 2014.

IBEF (Indian Brand Equity Foundation), Ministry of Commerce & Industry, Government of India. "About Haryana: Information on Industries, Geography, Economy & Growth." Updated November 9, 2021. www.ibef.org/states /haryana.aspx.

———. "Cement Industry in India." Updated December 17, 2021. www.ibef.org /industry/cement-india.aspx.

———. "Construction Equipment." September 2016. www.ibef.org/download /Construction-Equipment-September-2016.pdf.

———. "The Indian Infrastructural Sector: Investments, Growth and Prospects." January 2013. www.ibef.org/download/Infrastructure-Sector-040213.pdf.

ICEMA (Indian Construction Equipment Manufacturer's Association). "About ICEMA." Accessed March 10, 2020. www.i-cema.in.

ICICI Bank. "History." ICICI Group. Accessed March 10, 2020. www.icicibank .com/aboutus/history.page.

Ilaiah Shepherd, Kancha. *Why I Am Not a Hindu*. New Delhi: Sage, 2019.

Indian Express. "India 5th Largest Exporter of Black Money between 2002–11." December 12, 2013. http://archive.indianexpress.com/news/india-5th-largest -exporter-of- black-money-between-200211-report/1206798/.

Ingold, Tim. *The Life of Lines*. London: Routledge, 2015.

———. *Lines: A Brief History*. Oxon, UK: Routledge, 2007.

Irani, Lilly. *Chasing Innovation: Making Entrepreneurial Citizens in Modern India*. Princeton, NJ: Princeton University Press, 2019. https://escholarship .org/uc/item/3239b1qv#article_main.

J. C. Bamford Excavators Ltd. "Company Overview." Accessed November 24, 2014. www.jcbindia.com/company_overview.aspx.

Jain, Kajri. *Gods in the Bazaar: Economies of Indian Calendar Art*. Durham, NC: Duke University Press, 2007.

Jauregui, Beatrice. "Provisional Agency in India: *Jugaad* and Legitimation of Corruption." *American Ethnologist* 41, no. 1 (2014): 76–91.

Jeffery, Craig. *Timepass: Youth, Class, and the Politics of Waiting in India*. Stanford, CA: Stanford University Press, 2010.

Jeffery, Craig, and Stephen Young. "Jugad: Youth and Enterprise in India." *Annals of the Association of American Geographers* 104, no. 1 (2014) : 182–95. http://www.jstor.org/stable/24537744.

Jodhka, Surinder S. "Agrarian Changes and Attached Labour: Emerging Patterns in Haryana Agriculture." *Economic and Political Weekly* 29, no. 39 (1994): A102–6.

Jost, Patrik M., and Harjit Singh Sandhu. "The Hawala Alternative Remittance System and Its Role in Money Laundering." United States Treasury Department. Accessed February 27, 2020. www.treasury.gov/resource-center /terrorist-illicit-finance/Documents/FinCEN-Hawala-rpt.pdf.

Kanna, Ahmed. *Dubai: The City as Corporation.* Minneapolis: University of Minnesota Press, 2011.

Kant, Immanuel. *Observations on the Feeling of the Beautiful and Sublime and Other Writings.* Cambridge: Cambridge University Press, 2011. First published 1764.

Kar, Sohini. *Financializing Poverty: Labor and Risk in Indian Microfinance.* Stanford, CA: Stanford University Press, 2018.

Kasmir, Sharryn, and August Carbonella. "Dispossession and the Anthropology of Labor." *Critique of Anthropology* 28, no. 1 (2008): 5–25.

Kaul, Vivek. "Explained: How Vadra Gained DLF's Benevolence. Firstpost. October 11, 2012. www.firstpost.com/business/explained-how-vadra-gained -from-dlfs- benevolence-485471.html.

Kaviraj, Sudipto. "Filth and the Public Sphere: Concepts and Practices about Space in Calcutta." *Public Culture* 10, no. 1 (1997): 83–113. https://doi.org/10 .1215/08992363-10-1-83.

Khan, Naveeda. "The Acoustics of Muslim Striving: Loudspeaker Use in Ritual Practice in Pakistan." *Comparative Studies in Society and History* 53, no. 3 (2011): 571–94. www.jstor.org/stable/41241825.

Khubchandani, Kareem. "Snakes on the Dance Floor: Bollywood, Gesture, and Gender." *Velvet Light Trap* 77 (2016): 69–85. muse.jhu.edu/article/609055.

Kumar, Narayan. "Paupers & Princes of Realty: How Gurgaon Is Both the Land of Crorepatis and Cowherds." *Economic Times.* February 17, 2013. https:// economictimes.indiatimes.com/realty-trends/paupers-princes-of-realty-how -gurgaon-is-both-the-land-of-crorepatis-and-cowherds/articleshow /18534718.cms?from=mdr.

Kumar, Om. "Construction of the Ahir Identity and It's Modern Forms of Assertiveness in Gurugram." PhD diss., St. Xavier's College, 2020.

Kunreuther, Laura. "Sounds of Democracy: Performance, Protest, and Political Subjectivity." *Cultural Anthropology* 33 (2018): 1–31.

———. *Voicing Subjects: Public Intimacy and Mediation in Kathmandu.* South Asia across the Disciplines Series. Oakland: University of California Press, 2014.

Larkin, Brian. *Signal and Noise: Media Infrastructure and Urban Culture in Nigeria.* Durham, NC: Duke University Press, 2008.

Latour, Bruno. *Pandora's Hope: Essays on the Reality of Science Studies.* Cambridge, MA: Harvard University Press, 1999.

Lavie, S., Kirin Narayan, and Renato Rosaldo. Introduction to *Creativity/ Anthropology*, edited by S. Lavie, Kirin Narayan, and Renato Rosaldo. Ithaca, NY: Cornell University Press, 1993.

Lefebvre, Henri. *The Production of Space*. Cambridge. MA: Blackwell, 1991. First published 1974.

Levien, Michael. *Dispossession without Development: Land Grabs in Neoliberal India*. New York: Oxford University Press, 2018.

Liep, John. *Locating Cultural Creativity*. London: Pluto Press, 2001.

Low, Setha M. *Behind the Gates: Life, Security, and the Pursuit of Happiness in Fortress America*. New York: Routledge, 2003.

Low, S., and M. Maguire. *Spaces of Security: Ethnographies of Securityscapes, Surveillance and Control*. New York: New York University Press, 2019.

Low, S., and Neil Smith, eds. *The Politics of Public Space*. New York: Routledge, 2006.

Majumdar, Anindita. *Transnational Commercial Surrogacy and the (Un)Making of Kin in India*. New Delhi: Oxford University Press, 2017.

Make in India. Home page. Department of Industrial Policy & Promotion (DIPP), Ministry of Commerce, Government of India. Accessed May 30, 2018. www.makeinindia.com.

Mankekar, Purnima, and Akhil Gupta. "The Missed Period." *American Ethnologist* 46 (2019): 417–28. https://doi.org/10.1111/amet.12837.

Manning, P. "Spiritualist Signal and Theosophical Noise." *Journal of Linguistic Anthropology* 28 (2018): 67–92. https://doi.org/10.1111/jola.12177.

Manyanath, Nithin. "The Shameless Marriage: Thinking through Same-Sex Erotics and the Question of 'Gay Marriage' in India." In *Conjugality Unbound*, edited by Srimati Basu and Lucinda Ramberg. New Delhi: Women Unlimited, 2015.

Maruti Suzuki Workers Union. "An Appeal to Workers and Masses from Maruti Suzuki Workers Union." October 27, 2012. https://marutisuzukiworkersunion .wordpress.com/2012/10/27/an-appeal-to-workers-and-masses-from-maruti -suzuki-workers-union/.

Marx, Karl. "Capital." 1867. Marx/Engels Internet Archive. Accessed November 17, 2013. www.marxists.org/archive/marx/works/sw/index.htm.

———. "The Working Day, Section 3." 1867. Marx/Engels Internet Archive. Accessed March 8, 2020. www.marxists.org/archive/marx/works/1867-c1/ch10.htm.

Masco, Joseph. "Mutant Ecologies: Radioactive Life in Post–Cold War New Mexico." *Cultural Anthropology* 19 (2004): 517–50. https://doi.org/10.1525 /can.2004.19.4.517.

———. *The Nuclear Borderlands: The Manhattan Project in Post-Cold War New Mexico*. Princeton, NJ: Princeton University Press, 2006.

Massey, D. B. *Space, Place, and Gender*. Minneapolis: University of Minnesota Press, 1994.

Maurer, Bill. *Mutual Life, Limited: Islamic Banking, Alternative Currencies, Lateral Reason*. Princeton, NJ: Princeton University Press, 2011.

Mauss, Marcel. *The Gift: Forms and Functions of Exchange in Archaic Societies*. London: Cohen & West, 1966.

Mbembe, Achille. "The Aesthetics of Vulgarity." In *On the Postcolony*. Berkeley: University of California Press, 2001.

McGlotten, Shaka. "Ordinary Intersections: Speculations on Difference, Justice, and Utopia in Black Queer Life." *Transforming Anthropology* 20, no. 1 (2012): 45–66. https://doi.org/10.1111/j.1548-7466.2011.01146.x.

McGowan, Todd. *Capitalism and Desire: The Psychic Cost of Free Markets*. New York: Columbia University Press, 2016.

Mehrotra, Rahul. "Negotiating the Static and Kinetic Cities: The Emergent Urbanism of Mumbai." In *Other Cities, Other Worlds: Urban Imaginaries in a Globalizing Age*, edited by Andreas Huyssen. Durham, NC: Duke University Press, 2008.

Mehrotra, Rahul, and Felipe Vera. "Ephemeral Urbanism." In *The Post-Urban World: Emergent Transformation of Cities and Regions in the Innovative Global Economy.*, edited by T. Haas and H. Westlund. London: Routledge, 2017.

Mekha, Vigneshwar, and Adma Kamalakar Reddy. "Experiences of Cement Industry in India." *International Journal of Research in Geography* 4, no. 2 (2018): 72–78. http://dx.doi.org/10.20431/2454-8685.0402007.

Menon-Sen, Kalyani, and Gautam Bhan. *Swept Off the Map: Surviving Eviction and Resettlement in Delhi JJ Colony*. New Delhi: Yoda Books, 2008.

Menoret, Pascal. *Joyriding in Riyadh: Oil, Urbanism, and Road Revolt*. Cambridge: Cambridge University Press, 2014.

Merleau-Ponty, Maurice. *The Phenomenology of Perception*. Translated by Colin Smith. London: Routledge, 1962. First published 1945.

Metcalf, Thomas R. "The British and the Moneylender in Nineteenth-Century India." *Journal of Modern History* 34, no. 4 (1962): 390–97. www.jstor.org /stable/1880056.

Millar, Kathleen M. *Reclaiming the Discarded: Life and Labor on Rio's Garbage Dump*. Durham and London: Duke University Press. 2018.

Ministry of Commerce & Industry, Government of India. "Fact Sheet on Special Economic Zones." Special Economic Zones in India. Accessed February 26, 2020. http://sezindia.nic.in/upload/5dd4e2ab59d11Fact%20Sheet.pdf.

Ministry of External Affairs, Government of India. "India in Business, Haryana." National Informatics Center. Accessed November 13, 2016. http:// indiainbusiness.nic.in/newdesign/index.php?param=statesinfo/26/837/1.

Ministry of Finance, Government of India. "Key Features of Budget, 2002–2003" and "Budget Speech, 2011–12." National Informatics Centre, Union Budget and Economic Survey. Accessed March 6, 2015. www.indiabudget.gov

.in/budget_archive/ub2002-03/bh/bh1.pdf and www.indiabudget.gov.in /budget2011-2012/ub2011-12/bs/bs.doc.
———. "White Paper on Black Money." Department of Revenue. Accessed February 14, 2022. https://dor.gov.in/sites/default/files/FinalBlackMoney.pdf.
Ministry of Labour and Employment, Government of India. "The Building and Other Construction Workers (Regulation of Employment and Conditions of Service) Act, 1996." Maharashtra Industry, Trade and Investment Facilitation Cell. Accessed March 7, 2020. https://maitri.mahaonline.gov.in/pdf /building-and-other-construction-workers-act-1996.pdf
———. "The Child Labour (Prohibition and Regulation) Act, 1986." Ministry of Labour and Employment. Accessed March 7, 2020. https://labour.gov.in /sites/default/files/act_2.pdf.
Ministry of Law and Justice, Government of India. "The Gazette of India, Extraordinary: The Maternity Benefit (Amendment) Act, 2017." March 28, 2017. https://labour.gov.in/sites/default/files/Maternity%20Benefit%20 Amendment%20Act%2C2017%20.pdf.
———. "The Gazette of India, Extraordinary: The Special Economic Zones Act, 2005." Accessed February 14, 2022. http://sezindia.nic.in/upload/uploadfiles /files/SEZAct2005.pdf.
Ministry of Steel, Government of India. "Development of Indian Steel Sector since 1991." December 2018. https://steel.gov.in/sites/default/files/development _Since1991_27December2018.pdf.
Missing Basti Project, The. Home page. Accessed September, 13, 2021. https:// missingbasti.com/.
Mitchell, Timothy. *Colonizing Egypt*. Berkeley: University of California Press, 1988.
———. *Rule of Experts: Egypt, Techno-Politics, Modernity*. Berkeley: California University Press, 2002.
Mitra, Devashish. "Indian Labor Regulations Take Small Steps in the Right Direction." *World Bank Blogs*. February 1, 2016. https://blogs.worldbank.org /jobs/indian-labor-regulations-take-small-steps-right-direction.
Money Control. "Company History: Housing Development and Finance Corporation." Accessed February 16, 2022. www.moneycontrol.com/company -facts/hdfc/history/HDF.
Moore, Donald. *Suffering for Territory: Race, Place, and Power in Zimbabwe*. Durham, NC: Duke University Press, 2005.
Moten, Fred. *In the Break: The Aesthetics of the Black Radical Tradition*. Minneapolis: University of Minnesota Press, 2003.
Mukherjee, Sharmistha. "India Pips Germany, Ranks 4th Largest Auto Market Now." *Economic Times*, March 24, 2018. https://economictimes.indiatimes .com/industry/auto/india-pips-germany-ranks-4th-largest-auto-market-now /articleshow/63438236.cms.

Munn, Nancy. *The Fame of Gawa: A Symbolic Study of Value Transformation in a Massim Society.* Durham, NC: Duke University Press, 1992.

Muñoz, José Esteban. "Ephemera as Evidence: Introductory Notes to Queer Acts." *Women & Performance: A Journal of Feminist Theory* 8, no. 2 (1996): 5–16. https://doi.org/10.1080/07407709608571228.

Murphy, Michelle. *The Economization of Life.* Durham, NC: Duke University Press, 2017.

Murthy, Laxmi, and Meena Seshu. "The Feminist and the Sex Worker." In *The Business of Sex.* New Delhi: Zubaan, 2013.

Myers, Fred D. *The Empire of Things: Regimes of Value and Material Culture.* Santa Fe, NM: School of American Research Press, 2002.

Nair, Janaki. *The Promise of the Metropolis: Bangalore's Twentieth Century.* Delhi: Oxford University Press, 2005.

NASA Earth Observatory, "Urban Growth of New Delhi." September 27, 2018. https://earthobservatory.nasa.gov/images/92813/urban-growth-of-new -delhi.

Nakassis, Constantine, and Llerena Searle. "Introduction: Social Value Projects in Post-liberalisation India." *Contributions to Indian Sociology* 47, no. 2 (2013): 169–83. https://doi.org/10.1177/0069966713482962.

Nash, June, and Mariá Patricia Fernández-Kelly. *Women, Men, and the International Division of Labor.* Albany: State University of New York Press, 1983.

National Crime Records Bureau. "Table 3A.3 Women & Girls Victims of Rape (Age Group-wise)—2019." Accessed July 26, 2021. https://ncrb.gov.in/sites /default/files/crime_in_india_table_additional_table_chapter_reports /Table%203A.3_2.pdf.

National Information Centre. "List of Notified SEZ." July 31, 2021. http:// sezindia.nic.in/upload/uploadfiles/files/Notified%20SEZs%20360%2B7 %2B12.PDF.

———. "Bharatmala Pariyojana—Phase I." Accessed March 7, 2020. http:// pibphoto.nic.in/documents/rlink/2017/oct/p2017102504.pdf.

Navaro-Yashin, Yael. *The Make-Believe Space: Affective Geography in a Post-War Polity.* Durham, NC: Duke University Press, 2012.

NCRPB (National Capital Region Planning Board), Ministry of Housing and Urban Affairs, Government of India. *National Capital Region Growth and Development.* New Delhi: Har-Anand Publications, 1999. First published 1996.

———. "NCR Constituent Areas." Accessed March 8, 2020. http://ncrpb.nic.in /ncrconstituent.html.

Negri, Antonio, and Michael Hardt. "Value and Affect." *boundary 2* 26, no. 2 (1999): 77–88. www.jstor.org/stable/303792.

Nielsen, K. B., and A. G. Nilson. "Law Struggles, Lawmaking, and the Politics of Hegemony in Neoliberal India: Towards a Critical Perspective on the 2013 Land Acquisition Act." In *The Land Question in India: State, Dispossession, and Capitalist Transition*, edited by Anthony P. D'Costa and Achin Chakraborty. New Delhi: Oxford University Press, 2017.

Nye, David E. *American Technological Sublime*. Cambridge: Massachusetts Institute of Technology Press, 1996.

Ojha, Mayank. "Nested Cohabitation: The Modern City and Urban Villages." Academia. 2011. www.academia.edu/6161360/NESTED_COHABITATION_THE_MODERN_CITY_and_URBAN_VILLAGES.

Oldenberg, Veena T. *Gurgaon: From Mythic Village to Millenium City*. New Delhi: HarperCollins, 2018.

O'Neill, Kevin Lewis. "Hands of Love: Christian Outreach and the Spatialization of Ethnicity." In *Securing the City: Neoliberalism, Space and Insecurity in Postwar Guatemala*, edited by Kevin Lewis O'Neill and Kedron Thomas. Durham, NC: Duke University Press, 2011.

Ong, Aihwa. "The Gender and Labor Politics of Postmodernity." *Annual Review of Anthropology* 20 (1991): 279–309. www.jstor.org/stable/2155803.

———. *Spirits of Resistance and Capitalist Discipline: Factory Women in Malaysia*. Albany: State University of New York Press, 1987.

Orsini, Fransesca, ed. *Love in South Asia: A Cultural History*. Cambridge: Cambridge University Press, 2006.

Oxfam International. "India: Extreme Inequality in Numbers." Accessed October, 4. 2021. www.oxfam.org/en/india-extreme-inequality-numbers.

Oxford English Dictionary, 2nd ed., 1989. S.v. "Ephemeral." Accessed June 1, 2018. https://en.oxforddictionaries.com/definition/ephemeral.

Pande, Amrita. *Wombs in Labor: Transnational Commercial Surrogacy in India*. New York: Columbia University Press, 2014.

Pandey, Anjoo. "Importance of Cement Industry in India." *International Journal of Marketing and Technology* 7, no. 8 (August 2017). www.ijmra.us/project%20doc/2017/IJMT_AUGUST2017/IJMRA-12116.pdf.

Pandey, Gyan. *Bonded Histories: Genealogies of Labor Servitude in Colonial India*. Cambridge: Cambridge University Press, 2003.

———. *A History of Prejudice: Race, Caste, and Difference in India and the United States*. New York: Cambridge University Press, 2013.

Pandian, Anand. *Crooked Stalks: Cultivating Virtue in South India*. Durham, NC: Duke University Press, 2009.

Parreñas, Juno. *Decolonizing Extinction: The Work of Care in Orangutan Rehabilitation*. Durham, NC: Duke University Press, 2018.

Parry, Jonathan. "'The Crisis of Corruption' and 'the Idea of India': A Worm's Eye View." In *The Morals of Legitimacy*, edited by I. Pardo. New York: Berghahn Books, 2000.

———. "Sex, Bricks and Mortar: Constructing Class in a Central Indian Steel Town." *Modern Asian Studies* 48, no. 5 (2014): 1242–75. https://doi.org/10.1017/S0026749X1400002X.

Patnaik, Prabhakar. "Demonetization: Witless and Anti-People." The Citizen. November 9, 2016. www.thecitizen.in/index.php/NewsDetail/index/1/9151 /Demonetization-Witless-and-Anti- People.

Perez, Federico. "Urbanism as Warfare." PhD diss., Harvard University, 2011.

Peterson, Kristin. *Speculative Markets: Drug Circuits and Derivative Life in Nigeria*. Durham, NC: Duke University Press, 2014.

Peterson, Marina. "Atmospheric Sensibilities: Noise, Annoyance, and Indefinite Urbanism." *Social Text 35*, no. 2 (2017): 69–90. https://doi.org/10.1215 /01642472-3820545.

Peterson, Marina, and Jesse Shipley, ed. "Audio Work: Labor, Value, and the Making of Musical Aesthetics." Special issue, *Journal of Popular Music Studies* 24, no. 4 (2012). https://doi.org/10.1111/jpms.12000.

Pilo', Francesca, and Rivke Jaffe. "The Political Materiality of Cities." *City & Society* 32, no. 1 (2020): 8–22.

Pinto, Sarah. *Daughters of Parvati: Women and Madness in Contemporary India*. Philadelphia: University of Pennsylvania Press, 2014.

———. *Where There Is No Midwife*. New York: Berghahn Books, 2008.

Planning Commission. *Eleventh Five Year Plan (2007–2012) Agriculture, Rural Development, Industry, Services and Physical Infrastructure*. Volume III. New Delhi: Oxford University Press, 2008. https://niti.gov.in/planning commission.gov.in/docs/plans/planrel/fiveyr/11th/11_v3/11th_vol3.pdf.

———. *Twelfth Five Year Plan (2012–2017): Faster, More Inclusive Sustainable Growth*. Volume I. New Delhi: Sage Publications, 2013. https://niti.gov.in /planningcommission.gov.in/docs/plans/planrel/fiveyr/12th/pdf/12fyp _vol1.pdf.

Povinelli, Elizabeth. "Routes/Worlds." *e-flux Journal*, no. 27 (2011). www.e-flux .com/journal/27/67991/routes-worlds/.

———. *The Empire of Love: Toward a Theory of Intimacy, Genealogy, and Carnality*. Durham, NC: Duke University Press, 2006.

Prasad, S. N. "Case Study: Labour Unrest at Manesar Plant of Maruti Suzuki in 2012: A Perspective." Shri Dharmasthala Manjunatheshwara Institute for Management Development (SDMIMD). Accessed March 10, 2020. www.sdmimd.ac.in/SDMRCMS/cases/CIM2012/9.pdf.

PRS Legislative Research. "All about the Lokpal Bill." Accessed June 6, 2016. https://prsindia.org/articles-by-prs-team/all-you-wanted-to-know-about-the -lokpal-bill.

Qazi, Moin. "Inside the World of Indian Moneylenders." The Diplomat Media Inc. March 31, 2017. https://thediplomat.com/2017/03/inside-the-world-of -indian-moneylenders/.

Rabinow, Paul. *French Modern: Norms and Forms of the Social Environment*. Chicago: Chicago University Press, 1995.

Rademacher, A., and K. Sivaramakrishnan. *Ecologies of Urbanism in India: Metropolitan Civility and Sustainability*. New York: Columbia University Press, 2013.

Radjou, Navi, Jaideep Prabu, and Simone Ahuja. *Jugaad Innovation: A Frugal and Flexible Approach to Innovation in the 21st Century*. Foreword by Kevin Roberts. San Francisco, CA.: Jossey-Bass, 2012.

Raheja, Gloria. *The Poison in the Gift: Ritual, Prestation, and the Dominant Caste in a North Indian Village*. Chicago: University of Chicago Press, 1988.

Raheja, Gloria Goodwin, and Ann Grodzin Gold. *Listen to the Heron's Words: Reimagining Gender and Kinship in North India*. Berkeley: University of California Press, 1994.

Rai, Amit. *Jugaad Time: Ecologies of Everyday Hacking in India*. ANIMA: Critical Race Studies Otherwise. Durham, NC: Duke University Press, 2019.

Rajput, Rashmi, Surabhi Malik, and Abhinav Bhatt. "Mantralya Fire: Crime Branch to Begin Probe Today; Forensic Experts to Inspect Premises." NDTV Convergence Limited. June 22, 2012. www.ndtv.com/mumbai-news/mantralaya-fire-crime-branch-to-begin-probe-today-forensic-experts-to-inspect-premises-489347.

Ralph, Laurence. *Renegade Dreams: Living through Injury in Gangland Chicago*. Chicago: University of Chicago Press, 2014.

Ramberg, Lucinda. *Given to the Goddess: South Indian Devadasis and the Sexuality of Religion*. Durham, NC: Duke University Press, 2014.

———. "When the Devi Is Your Husband: Sacred Marriage and Sexual Economy in South India." *Feminist Studies* 37, no. 1 (2011): 28–60. www.jstor.org/stable/23069882.

Rancière, Jacques. *The Aesthetic of the Unconscious*. Malden, MA: Polity Press, 2009.

———. *The Politics of Aesthetics: The Distribution of the Sensible*. London: Continuum, 2004.

Rao, Anupama. *The Caste Question: Dalits and Politics in Modern India*. Berkeley: University of California Press, 2009.

Rao, Hitendra. "Manesar Land Release: Supreme Court Asks Haryana to Stop Construction till May 8." *Hindustan Times*. Updated April 24, 2015. www.hindustantimes.com/punjab/manesar-land-release-supreme-court-asks-haryana-to-stop-construction-till-may-8/story-moMWxF3TRhXhtJIDHr5VsN.html.

Rao, K. N. P. "A Brief History of the Indian Iron and Steel Industry." National Metallurgical Laboratory India. Accessed March 10, 2020. http://eprints.nmlindia.org/5558/1/1-7.PDF.

Rao, Nikhil. *House but No Garden: Apartment Living in Bombay's Suburbs*. Minneapolis: University of Minnesota Press, 2013.

Rao, Vyajayanthi. 2007 "Proximate Distances: The Phenomenology of Density in Mumbai." *Built Environment* 33, no. 2 (2007): 227–48. www.jstor.org /stable/23289578.

Rawat, Ramnarayan. *Reconsidering Untouchability: Chamars and Dalit History in North India*. Bloomington: Indiana University Press, 2011.

Ray, Surya Sarathi. "Modi Government Is Working on New Labour Law Protecting Dignity of Workers." *The Indian Express*. April 23, 2018. www.financialexpress.com/economy/modi-government-is-working-on-new -labour-law-protecting-dignity-of-workers-details-here/1141909/.

RBI (Reserve Bank of India). "Foreign Exchange Management (Transfer or Issue of Security by a Person Resident outside India) (Thirteenth Amend-ment) Regulations, 2016." September 9, 2016. https://rbi.org.in/Scripts /NotificationUser.aspx?Id=10606&Mode=0.

———. "Master Circular on Finance for Housing Schemes-UCBs." July 1, 2009. https://rbi.org.in/Scripts/BS_ViewMasCirculardetails.aspx?id=5124#2.

———. "Press Note 2." August 17, 2005. https://rbi.org.in/Scripts/BS_Circular IndexDisplay.aspx?Id=2449.

———. "Table 26: Gross State Value Added by Economic Activity." In *Handbook of Statistics on Indian States*. November 24, 2021. https://m.rbi.org.in/scripts /PublicationsView.aspx?id=20685.

Reddy, Akhileshwari. "New Labor Codes: What Changes for Interstate Migrants?" Vidhi Center for Legal Policy blog. November 25, 2020. https:// vidhilegalpolicy.in/blog/new-labour-codes-what-changes-for-interstate -migrants/.

Ring, Laura. *Zenana: Everyday Peace in a Karachi Apartment Building*. Bloomington: Indiana University Press, 2006.

Roy, Abhijit. "The Middle-Class in India: From 1947 to the Present and Beyond." *Asian Politics* 23, no. 1 (2018): 6. www.asianstudies.org/publications/eaa /archives/the-middle-class-in-india-from-1947-to-the-present-and-beyond/.

Roy, Ananya. "Urban Informality: Toward an Epistemology of Planning." *Journal of the American Planning Association* 71, no. 2 (2005): 147–58. https://doi.org/10.1080/01944360508976689.

———. *Urban Informality: Transnational Perspectives from the Middle East, South Asia, and Latin America*. Lanham, MD: Lexington Books, 2004.

———. "Why India Cannot Plan Its Cities: Informality, Insurgence and the Idiom of Urbanization." *Planning Theory* 8, no. 1 (2009): 76–87.

Roy, Sharmindra Nath, Manish, and Mukta Naik. *Migrants in Construction Work: Evaluating their Welfare Framework*. New Delhi: Center for Policy Research, 2017. www.cprindia.org/system/tdf/policy-briefs/Evaluating %20the%20welfare%20framework%20for%20building%20and%20other %20construction%20workers%20in%20india%201109%20(1).pdf?file=1& type=node&id=6423&force=1.

Rubin, Gayle. "The Traffic in Women: Notes on the 'Political Economy' of Sex."
    In *Toward an Anthropology of Women,* edited by Rayna R. Reiter. New York:
    Monthly Review Press, 1975.

Sahni, Sonia. "Real Estate Sector—The India Story." ABN Ambro Bank.
    Accessed April 18, 2015. www.prres.net/papers/Sonia%20_Real_Estate
    _Sector_The_India_Story.pdf.

Saini, Manveer. "Haryana Khap Blames Consumption of Chowmein for Rapes."
    Times of India. Updated October 16, 2012. http://timesofindia.indiatimes
    .com/india/Haryana-khap-blames-consumption-of- chowmeinfor-rapes/
    articleshow/16829882.cms.

Saito, Yoriko. *Everyday Aesthetics.* Oxford: Oxford University Press, 2008.

Salzburg, Rosa. *Ephemeral City: Cheap Print and Urban Culture in Renais-
    sance Venice.* Manchester, UK: Manchester University Press, 2014.

Santo, Diana Espirito. "Fluid Divination: Movement, Chaos, and the Genera-
    tion of 'Noise' in Afro-Cuban Spiritist Oracular Production." *Anthropology of
    Consciousness* 24, no. 1 (2013): 32–56. https://doi.org/10.1111/anoc.12006.

Sassen, Saskia. *The Global City: New York, London, Tokyo.* Princeton, NJ:
    University of Princeton Press, 2001.

Schomer, Karine. "Getting to Mars through 'Jugaad.'" *The Hindu.* Updated
    October 18, 2016. www.thehindu.com/opinion/op-ed/getting-to-mars
    -throughjugaad/article6479048.ece.

Scott, James C. *Seeing Like a State: How Certain Schemed to Improve the
    Human Condition Have Failed.* New Haven, CT: Yale University Press,
    1999.

Scott, Joan W. "Fantasy Echo: History and the Construction of Identity."
    Critical Inquiry 27, no. 2 (2001): 284–304. www.jstor.org/stable/1344251.

Searle, Llerna Guiu. *Landscapes of Accumulation: Real Estate and the Neo-
    liberal Imagination in Contemporary India.* Chicago: University of Chicago
    Press, 2016.

Sennett, Richard. *The Craftsman.* New Haven, CT: Yale University Press,
    2008.

Seth, Shivom. "Indian Farmers Shun Volatile Gold, Buy Land Instead." Septem-
    ber 5, 2013. www.moneyweb.co.za/archive/indian-farmers-shun-volatile
    -gold-buy-land-instead/.

Sethi, Aarti. "Mahadev's Gift: Men, Bullocks and the Community of Cultivation
    in Central India." *South Asia: Journal of South Asian Studies* 42, no. 6
    (2019): 1173–91. https://doi.org/10.1080/00856401.2019.1684051.

Shah, Mihir. "The Crowning of the Moneylender." *The Hindu.* Updated May 13,
    2011. www.thehindu.com/todays-paper/tp-opinion/the-crowning-of-the
    -moneylender/article2015255.ece.

Shah, Svati. *Street Corner Secrets: Sex, Work and Migration in the City of
    Mumbai.* Durham, NC: Duke University Press, 2014.

Shapiro, Nicholas. "Attuning to the Chemosphere: Domestic Formaldehyde, Bodily Reasoning, and the Chemical Sublime." *Cultural Anthropology* 30, no. 3 (2015): 368–93. https://doi.org/10.14506/ca30.3.02.

Sharma, Ankit. "YearEnder: Cases That Shook Indian Real Estate in 2018." *Economic Times* Realty. Updated December 31, 2018. https://realty .economictimes.indiatimes.com/news/industry/yearender-cases-that-shook -indian-real-estate-in-2018/67288294.

Sharma, Ravi Teja. "Slowdown in Real Estate Forces Builders to Cut Prices and Dole out Freebies." *Economic Times* India. Updated September 2, 2013. https://m.economictimes.com/wealth/personal-finance-news/slowdown-in -real-estate-forces-builders-to-cut-prices-and-dole-out-freebies/articleshow /22216644.cms.

Sharma, Ravi Teja, and Manmohan Rai. "Yamuna Expressway: Samajwadi Party Government Unwilling to Give Nod to Project Awarded by Former BSP Government." *Economic Times* India. Updated July 5, 2012. https://economic times.indiatimes.com/news/economy/infrastructure/yamuna-expressway -samajwadi-party-government-unwilling-to-give-nod-to-project-awarded-by -former-bsp-government/articleshow/14683368.cms?utm_source=content ofinterest&utm_medium=text&utm_campaign=cppst.

Shipley, Jesse Weaver. *Living the Hiplife: Celebrity and Entrepreneurship in Ghanian Popular Music.* Durham, NC: Duke University Press, 2013.

Shipton, Parker. *Mortgaging the Ancestors.* New Haven, CT: Yale University Press, 2009.

Siddiqui, Anooradha. "Ephemerality." *Comparative Studies of South Asia, Africa, and the Middle East* 40, no. 1 (2020): 24–34. https://doi.org/10.1215 /1089201X-8186005.

Simone, AbdouMaliq. "People as Infrastructure: Intersecting Fragments in Johannesburg." *Public Culture* 16, no. 3 (2004): 407–29. muse.jhu.edu/article /173743.

Singh, Bhagat, and B. K. Dutt. "Full Text of Statement of S. Bhagat Singh and B.K. Dutt in the Assembly Bomb Case." Shahid Bhagat Singh. Accessed June 15, 2021. www.shahidbhagatsingh.org/index.asp?link=june6.

Singh, Bhrigupati. *Poverty and the Quest for Life: Spiritual and Material Striving in Rural India.* Chicago: University of Chicago Press, 2015.

Singh, K. P., and Ramesh Menon. *Whatever the Odds: The incredible Story behind DLF.* Noida: HarperCollins, 2011.

Singh, Kautilya. "Uttarakhand Bans Trishul, Spears for Kanwar Yatra." *Economic Times.* Updated July 13, 2014. http://timesofindia.indiatimes.com /city/dehradun/Uttarakhand-bans-trishul-spears-for-Kanwar-yatra /articleshow/38272525.cms.

Siwach, Sukhbir. "Ashok Khemka Questioned Amendment to Land Ceiling Act." *Times of India.* October 23, 2012. http://timesofindia.indiatimes.com

/india/Ashok-Khemka-questioned-amendment-to-Land-Ceiling-Act /articleshow/16921295.cms.

Smith, Nicholas, Russell. "Urban Furnace: The Making of a Chinese City." PhD diss., Harvard University, 2015.

Solanki, Gopika. "Registering Marriage: Debating Legislative and Judicial Efforts." In *Conjugality Unbound*, edited by Srimati Basu and Lucinda Ramberg. New Delhi: Women Unlimited, 2015.

Solomon, Harris. *Metabolic Living: Food, Fat, and the Absorption of Illness in India*. Durham, NC: Duke University Press, 2016.

Sontag, Susan. *Styles of Radical Will*. New York: Picador, 1969. First published 1966.

Sopranzetti, Claudio. *Owners of the Map: Motorcycle Taxis Drivers, Mobility, and Politics in Bangkok*. Oakland: University of California Press, 2017.

Sreenivasan, T. P. "In Gold's Own Country." *New York Times*. December 24, 2012. https://india.blogs.nytimes.com/2012/12/24/kerala-golds-own-country/.

Srinivas, M. N. "The Dominant Caste in Rampura." *American Anthropologist* 61, no. 1 (1959): 1–16. https://doi.org/10.1525/aa.1959.61.1.02a00030.

Srinivas, Tulasi. *The Cow in the Elevator: An Anthropology of Wonder*. Durham, NC: Duke University Press, 2018.

Srivastava, Sanjay. *Entangled Urbanism: Slum, Gated Community and Shopping Mall in Delhi and Gurgaon*. New Delhi: Oxford University Press, 2014.

Steedly, Mary, and Patricia Spyer, eds. *Images That Move*. Santa Fe, NM: School for Advanced Research Press, 2013.

Steedly, Mary M. *Hanging without a Rope*. Princeton, NJ: Princeton University Press, 1993.

Stein, Felix." "Selling Speed: Management Consultants, Acceleration, and Temporal Angst." *Political and Legal Anthropology Review* 41, no. S1 (2018): 103–17. https://doi.org/10.1111/plar.12256.

Stewart, Kathleen. "Atmospheric Attunements." Rubric & UNSWriting. Accessed February 24, 2022. https://unswrubric.files.wordpress.com/2010/04 /atmosphericattunements.pdf.

Stoler, Ann, ed. *Imperial Debris: On Ruins and Ruination*. Durham, NC: Duke University Press, 2013.

Stoller, Paul. "Sound in Songhay Cultural Experience." *American Ethnologist* 11 (1984): 559–70. https://doi.org/10.1525/ae.1984.11.3.02a00090.

Stout, Noelle. *After Love: Queer Intimacy and Erotic Economies in Post-Soviet Cuba*. Durham, NC: Duke University Press, 2014.

———. *Dispossessed: How Predatory Bureaucracy Foreclosed on the American Middle Class*. Stanford, CA: California University Press, 2019.

———. "Petitioning a Giant: Debt, Reciprocity, and Mortgage Modification in the Sacramento Valley." *American Ethnologist* 43, no. 1 (2016): 1–14. https:// doi.org/10.1111/amet.12270.

Subramanian, Ajantha. *The Caste of Merit: Engineering Education in India.* Cambridge, MA: Harvard University Press, 2019.

Tamarkin, Noah. *Genetic Afterlives: Black Jewish Indigeneity in South Africa.* Durham, NC: Duke University Press, 2020.

Tarlo, Emma. *Unsettling Memories: Narratives of the Emergency in Delhi.* Berkeley: University of California Press, 2003.

Tata Steel. "Evolution Story." Accessed March 10, 2020. www.tatasteel100.com /story-of-steel/index.asp.

Thakur, Joydeep. "Scientists Wage War on Colonial Kikar, Reclaim Delhi's Forest Land." *Hindustan Times.* Updated April 25, 2017. www.hindustan times.com/delhi/scientists-wage-war-on-colonial-kikar-reclaim-delhi-s -forest-land/story-v6mCQjbUFsETVXavXWaoUP.html.

Thorner, Daniel. "The All-India Rural Credit Survey: Viewed as Scientific Enquiry." *Economic and Political Weekly* 12, nos. 23–25 (1960). www.epw.in /system/files/pdf/1960_12/23-24-25/the_allindia_rural_credit_survey viewed_as_a_scientific_enquiry.pdf.

Times News Network. "Kejriwal Escalates Attack on Robert Vadra-DLF-Haryana 'nexus.'" October 10, 2012. https://timesofindia.indiatimes.com /india/kejriwal-escalates-attack-on-robert-vadra-dlf-haryana-nexus /articleshow/16744988.cms?from=mdr.

Trawick, Margaret. *Notes on Love in a Tamil Family.* Berkeley: University of California Press, 1992.

Trouillot, Michel-Rolph. *Silencing the Past: Power and the Production of History.* Boston: Beacon Press, 1995.

Turner, Victor. *The Ritual Process: Structure and AntiStructure.* Ithaca, NY: Cornell University Press, 1982. First published 1969.

Tsing, Anna L. "Unruly Edges: Mushrooms as Companion Species for Donna Haraway." *Environmental Humanities* 1 (2012): 141–54. https://doi.org/10 .1215/22011919-3610012.

Union Budget, Government of India. "Union Budget Highlights 2016–2017." Accessed March 7, 2020. www.indiabudget.gov.in/budget2016-2017/ub2016 -17/bs/bs.pdf.

Upadhyaya, Sanjay, and Pankaj Kumar. *Amendments in Labour Laws and Other Labour Reform Initiatives Undertaken by State Governments of Rajasthan, Andhra Pradesh, Haryana and U.P.: An Analytical Impact Assessment.* Delhi: V.V. Giri National Labour Institute. 2017. https://vvgnli .gov.in/sites/default/files/122-2017%20-%20Sanjay%20Upadhyaya.pdf.

Vaidya, Anand. "India's Forest Rights Act, Collective Action, and the Anthropology of the Everyday." PhD diss., Harvard University, 2014.

Vaishnav, Milan. *When Crime Pays: Money and Muscle in Indian Politics.* Noida: HarperCollins, 2017.

Vanaik, Anish. *Possessing the City: Property and Politics in Delhi, 1911–1947*. New York: Oxford University Press, 2020.

Vasavi, A. R. *Shadow Space: Suicides and the Predicament of Rural India*. Gurgaon: Three Essays Collective, 2012.

Vellinga, Marcel. "Review Essay." Review of *Anthropology and the Materiality of Architecture*, by Signe Howell, Stephen Sparkes, Victor Buchli, and Daniel Miller. *American Ethnologist* 34, no. 4 (2007): 756–66. www.jstor.org/stable /4496850.

Venkatesh, Sudhir. "'Doin' the Hustle.'" *Ethnography* 3, no. 1 (2002): 91–111. https://doi.org/10.1177/1466138102003001004.

Vidal, John. "As Flood Waters Rise, Is Urban Sprawl as Much to Blame as Climate Change?" *The Guardian*. September 2, 2017. www.theguardian.com /world/2017/sep/02/flood-waters-rising-urban-development-climate-change.

Vijayakumar, Gowri. 2019. "Sexual Laborers and Entrepreneurial Women: Articulating Collective Identity in India's HIV/AIDS Response." *Social Problems* 67, no. 3 (2020): 507–26. https://doi.org/10.1093/socpro/spz031.

Virilio, Paul. *Speed and Politics*. Los Angeles: Semitext(e), 1977.

Wadley, Susan S. *Struggling with Destiny in Karimpur, 1925–1984*. Berkeley: University of California Press, 1994.

Wahi, Namita. *The Right to Property and Economic Development in India*. PhD diss., Harvard University, 2014.

Walley, Cristine J. Introduction to *Exit Zero: Family and Class in Postindustrial Chicago*. Chicago: University of Chicago Press, 2014. https://doi.org/10 .7208/chicago/9780226871813.001.0001.

———. "It All Came Tumbling Down: My Father and the Demise of Chicago's Steel Industry." In *Exit Zero: Family and Class in Postindustrial Chicago*. Chicago: University of Chicago Press, 2014. https://doi.org/10.7208/chicago /9780226871813.001.0001.

———. "A World of Iron and Steel: A Family Album." In *Exit Zero: Family and Class in Postindustrial Chicago*. Chicago: University of Chicago Press, 2014. https://doi.org/10.7208/chicago/9780226871813.001.0001.

Walsh, Andrew. "In the Wake of Things: Speculating in and about Sapphires in Northern Madagascar." *American Anthropologist* 106, no. 2 (2004): 225–37. www.jstor.org/stable/3566960.

Weber, Max. *The Protestant Ethic and the Spirit of Capitalism*. London: Routledge, 1930.

Weber, Max, T. Parsons, and A. M. Henderson. *The Theory of Social and Economic Organization*. New York: Oxford University Press, 1947.

Weber, Nicholas Fox. *Le Corbusier: A Life*. New York: Knopf, Borzoi, 2008.

Weiner, Annette B. *Inalienable Possessions: The Paradox of Keeping-While Giving*. Berkeley: University of California Press, 1992.

Weinstein, Liza. *The Durable Slum: Dharavi and the Right to Stay Put in Globalizing Mumbai*. Globalization and Community Series. Minneapolis: University of Minnesota Press, 2014.

Weiss, Brad. 2002. "Thug Realism: Inhabiting Fantasy in Urban Tanzania." *Cultural Anthropology* 17, no. 1 (2002): 93–124. www.jstor.org/stable/656674.

West, Cornel, and Suraj Yengde. "A Shared History of Struggle Should Unite India's Dalits and African Americans in the Fight for Equality." *The Root*. June 12, 2017. www.theroot.com/a-shared-history-of-struggle-should-unite-india-s-dalit-1795973401.

Weston, Kath. *Animate Planet: Making Visceral Sense of Living in a High-Tech Ecologically Damaged World*. Durham, NC: Duke University Press, 2017.

Wilson, Ara. *The Intimate Economies of Bangkok: Tomboys, Tycoons, and Avon Ladies in the Global City*. Berkeley: University of California Press, 2004.

Wilson, Elizabeth. *Gut Feminism*. Durham, NC: Duke University Press, 2015.

Woods, Mary N. *Women Architects in India: Histories of Practice in Mumbai and Delhi*. New York: Routledge, 2016.

World Bank Group. "GDP (Current US$)—India." Accessed December 18, 2018. https://data.worldbank.org/indicator/NY.GDP.MKTP.CD?locations=IN.

———. "Structural Adjustment in India." Accessed June 15, 2021. https://documents1.worldbank.org/curated/en/923271468750298112/pdf/28681.pdf.

World Income Distribution. "Evolution of Average Income, India 1922–2018." Accessed March 8, 2020. https://wid.world/country/india/, paragraph 4.

Yang, Anand. *Bazaar India: Markets, Society, and the Colonial State in Bihar*. Berkeley: University of California Press, 1999.

Yengde, Suraj. "Being a Dalit." In *Caste Matters*. New York: Penguin Books, 2019. Kindle.

Zaloom, Caitlin. "The Evangelical Finance Ethic." *American Ethnologist* 43, no. 2 (2016): 325–38. https://doi.org/10.1111/amet.12308.

Zee, Jerry C. "Holding Patterns: Sand and Political Time at China's Desert Shores." *Cultural Anthropology* 32, no. 2 (2017): 215–41. https://doi.org/10.14506/ca32.2.06.

Zee Media Bureau. "India Remembers Maulana Hasrat Mohani Who Gave the Revolutionary Slogan 'Inquilab Zindabad.'" Zee Media Corporation Ltd. Updated January 2, 2017. https://zeenews.india.com/india/india-remembers-maulana-hasrat-mohani-who-gave-the-revolutionary-slogan-inquilab-zindabad_1963758.html.

Zhang, Li. *In Search of Paradise: Middle Class Living in a Chinese Metropolis*. Ithaca, NY: Cornell University Press, 2010.

Ziipao, Rocky R. *Infrastructure of Injustice: State and Politics in Manipur and North East India*. New Delhi: Routledge, 2020.

Žižek, Slavoj. *The Sublime Object of Ideology*. London: Verso, 1989.

Index

acoustic rationalization, 116, 125, 134–36, 231n6

aesthetics, 7, 139, 204, 213n10, 216n43. *See also* ephemeral

affect, 7, 21, 212–13n9; affective labor 199, 241n31; excess, 175; value 185–86; whiteness of 139, 235n2. *See also* atmospheres, ephemeral, sound.

agriculture, 135; decline of, 42–44, 219n24; farm laws 219n25; labor 27, 141; land, 41, 90, 95, 229n15; landscapes 59, 92. *See also* Green Revolution

Ahirs, 14, 37; 218n13

alcohol: alcoholism, 43, 48, 51, 132; industries, 64, 80

Anna Hazare, 56, 134–35, 221n3

architecture: affect 174–75, 199–200; architects, 6, 20, 100, 102, 105–7; care or nurture, 198–99; desire 178–181, 184; drawings, 86–87; economy or expansion, 19, 59–61, 67; education, 14–18; ephemeral, 3–5, 7–11, 147, 203, 205; home, 191–95; inequity, 160; informal, 17; money laundering, 71–72, 77; networks, 36, 38–39, 51–52, 103–4, 185; New Delhi of, 88–89; power, 107–9, 111, 196. *See also* construction, design, drawings, labor

artisanship. See *karigar*

Arvind Kejriwal, 56

atmospheres: caste or kinship, 12–14, 39, 147; debates on, 212n8; ephemeral, 3–5, 7, 9–10, 20–22, 139, 204; infrastructure, 34–35, 39; love 199; political consciousness, 170; value, 81, 141; whiteness of 235n2; work zones, 138–39. *See also* ephemeral

AutoCAD, 102–6

awaaz/ awaj, 114. *See also* noise

Baniyas, 8, 35, 178

Banjaras, 76–77, 176–78

bazaar, 181, 184–86, 223–24n36, 240n16

bribes: black money, 56–57; construction finance, 73–81. *See also* finance

brokers: kinship, 37; 73–75, 94–96; land dealings, 41, 73–74, 80, 94–96

care: childcare, 198; nurturing, 198, 216n43; work, 102, 110, 146;

caste, 12–14; ephemeral atmospheres 24; exogamy and endogamy, 220n33; experience of poverty, 29, 42, 151; identity, 214–15n23; inequity, 80, 147, 169; kinship or networks, 35–39, 84; knowledge, 16,

speculation, 221n9; real estate, 36, 40–42, 46, 94–95, 75, 159–60
speed, 114–16, 120–25, 134–36, 202, 233nn28, 29. *See also tez*
State, 28–33, 42–43, 60, 80, 164–70, 201–2, 218n9. *See also* planners, politicians
strike, 135, 163–64, 168–69
subcontracting. *See* contracting
sublime, 57–59, 83–84, 226–27n78

technology, 132; drawing, 103–4; history, 119–21, 132; mobility, 27–31; technoaesthetics, 7, 58, 115–16. *See also* machines
tension (tenshun), 162–63, 186–88, 195, 199, 237n25
tez / tezi, 127–30. *See also* speed

thekedar. *See* contractors
tower crane, 125–30
training, 15–16, 28, 74. *See also* learning, *tez*

unions, 100, 162–66, 168–69

Vadra, Robert, 69
value, 77, 81, 92, 105, 157, 181, 185

wages, 76–77, 141–45, 147, 160–61
Weber, Max, 148. See also *acoustic rationalization*
women's work. *See* gender

Yamuna Expressway, 46, 48
Youth, 48, 132, 150–51, 156–57

Founded in 1893,
UNIVERSITY OF CALIFORNIA PRESS
publishes bold, progressive books and journals
on topics in the arts, humanities, social sciences,
and natural sciences—with a focus on social
justice issues—that inspire thought and action
among readers worldwide.

The UC PRESS FOUNDATION
raises funds to uphold the press's vital role
as an independent, nonprofit publisher, and
receives philanthropic support from a wide
range of individuals and institutions—and from
committed readers like you. To learn more, visit
ucpress.edu/supportus.

www.ingramcontent.com/pod-product-compliance
Lightning Source LLC
Chambersburg PA
CBHW020842270326
41928CB00006B/511